DAY
SKIPPER

3rd Edition

Pat Langley-Price
and Philip Ouvry

Adlard Coles Nautical
LONDON

Published by Adlard Coles Nautical
an imprint of A & C Black
Publishers Ltd
37 Soho Square, London W1D 3QZ
www.adlardcoles.com

First edition published by
Adlard Coles 1988
Second edition published by
Adlard Coles Nautical 1991
Reprinted 1993
Revised 1996
Reprinted 1998, 2000, 2001
Third edition 2003

ISBN 0-7136-6223-9

A CIP catalogue record for this
book is available from the British
Library.

A & C Black uses paper produced
with elemental chorine-free pulp,
harvested from managed sustain-
able forests

Typeset in 10 on 13pt Stone Sans

Printed and bound in Great Britain
by The Cromwell Press

Design by Susan McIntyre

Note: While all reasonable care has
been taken in the preparation of
this publication, the publisher takes
no responsibility for the use of the
methods or products described in
the book.

CONTENTS

INTRODUCTION

The aim of this book is to enable the first time skipper to learn enough about pilotage and navigation to make short coastal passages safely; in other words to be a Day Skipper.

Pilotage is the ability to sail from place to place along a coastline using what you can see. Entering a harbour or an anchorage, and making a passage close inshore, is done by identifying potential hazards and working out a safe route to avoid dangers. *Navigation*, on the other hand, is the art of guiding the boat safely where marks are few or non-existent by using charts and instruments. The boat's position needs to be checked at regular intervals, particularly in poor visibility or near a coast.

Modern electronic aids to navigation make navigation simple. However, in the event of instrument failure, a skipper must still be able to work out the course to steer, and plot a position. In particular he or she should be able to recognise what the features on a chart look like in reality.

The skipper also needs to know heights of tide and tidal streams, weather indications and forecasts, so as to determine whether it is safe to make a passage and the best time to start.

As skipper, you are also responsible for the care and safety of the boat and crew, so must be able to deal with emergency situations such as man overboard, accidents, fires, etc, and must know how to summon assistance. All the necessary details are included in this book.

The syllabus for the Royal Yachting Association shorebased course is included. Each item in the syllabus is fully discussed and there are question papers with answers after each chapter.

We hope that using *Day Skipper* will help you to sail and navigate safely, confidently and enjoyably. We would be pleased to hear your comments (through the publisher) on any aspect of the book.

Pat Langley-Price and Philip Ouvry

Acknowledgements

Chart extracts are reproduced with permission under licence from the UK Hydrographic Office and the Controller of HMSO. Extracts and tidal data are reproduced from Macmillan Reeds Nautical Almanac 2002 with permission from Nautical Data Ltd.

Special thanks go to Piers Mason of Nautical Data Ltd; Helen Deaves of Stanfords Charts; Captain John Milner of Poole Harbour Commissioners; Mike McEnnerney of Photolink.

Additonal photo credits: UK Met Office; HM Coastguard; Silva; Ritchie; KVH; Magellan; Yeoman Navigator; Firdell Radar Reflectors Ltd; Raytheon; ICOM; ICS Electronics; McMurdo.

Personal thanks: Carole Edwards, Senior Editor, Adlard Coles Nautical.

RYA SHOREBASED COURSE SYLLABUS

Day Skipper is an elementary course in seamanship, navigation and meteorology. It is intended as an integral part of the overall training for the Competent Crew and Day Skipper/Watch Leader and as an introductory course to the more advanced Coastal Skipper/Yachtmaster Offshore shorebased course.

Nautical terms
- Parts of a boat, and hull.
- General nautical terminology.

Ropework
- Knowledge of the properties of synthetic ropes in common use.
- Ability to make, and knowledge of the use of: • Figure-of-eight • Bowline • Clove hitch • Reef knot • Single and double sheet bend • Rolling hitch • Round turn and two half hitches
- Securing to cleats, use of winches and general rope handling.

NB Knots are not now officially included in the Day Skipper syllabus but knowledge of these basic knots is essential for good seamanship.

Anchorwork
- Characteristics of different types of anchor.
- Considerations to be taken into account when anchoring.

Safety
- Knowledge of the safety equipment to be carried, its stowage and use (RYA Booklet C8).
- Fire precautions and fire fighting.

- Use of personal safety equipment, harnesses and lifejackets.
- Ability to send a distress signal by VHF radiotelephone.
- Basic knowledge of rescue procedures including helicopter rescue.

International Regulations for Preventing Collisions at Sea
- Full knowledge of steering and sailing rules (numbers 5, 7, 8, 9, 10 and 12–19).
- Working knowledge of general rules (all other rules).

Definition of position, course and speed
- Latitude and longitude
- Knowledge of standard navigational terms.
- True bearings and courses.
- The knot (speed).

Navigational charts and publications
- Information shown on charts, chart symbols, representation of direction and distance.
- Navigational publications in common use.
- Chart correction.

Navigational drawing instruments
- Use of parallel rulers, dividers and proprietary plotting instruments.

Compasses
- Application of variation; awareness of deviation and its causes.
- Use of a hand-bearing compass.

Position
- Dead reckoning and estimated position including an awareness of leeway.
- Techniques of visual fixing.
- Satellite derived positions.
- Use of waypoints to fix position.
- Course to steer.

Tides and tidal streams
- Tidal definitions, levels and datum.
- Tide tables.
- Use of Admiralty method of determining tidal height at standard ports and awareness of corrections for secondary ports.
- Use of tidal diamonds and tidal stream atlases for chartwork.

Visual aids to navigation
- Lighthouses and beacons, light characteristics.

Meteorology
- Sources of broadcast meteorological information.

- Knowledge of terms used in shipping forecasts, including the Beaufort scale, and their significance to small craft.
- Basic knowledge of highs, lows and fronts.

Passage planning
- Preparation of navigational plan for short coastal passages.
- Meteorological considerations in planning short coastal passages.
- Use of waypoints on passage.
- Importance of confirmation of position by an independent source.
- Keeping a navigational record.

Navigation in restricted visibility
- Precautions to be taken and limitations imposed by fog.

Pilotage
- Use of transits, leading lines and clearing lines.
- IALA system of buoyage for Region A.
- Use of sailing directions.
- Pilotage plans and harbour entry.

Responsible seamanship
- Avoidance of pollution.
- Protection of the marine environment.

1 ■ WHAT IS A CHART?

A chart is a sailor's map. He uses it to identify his position and his destination; and the best route between the two.

Fig 1.1 shows the earth overlaid with imaginary lines of latitude and longitude. Lines of latitude known as *parallels of latitude* are equally spaced either side of the equator. Latitude is 0° at the equator increasing north and south to 90° at each pole. Lines of longitude, known as *meridians of longitude*, converge at the north and south poles. The meridian passing through Greenwich, London is the datum meridian for longitude. Longitude is 0° at Greenwich increasing to 180° east and west of the Greenwich meridian. The latitude and longitude scales are used to define a position and are graduated into units called degrees (°) with sub-divisions into minutes (') and tenths of a minute. There are 60 minutes in one degree. Sixty degrees, ten point five minutes would be written: 60° 10'.5. Like a grid, co-ordinates from both scales are used to identify a position.

Nautical miles

The meridians of longitude converge towards the poles so the latitude scale is used to measure distance, one minute of latitude being equivalent to one nautical mile (M). A nautical mile – 6076 feet or 1852 metres – is not equal to a statute mile – 5280 feet.

Fig 1.1 Latitude and longitude.

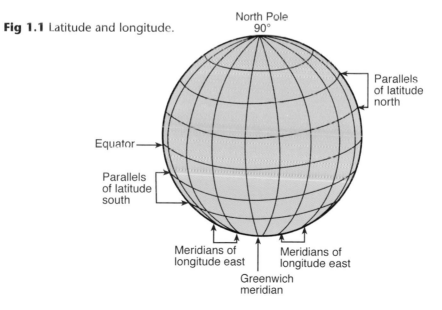

How is a chart made?

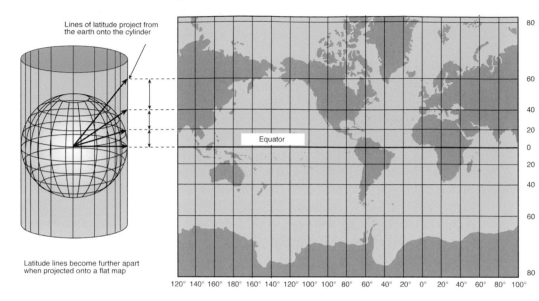

Fig 1.2 Mercator projection.

A chart is an image of the earth's curved surface projected onto a flat area. One of the main forms of projection is called *Mercator*. This is the usual projection for the type of charts you will be using. It has its limitations, however. If you want to sail at latitudes greater than 70° or further than 600 miles, you need to use a chart with a *gnomonic* projection.

Mercator projection
Due to the method of projection for this type of chart, an east–west distortion occurs and parallels of latitude are spaced increasingly further apart as the distance from the equator increases. A straight line plotted on the chart crosses all meridians at the same angle. This line is called a *rhumb line*.

With a Mercator projection, as latitude increases the scale increases, so distance must *always* be measured from the latitude scale level with the boat's position (Fig 1.3). Distances are always in nautical miles, and speeds or rates are in knots, which are nautical miles per hour.

Gnomonic projection
A gnomonic chart is produced by using a projection of the Earth's surface from the centre to a tangential plane. On a gnomonic projection, a straight line represents the shortest distance on the Earth's surface. On polar gnomonic charts the north and south poles are the tangential points.

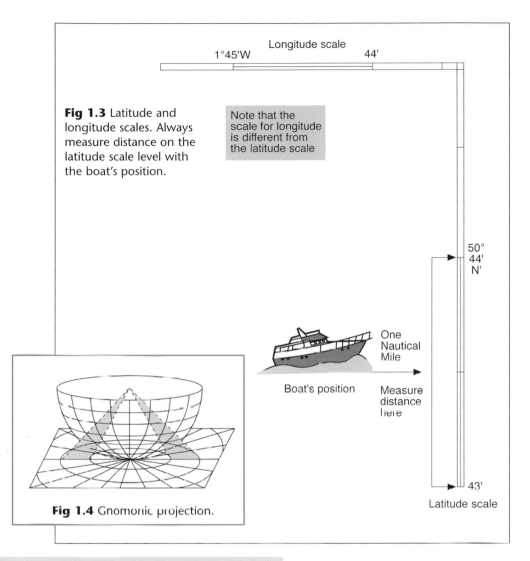

Longitude scale

1°45'W   44'

Fig 1.3 Latitude and longitude scales. Always measure distance on the latitude scale level with the boat's position.

Note that the scale for longitude is different from the latitude scale

50°
44'
N'

One Nautical Mile

Boat's position

Measure distance here

Fig 1.4 Gnomonic projection.

43'

Latitude scale

Information on the chart

Fig 1.5 shows a portion of Stanford's chart 12, which covers the area from the Needles, Isle of Wight, to Start Point. The title is: *The English Channel from the Needles to Start Point*. It is a small-scale chart which means that it shows a large area but not in much detail. It is used for reference and passage planning. The insert is an extract from Stanford's large scale chart 15 which shows Poole Harbour approaches. This is a Mercator projection chart consisting of a number of chartlets. It shows a portion of the same area as chart 12 but in much more detail, which is needed when you are approaching a harbour or anchorage as many of the necessary features or hazards are omitted on a small-scale chart.

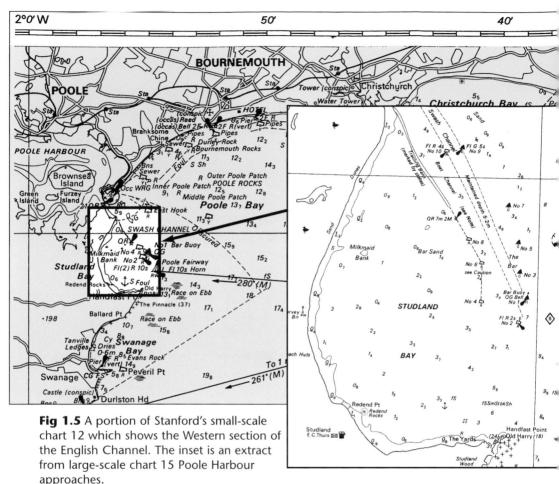

Fig 1.5 A portion of Stanford's small-scale chart 12 which shows the Western section of the English Channel. The inset is an extract from large-scale chart 15 Poole Harbour approaches.

Title and number This is shown on the chart and may be repeated on the outside cover. The title states the area covered: *Chart 15 Dorset Harbours and approaches.*

Legend This is the information printed under the title and includes projection, scale, and soundings.

Depths and heights The chart is metric so all depths and heights will be shown in metres.

Cautions These are warnings of particular hazards or navigational information usually printed near the title. Always read the cautions before using the chart.

Tidal streams These are tabulated at intervals each side of high water for the port indicated. On chartlet 3 this is Portsmouth; but on chartlet 4 it is Plymouth. They show the direction and rate of tidal streams for the area covered.

Rocks

Chart symbols for dangerous rocks are shown here together with a profile which gives you an idea of how they would look under water.

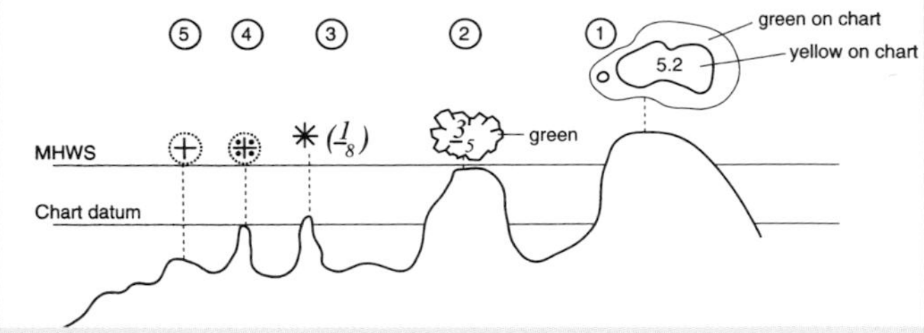

1 Rock (yellow on chart) which does not cover. The figure shown is the height above mean high water springs (MHWS).

2 This indicates a rock which covers and uncovers. The height above chart datum is given if known. The underlined figure indicates the drying height ie the rock is 3.5 metres above the level of chart datum.

3 A star (which could have a dotted circle round it) shows a small rock which, like 2 covers and uncovers.

4 A cross with dots in its angles shows a rock which is awash at chart datum level.

5 A cross without dots shows a rock of which the depth is unknown but could be a danger.

Compass rose This is a circular diagram showing compass points graduated from 0° through 360° and is used for navigation (see Fig 3.1, page 16).

Latitude and longitude scales The latitude scale is along the side borders of the chart and the longitude scale along the top and bottom borders.

Symbols and abbreviations Information is shown in an abbreviated form. An explanation of some of the symbols found on a chart is shown in Fig 1.6.

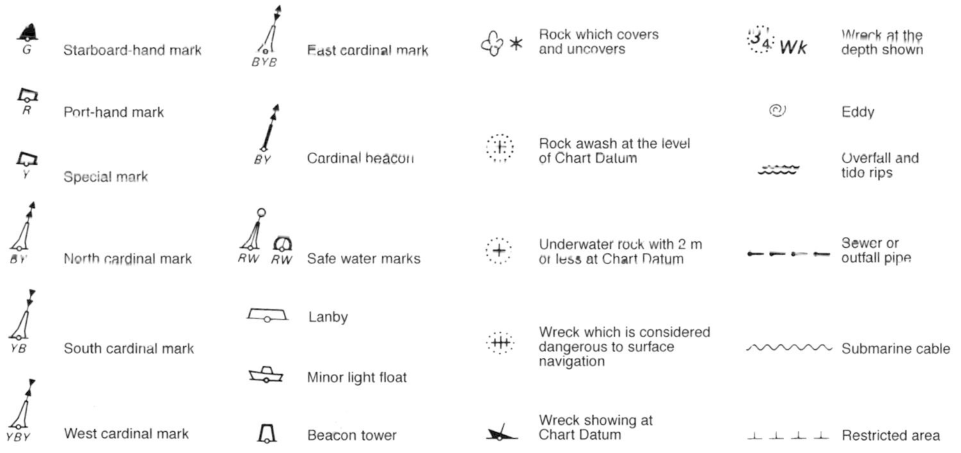

Fig 1.6 Chart symbols and abbreviations.

Who publishes charts?

There are various companies or organisations responsible for the publication of charts.

The United Kingdom Hydrographic Office at Taunton publishes Admiralty charts; coverage is worldwide. A full listing is found in the Catalogue of Admiralty Charts and other Hydrographic Publications. Of particular interest to small craft users are the Small Craft Folios, which consist of sets of charts for areas frequently used by yachtsmen.

Imray Laurie Norie and Wilson produce a series of charts for yachtsmen for the waters around the British Isles and northwest Europe. C *charts* are for offshore passage making. *Y charts* are large scale on smaller-sized sheets giving coverage of harbours, estuaries and rivers and include a number of coastal charts.

Stanfords coverage is northwest Europe. Harbour charts are available for some areas, consisting of several chartlets of harbours and stretches of intervening coastline. Chart 15 is an example.

Admiralty charts are available from registered chart agents. Yacht chandlers may sell local Admiralty charts and also Imray and Stanfords charts.

Corrections

If charts are to be reliable they must be regularly corrected to include additional or changed navigational information.

Corrections can be made to Admiralty charts by returning the charts to the chart agent, or by applying the corrections found in *Admiralty Notices to Mariners, Weekly Edition*. Notices are numbered in sequence throughout the year listing affected charts, and giving the correction and the number of the previous notice affecting the same chart. General information is available on website www.hydro.gov.uk or specifically for leisure craft on www.admiraltyleisure.co.uk.

Imray charts can be corrected by paying a small amount for the Imray *Bulletin of Corrections* published quarterly. Individual notices are available free of charge. Charts may be returned to Imray for correction. There is also information available on website www.imray.com.

Corrections to Stanfords charts can be found on website (updated monthly) www.allweathercharts.co.uk. Correction sheets are available free of charge but there is a charge for hand corrections.

HM Coastguard and NAVTEX broadcast important navigation warnings.

When a chart has been corrected the number of the notice concerned should be written in the bottom left-hand margin of the chart.

If corrections are extensive a new chart is issued.

Nautical publications

Hydrographic publications

Sailing Directions (Pilots) NP1-72. These are published by the UK Hydrographic Office and are used in conjunction with Admiralty charts for planning a passage. They include details of land features, off-lying dangers, tidal streams and currents, buoyage systems, port entrances and channels. Correction by revision, supplements or *Admiralty Notices to Mariners*.

Symbols and Abbreviations 5011 This chart published in booklet form contains symbols and abbreviations used on Admiralty charts. It is updated by re-issue.

Tidal Stream Atlases These are in pictorial form and show diagrams of tidal streams throughout a tidal cycle.

Admiralty Tide Tables Three volumes cover the entire world, giving information on times and heights of tides at standard ports throughout the world. They include tidal curves for predicting heights of tide at intermediate times. For secondary ports, differences from the standard port are tabulated.

Admiralty List of Radio Signals There are several volumes giving worldwide coverage. Of particular interest to small craft users are three volumes for leisure craft (NP 289, 290 and 291) which cover the United Kingdom, the Mediterranean, Baltic and Caribbean areas. They include details of marine capacity and limiting depths available. All are corrected by *Admiralty Notices to Mariners, Weekly Edition*.

Admiralty List of Lights and Fog Signals Worldwide coverage is given in several volumes. Volume A (NP74) covers the British Isles and Northern Coasts of France. Corrected by *Admiralty Notices to Mariners, Weekly Edition*.

Commercial publications

Almanacs

Various private companies publish nautical almanacs annually giving port information, times and heights of tides, tidal stream diagrams, radio services, lists of lights and many other details. The following publications will be of use to small craft owners: *The Macmillan Reeds Nautical Almanac*; *Practical Boat Owner Small Craft Almanac*; *Macmillan Reeds Channel Almanac*; *Macmillan Reeds Western Almanac*; *Macmillan Reeds Eastern Almanac*.

Sailing directions

There is also a wide variety of sailing directions or pilots published by private companies, giving information specific to small boat users. Many of these are the result of private surveys by the authors concerned. They are, however, written from the yachtsman's point of view, and have a long and fine reputation for usability and value for money. They may seem expensive but can save their value many times over in use. Although they are corrected at regular intervals, they should always be used in conjunction with up-to-date navigational charts.

The Cruising Almanac covers all yachting destinations in northern Europe. It is prepared by the Cruising Association and published by Imray. It is revised every two years.

A fuller explanation of much of the above information is given in later chapters.

QUESTIONS

Use chart 15 to answer these questions

1.1   What is the main difference between chart 15 and the portion of chart 12 (Fig 1.6)?

1.2   What is the title of chart 15?

1.3   What are the figures:
   a)   down the side border of the chart;
   b)   along the top and bottom of the chart?

1.4   How can a specific position be identified on chart 15?

1.5   What is a knot?

1.6   Why is it important to measure distance from the latitude scale in the area of the boat's position?

1.7   What are the properties of a Mercator projection chart?

1.8   Why is it not possible to use Mercator projection charts for polar regions and for passages over 600M?

1.9   What is the datum meridian for longitude?

1.10   How would you write in figures: Fifty degrees, thirty-eight point five minutes?

2 ■ USING A CHART

You use plotting instruments on a chart to measure latitude and longitude, plot a course or position line and measure distance.

Instruments

Plotting instruments are principally proprietary versions of protractors, course plotters, parallel rules and dividers. The photo below shows a Portland course plotter, a Captain Fields parallel rule, and brass dividers. You will also need a 2B pencil and eraser.

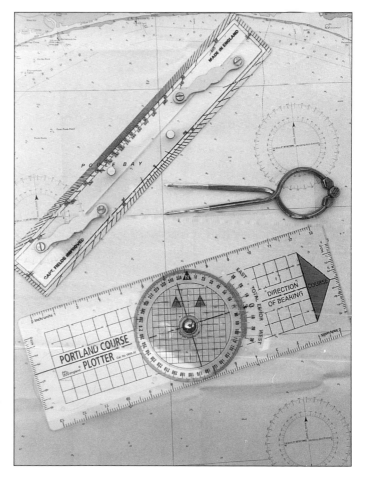

Chart plotting instruments: ▶
from the top: Captain Fields pattern parallel rule; brass dividers; Portland course plotter.

Position

Your position can be represented either as latitude and longitude or by its compass bearing and distance from a known point (see pages 11 and 12).

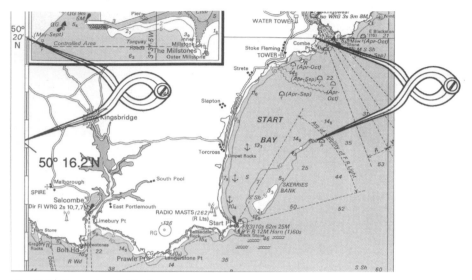

Fig 2.1 Measuring latitude.

Latitude and longitude

Fig 2.1 shows you how to measure latitude using dividers. To find the latitude of the red bell buoy in Start Bay, place one point of the dividers on the buoy and the other on the nearest parallel of latitude which is 50° 20′N. Keeping the dividers the same distance apart, transfer them to the latitude scale. Place one point on the same parallel of latitude 50° 20′N and the other will indicate the latitude of the buoy which is 50° 16.2′N.

You find the longitude of the buoy in a similar way using a meridian and the longitude scale (Fig 2.2). Place one point of the dividers on the buoy and the other on the nearest meridian of longitude which is 3° 30′W. Keeping the dividers the same distance apart, transfer them to the longitude scale. Place one point on the same meridian of longitude 3° 30′W and the other to intersect the longitude scale at 3° 33.9′W which is the longitude of the red bell buoy.

To plot a position given its latitude and longitude, you reverse this procedure.

Provided the position is close enough to the edge of the chart, a protractor, plotter or parallel rule can be used to measure and plot latitude and longitude.

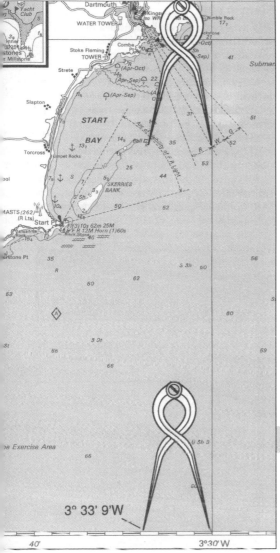

3° 33' 9"W

40'

3°30'W

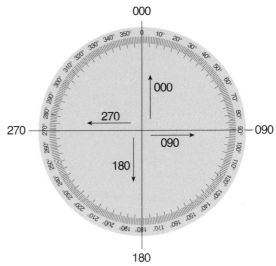

Fig 2.2 Measuring longitude.

Fig 2.3 Direction from a compass rose.

Finding direction

You use a plotter, protractor or parallel rule to measure direction.

Protractor
Fig 2.3 shows a compass rose. If you imagine you are standing at the centre of the compass rose and the course you want is 090°T, then look in the direction of 090° and you will see which way to plot the direction.

Course plotter
Fig 2.4 shows a course plotter. You want to plot a course of 056°T so you dial it on the rotating disk so that it coincides with the 0 on the small scale. Line up one of the gridlines on the disk with an adjacent meridian (or parallel of latitude). The edges of the plotter then show the course line that you want: 056°T. Bearings are plotted in the same manner to give position lines.

Fig 2.4 Direction using a course plotter.

Edge of plotter shows course 056°T

Dial 056° on disk

If you want to find the direction of a course plotted on a chart, you reverse the procedure. Line up the edge of the plotter along the course line and rotate the disk until the gridlines are lined up with an adjacent meridian (or parallel of latitude) and the N on the disk corresponds to a northerly direction on the chart. Read off the course opposite the 0 on the small scale

Bearings are plotted in the same way to give *position lines*. On some plotters, it is possible to allow for variation and therefore plot magnetic courses (see Chapter 4) and bearings direct.

Parallel rule

A parallel rule consists of two identical sections joined together by two moveable bars so that when the rule is moved or 'walked' across the chart the two edges are always parallel. It can be used in conjunction with the compass rose to plot and measure direction. The disadvantage of this instrument is that it requires a large chart table to operate without slipping

A Captain Fields parallel rule (see page 9) includes a graduated protractor which enables it to be used with only a meridian of longitude and independent of a compass rose. This reduces the need to walk it across the chart.

The photograph shows the groyne off Hengistbury Head; on the right you can see a port-hand can beacon. See Fig 2.5 Measuring distance.

Measuring distance

You also use dividers to measure distance. Distance is measured in nautical miles. *One nautical mile is the equivalent to one minute of latitude* and is always measured along the latitude scale opposite the area where you are sailing.

Two exercises to measure distance

Look at Fig 2.5. To measure the distance from point A to the beacon at the end of the groyne off Hengistbury Head, open the dividers and put one point on each of the two positions. Keeping the dividers the same distance apart, transfer them to the latitude scale alongside. They span one complete graduation and 0.95 of the next. One graduation equals one nautical mile so the distance from Point A to the beacon is 1.95 nautical miles. In practice, distances are plotted to the nearest tenth of a nautical mile so it would be recorded as 2 nautical miles (2.0M)

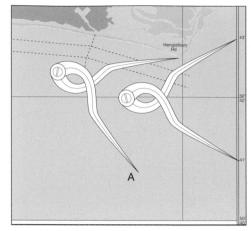

Fig 2.5 Distance off.

Next look at Fig 2.6. In this case the dividers are not large enough to span the complete distance between points A and B. To measure longer distances, the dividers are opened out to a convenient distance, say 2.0 nautical miles. After two spans, the remaining distance is 1.6M so the total distance from point A to point B is 5.6M (2 + 2 + 1.6)

To plot a distance you just reverse the procedure. The distance you want is set on the dividers using the latitude scale opposite the area of interest. Place one point of the dividers on the starting position and the other along the course line in the direction you want to go.

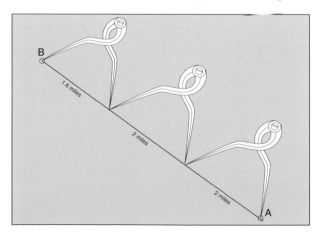

Fig 2.6 Measuring longer distances.

Sailing along the coast, a church spire, a conspicuous building or a tower, provided they are marked on the chart, are used to identify position.

QUESTIONS

Use chart 15, chartlet 3, Poole Bay, and chartlet 4, Poole Harbour

2.1   What is in position 50° 39'.3N 1° 55'.3W?

2.2   From a position 1.0M south of the beacon at the end of the groyne off Hengistbury Head what is the direction and distance of the yellow buoy off Boscombe Pier? How close does this course pass to the yellow buoy in the Foul Ground off Boscombe?

2.3   What is the latitude and longitude of a position 130°T from Bournemouth Pierhead? From this position what is the bearing and range of Bournemouth Pier?

2.4   From Poole entrance Bar Buoy No 1, what is the bearing and range (distance) of the beacon at the end of the groyne off Hengistbury Head? At a speed of 3.2k, how long would it take to reach the beacon assuming negligible tidal stream?

2.5   From Poole Entrance Buoy No 2, what is the direction and distance to Channel Buoy No 12 (Fl R) off Hook Sand? What special information is there on the chart concerning navigation in the Swash Channel?

3 ▪ WHAT AFFECTS THE COMPASS?

Compasses

To steer a boat in a given direction, you use an instrument called a compass. A compass can also be used to sight land and seamarks to fix the boat's position.

A compass needle points towards magnetic north, not towards true or geographic north. The magnetic north pole is about 1000 nautical miles from the geographical North Pole: it is situated in the area of Hudson Bay, Canada. In practice, to find direction we use a compass, which contains a needle-shaped magnet suspended so that it is free to rotate horizontally. This magnet rotates until it points towards magnetic north.

Variation

Courses plotted on the chart refer to true north but the compass needle points to magnetic north, so an adjustment has to be made between the course on the chart and that steered by the boat.

Look at the compass rose (Fig 3.1). This consists of two circles graduated through 360°. The inner magnetic circle does not line up exactly with the outer

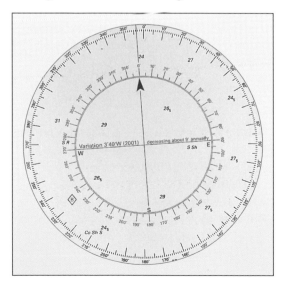

Fig 3.1 Applying variation. The compass rose will tell you the variation to apply.

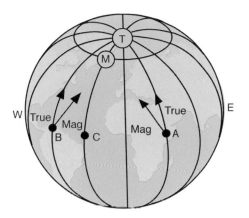

Fig 3.2 Variation changes with geographical position.

*This type of bracket-mounted steering com-
pass is a popular choice with yachtsmen as
it can be fitted at almost any location and
can be easily removed for safe storage.*

true one but differs by about 3°. This angular difference between true north
and magnetic north is called *variation*. It changes yearly. In this example, you
will see that the variation is 3° 40′ W decreasing about 9′ annually.

Variation also depends on geographical position and can be as much as 30°
in certain areas of the world where small craft are likely to go (Fig 3.2)

Variation is added or subtracted dependent upon whether it is east or
west. An aid to the memory is:

True to magnetic *add* variation west
Magnetic to true *subtract* variation west

Example			
True course	265°T	Magnetic course	148°M
Variation	+ 5°W	Variation	− 7°W
Magnetic course	270°M	True course	141°T

To indicate a magnetic course or bearing, the letter 'M' is placed after the
figures.

For variation east the rule is opposite to that for variation west:

True to magnetic *subtract* variation east
Magnetic to true *add* variation east

Example

True course	111°T	Magnetic course	344°M
Variation	– 3°E	Variation	+ 5°E
Magnetic course	108°M	True course	349°T

Deviation

A compass can also be affected by the close proximity of ferrous metal, electrical circuits and electronic equipment containing magnets. All of these produce magnetic fields, which may cause the compass magnet to deflect from magnetic north. Any such deflection is called *deviation*.

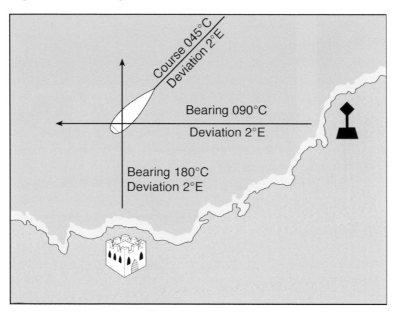

Fig 3.3 Deviation alters with the change of heading of a boat.

The steering compass

The compass used by the helmsman is known as the *steering compass*. It is in a fixed position.

The placing of the steering compass is important; it should be fixed so that the compass *heading* is clearly visible to the helmsman, and it must be firmly secured and in a safe position where it will not be damaged in heavy weather or by clumsy crew members. It should be well away from any deflecting influences, and the *lubber line* (the mark on the fixed part of the compass indicating the heading) must be accurately aligned with the fore-and-aft line of the boat.

It is possible to compensate partly for any permanent magnetic influence by the location of magnetized needles adjacent to the compass; however, this is a specialised task carried out by a qualified compass adjuster. The adjuster will manoeuvre the boat round in a circle, measuring at regularly spaced headings the deviation of the steering compass: this procedure is known as *swinging the compass*. Any remaining deviation will be tabulated for each compass heading in a deviation table. If the compass is re-sited, another compass swing is necessary. Deviation alters with a change of heading of the boat (Fig 3.3).

A deviation table will show the deviation to be applied for different headings of the boat (Fig 3.4). Deviation can be either east or west of magnetic north and corrections are applied using the same rules as for variation.

Compass heading	Deviation	Compass heading	Deviation
000°	$4\frac{1}{2}$°W	180°	5°E
020°	4°W	200°	$4\frac{1}{2}$°E
040°	3°W	220°	$3\frac{1}{2}$°E
060°	0°	240°	0°
080°	2°E	260°	$2\frac{1}{2}$°W
100°	3°E	280°	$3\frac{1}{2}$°W
120°	4°E	300°	4°W
140°	$4\frac{1}{2}$°E	320°	5°W
160°	5°E	340°	5°W

Fig 3.4 Deviation table.

Placing the letter 'C' after the figures indicates a compass reading that has not been corrected for deviation or variation.

Example			
Compass course	300°C	True course	114°T
Deviation	– 4°W	Variation	+ 6°W
Magnetic course	296°M	Magnetic course	120°M
Variation	– 5°W	Deviation	– 4°E
True course	291°T	Compass course	116°C

Compass error

If variation and deviation are aggregated together, the result is known as compass error.

Example

Variation	6°W	True course	057°T
Deviation	− 4°E	Compass error	+ 2°W
Compass error	2°W	Compass course	059°C

Hand-bearing compass

For taking bearings of landmarks, buoys, and other vessels in the vicinity you should use a separate hand-held compass. As it is not fitted in a permanent position, there can be no deviation table for it so you must use it in positions on a boat where there is negligible deviation. Any bearings taken with a hand-bearing compass are magnetic bearings.

If the course indicated on the steering compass is suspect, you can check it against the direction of the boat's heading using the hand-bearing compass. With the boat on a steady course, line up the hand-bearing compass with the fore-and-aft line of the boat and compare the readings of the two compasses.

Example

Steering compass	340°C
Hand-bearing compass	346°M
Deviation	6°E

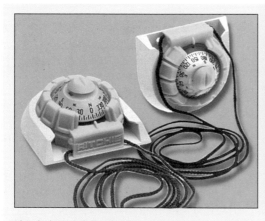

This lightweight, robust compass can be used as a hand-bearing compass or fitted in a bracket on a bulkhead.

A hand- bearing compass is used to take bearings of shore marks and buoys. A useful check on the accuracy of your steering course is to take a back bearing of a known mark that you have passed. PHOTO: JOHN GOODE.

This electronic digital compass has a memory to store the course you require as a reference heading.

The display (below) shows you how far off course you are from the latest reference heading. Degrees to port show up as segments on the left side of centre and degrees to starboard show up as segments on the right side. Plus or minus signs appear to show whether you are higher or lower than the reference heading.

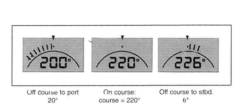

Off course to port 20°   On course: course = 220°   Off course to stbd. 6°

In addition to giving a digital read-out of your heading, this electronic compass shows the familiar compass points. You can also lock onto a course which changes the compass rose to a steering indicator (below) that clearly shows when you are off course.

Off course to port 20°   On course: course = 090°   Off course to stbd 4°

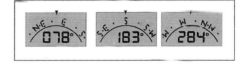

Electronic compass

An electronic or fluxgate compass combines a remote heading sensor with a heading display. The sensor electronically measures the direction of magnetic north from which the vessel's heading is derived. This heading can then interface with the other equipment.

Modern electronic compasses will measure and automatically compensate for deviation. The boat is steered steadily round in a circle, during which both the direction and strength of the magnetic field experienced by the compass is measured. Any inequality in the strength of the magnetic field on reciprocal headings is balanced out so that the deviation becomes negligible.

The rules for siting the sensor of an electronic compass are the same as those for a steering compass, except that it does not have to be visible. The compass safe distance is one metre.

QUESTIONS

3.1 What is the variation in Poole Bay in position 50° 39'N 1°43'W for the year 2005?

3.2 a) Correct the following true bearings to magnetic bearings:

Bearing	Variation
218°T	6°W
147°T	4°E
359°T	10°W

b) Correct the following magnetic bearings to true bearings:

Bearing	Variation
001°M	9°W
178°M	7°E
007°M	5°E

3.3 a) Correct the following magnetic bearings to compass bearings:

Bearing	Deviation
010°M	9°E
356°M	8°W
162°M	4°E

b) Correct the following compass bearings to magnetic bearings:

Bearing	Deviation
241°C	10°W
054°C	12°E
292°C	3°W

3.4 A boat is on a course of 120°C. The variation is 6°W; the deviation is shown in Fig 3.4. The following bearings are taken using the steering compass:

Tower	091°C
Church	167°C
Monument	330°C

a) What are the true bearings to plot?

b) What is the compass error?

3.5 What should be taken into consideration when siting a compass?

4 ■ TIDES

A tide is a vertical movement of water, which, around UK coasts, happens twice in approximately 25 hours (semi-diurnal tides). During this period two low waters and two high waters occur. In other parts of the world diurnal tides occur, and there is only one low water and one high water each day.

Tides are caused by the gravitational force of the moon and to a lesser extent the sun. The effect of the moon's gravity upon the Earth is not, however, uniform and the surface nearer the moon experiences a greater pull than the centre of the Earth. This makes the water at this point move towards the moon faster than the Earth itself, and the oceans on that side bulge towards the moon. On the other side of the Earth the pull is weaker still and the water is left slightly behind, bulging backwards. The sun exerts a similar pull upon the oceans but, because it is much further away from the Earth than the moon, the effect is not as great.

Spring and neap tides

When the sun and moon are in line relative to the Earth, their gravitational forces combine, causing the maximum tidal range known as a *spring* tide, when the high water is higher and the low water lower than at other times

When the sun and moon are at right angles relative to the Earth, their forces on the Earth are acting in opposition, and a minimum tidal range

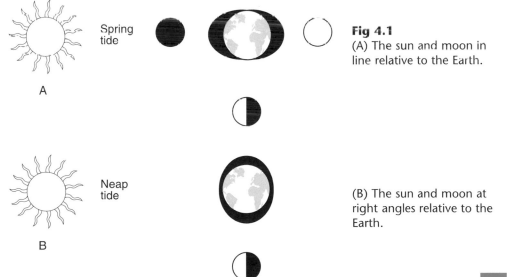

A

Spring tide

B

Neap tide

Fig 4.1
(A) The sun and moon in line relative to the Earth.

(B) The sun and moon at right angles relative to the Earth.

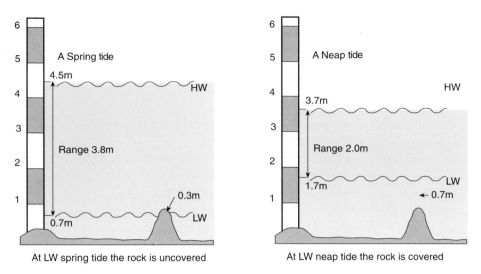

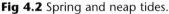

Fig 4.2 Spring and neap tides.

occurs. This is called a *neap* tide, in which the extremes of tide are less than at other times (see Fig 4.1).

Spring tides occur shortly after the new and the full moon, and neap tides occur shortly after the quarter moon. During a lunar month, following the moon's cycle of just over four weeks, two spring tides and two neap tides will occur.

Tidal terms

Equinoxes Twice a year the sun is directly over the equator, and at these times, especially if the moon is in line with the sun, larger than normal tides occur. The largest of these is the equinoctial spring tide which occurs twice a year around 21 March (vernal equinox) and 23 September (autumnal equinox).

Chart datum (CD) Chart datum is the level of the sea at or near the Lowest Astronomical Tide (LAT). For areas surveyed by the Hydrographer of the Navy, it is referred to the Ordnance Datum at Newlyn in Cornwall. LAT is the lowest level, taking into account astronomical conditions, to which the tide is ever expected to fall. Normally the sea will be above that level, but occasionally, when affected by high barometric pressure, strong winds or storm surges, it may fall below it. The depth of water below CD is shown on the chart by figures indicating depth in metres and decimetres. For example, a depth of 3 metres would be shown as 3, and a depth of 3.8 metres as 3_8

Drying height If part of the seabed, such as a rock or sandbank, projects above CD but is completely covered by the tide at high water, its height

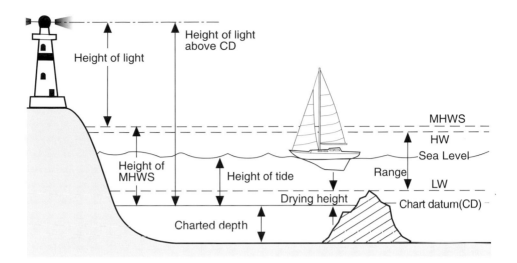

Fig 4.3 Datum levels.

above CD will be indicated by a figure with a line drawn under it: drying 2 metres would be shown as <u>2</u>.

Mean (average) datum levels These are the average heights above CD of all spring and neap high and low tides throughout the year:

Mean high water springs (MHWS)   Mean high water neaps (MHWN)
Mean low water springs (MLWS)   Mean low water neaps (MLWN)

These mean levels are indicated on some coastal charts, in Admiralty Tide Tables, almanacs and other nautical publications. The heights of features on land are measured above MHWS; not above CD.

Tidal range This is the difference in metres between the height of high water and the preceding or succeeding low water. The difference in height between MHWS and MLWS is the mean spring range, and the difference between MHWN and MLWN the mean neap range. If the range of any particular tide is compared with these ranges, it can be established whether the tide is spring, neap or an intermediate tide (you will need this information later for tidal calculations).

High water and low water (HW/LW) High water and low water are heights of tide measured above CD.

Duration The duration is the period of time between high and low water for a falling tide, or between low water and high water for a rising tide.

Rise The rise is the difference in height between any high water and CD.

Height of tide The height of tide is the vertical difference between sea level and CD at any given time.

Tidal curve The tidal curve is the change in sea level during a tidal cycle presented graphically in the tide tables.

Rule of twelfths

Sometimes if you want a quicker approximation of height of tide, you can use a simple arithmetical process called The Rule of Twelfths which is based on the assumption that the tide rises or falls as follows:

In the **first** hour the tide rises **one twelfth** of its range
In the **second** hour the tide rises **two twelfths** of its range
In the **third** hour the tide rises **three twelfths** of its range
In the **fourth** hour the tide rises **three twelfths** of its range
In the **fifth** hour the tide rises **two twelfths** of its range
In the **sixth** hour the tide rises **one twelfth** of its range

How much water is there?

You can find information on tides in the Admiralty Tide Tables, a yachtsman's almanac or local tide tables. There are tables which show for each day the times and heights of high water and low water at main ports (called *standard ports*). For other ports, known as *secondary ports*, the times and heights of high water and low water are found by corrections to the adjacent standard port times and heights. These corrections, known as *secondary port differences*, are found in separate sets of tables. Some local tide tables incorporate these differences.

The tables only give the height of the tide at the time of high water and low water. To find out the height of tide at other times, we use diagrams of *tidal curves*. There are tidal curves for each standard port; and, with certain exceptions, the same tidal curves are used for the associated secondary ports.

To show you how to use the tide tables and tidal curves, we will work through some examples. All heights are in metres and all times are indicated using a four-figure notation based on a 24-hour day. Times shown are in local mean time (UK: GMT). During summer months 1 hour must be added (UK: BST). (*Use the extracts provided at the back of the book.*)

If your boat is on a drying mooring, understanding the tides is an essential skill for calculating when you can depart from the mooring... and return to it.

Standard ports

To find the time for a given height of tide at a standard port
At what time (BST) at Dover during the afternoon of 10 August will the tide fall to a height of 3.0m? (Refer to the Dover Tide Tables, Extract 1, and the tidal curve diagram, Fig 4.4.)

For the period covering the afternoon of 10 August, extract from the tide tables for the port of Dover the times and heights of high water (HW) and low water (LW) and work out the range by subtracting the height of LW from the height of HW. Convert all times to BST.

	HW		LW		Range
	Time	*Height*	*Time*	*Height*	
Dover	1202 GMT	6.8	1939 GMT	0.7	6.1
Add 1 hour	+ 0100		+0100		
Dover	1302 BST		2039 BST		

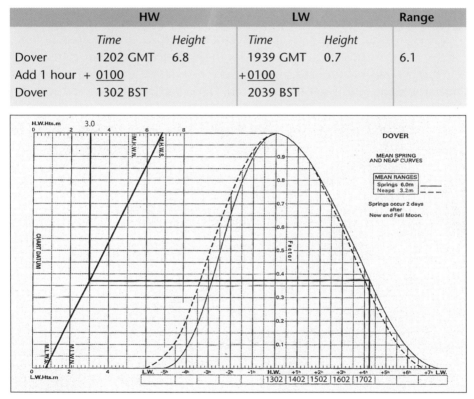

Fig 4.4 Dover tidal curve diagram.

1 Fill in on the time scale at the bottom of the tidal curve diagram the time of HW (1302) and hours before and after HW as required.
2 Mark the height of HW (6.8) on the top height scale (H.W.Hts.m) and the height of LW (0.7) on the bottom height scale (L.W.Hts.m).
3 Draw the range line between the HW mark and the LW mark.
4 Mark the height of tide required (3.0) on the top height scale and draw a line vertically downwards to the range line.

5 From the point of intersection on the range line draw a horizontal line to the right to cut the rising or falling curve as appropriate. It may be necessary to interpolate between the curves for spring and neap ranges. Compare the range (6.1) with the mean ranges shown in the top right-hand corner of the tidal curve diagram: springs 6.0m, neaps 3.2m. In this case the range (6.1) corresponds with the range for springs. Draw a line vertically downwards from the tidal curve to the time scale and read off the interval: HW +4h 12m. Apply this interval to the time of HW to give the time required of **1714**.

(Note: An interval is shown as before or after HW by the use of a – or + sign.)

To find the height of tide at a given time at a standard port

What will be the height of tide at Dover on 21 June at 0630 BST? (Refer to the Dover Tide Tables, Extract 1, and the tidal curve diagram, Fig 4.5.)

For the period including 0630 on 21 June, extract the times and heights of high water and low water from the tide tables for Dover and work out the range.

	LW		HW		Range
	Time	*Height*	*Time*	*Height*	
Dover	0225 GMT	1.4	0801 GMT	5.9	4.5
Add 1 hour	0100		+0100		(mid-
Dover	0325 BST		0901 BST		range)

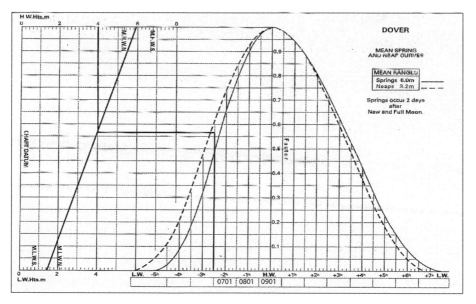

Fig 4.5 Dover tidal curve diagram.

Proceed as for the previous example as far as step 3.

4 Enter the time scale with the interval HW–2h 31m (0630) and draw a line vertically upwards to the tidal curve interpolating if necessary between the spring and neap curves.

5 From this point on the tidal curve, draw a horizontal line to the left to the range line.

6 From the point of intersection on the range line draw a line vertically upwards to the height scale and read off the height, which is 4.0m.

(Note: Although we have noted the time of LW, it is not required in any calculation so you can ignore it.)

Secondary ports

HW and LW times and heights for secondary ports are obtained by applying secondary port differences to standard port tabulations. You must do this before applying the correction for summer time (GMT to BST).

Suppose we need to find HW at Folkestone when HW Dover is at 0100 GMT. (*Refer to Extract 2.*) A difference of –20 minutes is tabulated for Dover HW times of 0000 and 1200, and a difference of –5 minutes for 0600 and 1800. The time interval between the tabulated time of 0000 and the required time of 0100 is 1 hour. The duration of the tide between 0000 and 0600 is 6 hours. From 0000 to 0100 is one-sixth of the duration. The range of the difference between –20 minutes and –5 minutes is 15 minutes. The correction to apply to the Dover HW time will be one-sixth of the range of the difference (2.5) applied to –20 minutes = 17.5 minutes. HW at Folkestone will be 0042 GMT.

$$\frac{\text{interval from HW}}{\text{duration of tide}} \times \text{range of difference} = \text{proportion of difference}$$

$$1/6 \times 15 = 2.5$$

Proportion of difference applied to tabulated figure:

$$20 - 2.5 = 17.5 \text{ (minus)}$$

It can also be done graphically (see Fig 4.6).

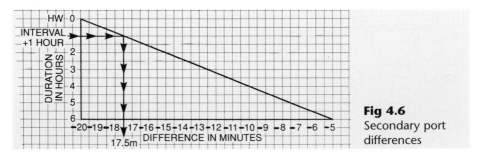

Fig 4.6
Secondary port differences

To find the time that the tide will reach a given height at a secondary port
At what time (BST) will the tide first fall to a height of 2.8m at Ramsgate on 4 July? (Refer to the Dover Tide Tables, Extract 1, and the tidal curve diagram, Fig 4.7, and Secondary Port Differences, Extract 3.)

For the period covering the falling tide on 4 July, extract the times and heights of high water and low water at the standard port, Dover. From the tide tables work out the range, then apply the tidal differences for the secondary port, Ramsgate.

	HW		LW		Range
	Time	*Height*	*Time*	*Height*	
Dover	0554 GMT	5.2	1239 GMT	2.2	3.0
Differences	+ 0030	− 1.3	+ 0017	− 0.7	(neaps)
Ramsgate	0624 GMT	3.9	1256 GMT	1.5	
Add 1 hour	+ 0100		+ 0100		
Ramsgate	0724 BST		1356 BST		

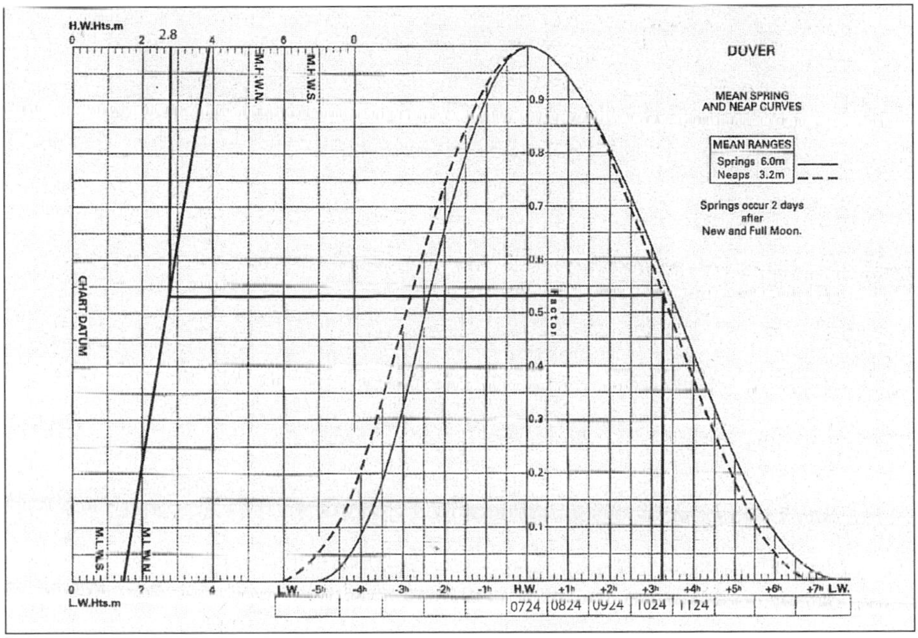

Fig 4.7 Dover tidal curve diagram.

The tidal curve diagram for the standard port is used as in the examples above, but you enter the times and heights of HW and LW at the secondary port on the diagram. We need the range at the *standard* port for interpolation between the spring and neap curves. The interval is HW + 3h 18m. The time required is 1042. You must make the time correction to BST *after* the differences for the secondary port have been applied.

To find the height of tide at a given time at a secondary port.
What will be the height of tide at Folkestone on 1 May at 0615 BST? (Refer to the Dover Tide Tables, Extract 1, and Secondary Port Differences, Extract 2, and the tidal curve diagram, Fig 4.8.)

	HW		LW		Range
	Time	*Height*	*Time*	*Height*	
Dover	0132 GMT	6.7	0901 GMT	0.9	5.8
Differences −	0016	+ 0.4	− 0010	− 0.1	(springs)
Folkestone	0116 GMT	7.1	0851 GMT	0.8	
Add 1 hour +	0100		+0100		
Folkestone	0216 BST		0951 BST		

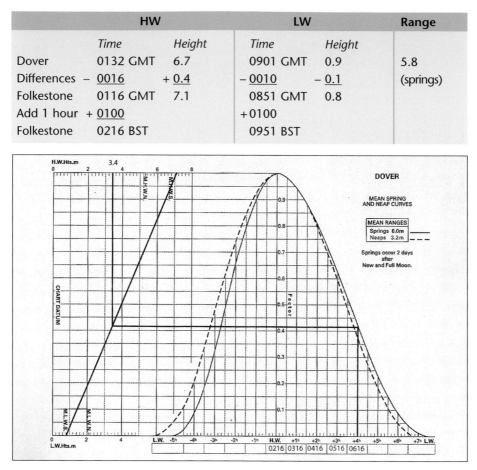

Fig 4.8 Dover tidal curve diagram.

Time (0615) is HW + 3h 59m. Height required: **3.4m**.

Solent ports (Swanage to Selsey)
Look at Fig 4.9, which is the tidal curve diagram for Lymington and Yarmouth, both of which come under the special classification of Solent ports. What are the differences between this diagram and the tidal curve diagram for Dover?

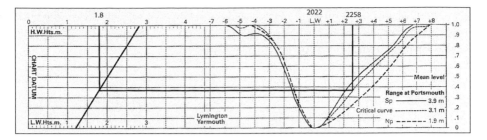

Fig 4.9 Lymington and Yarmouth tidal curve diagram.

There are two differences: Lymington and Yarmouth are both secondary ports, the standard port for the area being Portsmouth; and the time intervals are taken from LW, not HW.

In the area covered by the Solent ports the tides are complex with the result that HW can remain at a steady level (called a stand of the tide) or occasionally fall a little then rise again for a second HW. The tidal pattern varies considerably between ports adjacent to each other. Therefore it is much easier to determine the time of LW rather than HW and so tidal curve diagrams use LW as the datum. As the tidal patterns of the secondary ports are so different to those of the standard port, Portsmouth, and to each other, a complete series of tidal curve diagrams is necessary. Poole Harbour, though not formally a standard port, has its own set of tide tables.

A slightly modified procedure is used with the tidal curve diagram for Solent ports.

To find the time for a given height of tide at a Solent port
At what time in the evening of 17 May will the tide at Yarmouth rise to a height of 1.8m? (Refer to Fig 4.10 tidal curve diagram, Lymington and Yarmouth, the Portsmouth Tide Tables, Extract 4, and Secondary Port Differences, Extract 5, and the tidal curve diagram, Fig 4.9.)

For the afternoon of 17 May, extract the time and height of low water and the height of high water for the standard port, Portsmouth, and apply the tidal differences from Yarmouth.

	LW		HW	Range
	Time	Height	Height	
Portsmouth	1949 GMT	1.4	4.3	2.9
Differences	− 0027	− 0.2	−1.5	(mid
Yarmouth	1922 GMT	1.2	2.8	range)
Add 1 hour	+ 0100			
Yarmouth	2022 BST			

Fill in the time of LW and the heights of HW and LW. Compare the range on the tidal curve diagram to determine which curve to use. Proceed as for previous examples for secondary ports.

Interval: LW + 2h 36m.
Time required: **2258**.

To find the height of tide at a given time for a Solent port
What is the height of tide at Cowes on 5 June at 1715 BST. (Refer to the Portsmouth Tide Tables, Extract 4, the Secondary Port Differences, Extract 6, and the tidal curve diagram Fig 4.10.)

	LW		HW	Range
	Time	*Height*	*Height*	
Portsmouth	1237 GMT	1.8	4.0	2.2
Differences	– 0015	– 0.1	– 0.3	(neaps)
Cowes	1222 GMT	1.7	3.7	
Add 1 hour	+ 0100			
Cowes	1322 BST			

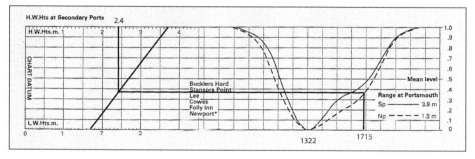

Fig 4.10 Cowes tidal curve diagram.

Interval: LW + 3h 53m.
Height of tide required: **2.4m**.

Clearances

When we know the height of tide at a particular location, examination of the depths of water and drying heights shown on the chart will enable us to determine the actual depth of water. If the draught of the boat is known, then we can work out the clearance between the bottom of the keel and the seabed (Fig 4.11).

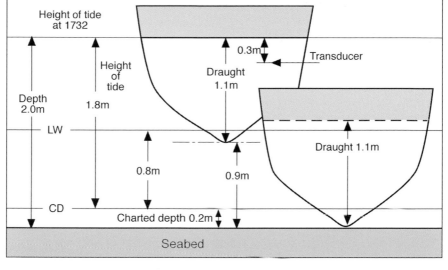

Fig 4.11 At 1732 the boat has a clearance above the seabed of 0.9m but at LW she will be aground.

If the information on the chart is dubious or lacking, the depth determined from the echo sounder or lead line can be used to estimate the charted depth. To allow for any rounding in the tidal calculation and for any abnormal weather conditions, a minimum clearance of 0.5m between the keel and the seabed is normally assumed.

Determining depths of water
A yacht whose draught is 1.3m anchors in the approaches to Lymington River at 1830 BST on 13 May. At that time the depth of water was 1.7m as measured on the echo sounder, which was sited 0.3m below the waterline. Will she be aground at low water; and how much anchor chain should she let out if she intends to remain overnight? Calm conditions are forecast.

	HW		LW		HW	Range
	Height	Time	Height	Height		
Portsmouth	4.4	1719 GMT	0.9	4.5	3.5	
Differences	1.5	– 0020	– 0.1	– 1.6	(nearly	
Lymington	2.9	1859 GMT	0.8	2.9	springs)	
Add 1 hour		+0100				
Lymington		1959 BST				

Referring to Fig 4.12, we can see that the height of tide at Lymington at 1830 on 13 May is 1.6m on a falling tide. LW is at 1959 and the height of tide at LW is 0.8m. If the echo sounder is 0.3m below the waterline and indicates

1.7m, then the actual depth of water at 1830 is 2.0m. The seabed is there-fore 2.0 − 1.6 = 0.4m below chart datum (this means the charted depth would be shown as 0_4). The height of tide at LW is 0.8m above chart datum or 0.8 + 0.4 = 1.2m above the seabed. As the yacht draws 1.3m, *she will be aground at LW*. At the following HW the height of tide will be 2.9m above chart datum or 2.9 + 0.4 = 3.3m above the seabed. The rule of thumb to determine the length of anchor chain to let out is 4 × maximum depth of water in calm weather or 4 × 3.3 = 13.2m; so 14m of anchor chain would be on the safe side.

In Lymington River a boat goes aground on a falling tide at 1830 BST on 13 May. At what time might she expect to refloat? (Refer to tidal curve diagram, Fig 4.12.)

In simple terms the question asks 'When will the height of tide return to the same level that it was at 1830?' On Fig 4.12 if we extend the horizontal line to the right, to midway between the spring and mid-range curves on the ris-ing tide, and then draw a line vertically upwards, this line will cut the time scale at LW + 2h 31m or 2230.

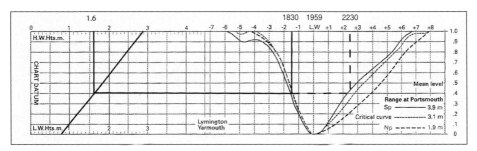

Fig 4.12 Lymington tidal curve diagram.

Heights of land features

All heights of land features are measured above the datum level of Mean High Water Springs (MHWS, Fig 4.3). Heights of features are in metres and are shown on the chart enclosed in brackets (18). The characteristics of lighthouses and lightships include the height of the light in metres above MHWS shown as a number followed by the letter 'm'. For Anvil Point light the characteristics are: Fl 10s 45m 24M. The height of the light is 45 metres above MHWS. The nominal range of the light is 24 nautical miles (24M). The nominal range of a light is the range at which it will be sighted when the normal meteorological visibility is 10M. It is really a measure of the brightness of the light.

This can be the result when you get your tidal sums wrong – and try to cut corners round a shingle bank.

Distance off when raising a light

The charted characteristics of a lighthouse show the height of the light above MHWS; which, for Anvil Point light, is 45m. The height of MHWS above chart datum can be determined from the tide datum levels shown on a chart. If the height of tide is also calculated, then the height of a light above sea level can be worked out. Tables can be found in yachtsmen's almanacs showing the 'distance off of a light when it is first seen (or raised) on the horizon'. To use these tables the observer must know his 'height of eye' above sea level, which, for a small craft, is usually 1.5m to 2.0m. For instance, at the time of high water, Anvil Point light would be raised from a boat with the height of the eye of the observer at 1.5m above sea level at a distance off of 16.5M.

At night, particularly if the conditions are cloudy, the loom (reflected beam) of the light from a lighthouse can be seen considerably beyond the point at which the light itself becomes visible, just as the streetlights of a port well over the horizon may appear as a dim glow in the sky.

TO FIND DISTANCE OFF LIGHTS RISING OR DIPPING

Height of Light		HEIGHT OF EYE												
		Metres												
		1.5	3	4.6	6.1	7.6	9.1	10.7	12.2	13.7	15.2	16.8	18.3	19.8
		Feet												
		5	10	15	20	25	30	35	40	45	50	55	60	65
m	ft													
12	40	9¾	11	11¾	12½	13	13½	14	14½	15	15½	15¾	16¼	16½
15	50	10¾	11¾	12½	13¼	14	14½	15	15½	15¾	16¼	16¾	17	17½
18	60	11½	12½	13½	14	14¾	15¼	15¾	16¼	16½	17	17½	17¾	18¼
21	70	12¼	13¼	14	14¾	15½	16	16½	17	17¼	17¾	18	18½	19
24	80	13	14	14¾	15½	16	16½	17	17½	18	18½	18¾	19¼	19½
27	90	13½	14½	15½	16	16¾	17¼	17¾	18¼	18½	19	19½	19¾	20¼
30	100	14	15	16	16½	17¼	17¾	18¼	18¾	19¼	19½	20	20½	20¾
34	110	14½	15¾	16½	17¼	17¾	18¼	19	19¼	19¾	20¼	20½	21	21¼
37	120	15¼	16¼	17	17¾	18¼	19	19½	20	20¼	20¾	21	21½	22
40	130	15¾	16¾	17½	18¼	19	19½	20	20½	20¾	21¼	21½	22	22½
43	140	16¼	17¼	18	18¾	19½	20	20½	21	21¼	21¾	22	22½	23
46	150	16¾	17¾	18½	19¼	19¾	20½	21	21¼	21¾	22¼	22½	23	23¼
49	160	17	18¼	19	19¾	20¼	20¾	21½	21¾	22¼	22¾	23	23½	23¾
52	170	17½	18½	19½	20	20¾	21¼	21¾	22¼	22¾	23	23½	24	24¼

Fig 4.13 Distance off a light

Anvil Point lighthouse.

Tidal streams

The vertical rise and fall of the tide is the result of the horizontal movement of water known as a tidal stream. For specific positions on each chart there is a table that gives the true direction towards which the tidal stream is flowing (the set of the tide), together with the rate of flow in knots (nautical miles per hour) for both spring and neap tides. This information is tabulated for the time of high water at the associated standard port and at hourly intervals before and after. A diamond shape enclosing a letter indicates the specific positions: these are known as tidal diamonds.

Tidal stream diamonds

If we refer to the tidal data on the chart for St Alban's Ledge, we see that for tidal diamond E, the tidal stream at HW (High Water) is tabulated as 081°T 1.7k for a spring tide and 081°T 0.9k for a neap tide. The rate for a tidal stream midway between a spring and a neap would be 1.3k.

For one hour before HW, the tidal streams are 063°T 0.8k and 0.4k for springs and neaps respectively. So the direction and rate of the tidal streams vary through the tidal cycle but for plotting it is assumed that the tidal streams change direction and rate hourly as tabulated, eg:

1100	1 hour before HW	063°T	0.8k
1200	HW	081°T	1.7k
1300	1 hour after HW	083°T	2.2k

Only at exactly 1200, the midpoint between 1130 and 1230, will the tidal stream be 081°T 1.7k. In practice we would regard the tidal stream as 081°T 1.7k throughout the whole hour.

Tidal stream atlas

Tidal streams are also represented pictorially in a *tidal stream atlas* or *tidal stream diagram* (Fig 4.14). Tidal stream atlases or diagrams are used either for passage planning or for pilotage. The arrow indicates the direction of flow. The figures are divided by the dot in the centre: the larger number representing the spring rate and the smaller the neap rate.

All the figures shown for rates are mean rates; the actual rate can vary considerably at exceptional spring tides.

Effects of tidal streams

There is normally no tidal stream information for areas close inshore. Sometimes you will find information on local effects in navigation guidebooks known as 'sailing directions' or 'pilots'.

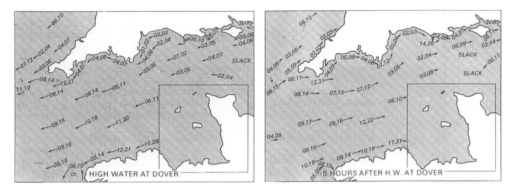

Fig 4.14 Extract from a tidal stream atlas.

Every opportunity should be taken to check tidal streams by observations of anchored vessels, buoys and lobster pots.

Generally a tidal stream flows more strongly in deep water; and in a bay it may sweep round in a contrary direction to the main stream. However, it tends to flow faster around headlands, sometimes causing severe tide races or overfalls where the water is very confused. It can also well up from an uneven bottom causing disturbed seas and eddies. These areas should be avoided particularly if the wind is blowing in the opposite direction to the tidal stream.

In a river or tidal estuary the strongest current or tidal stream, and the deepest water, lie on the outside of a bend; the inside frequently silts up. In the absence of any buoys, beacons or withies, do not cut the corners on bends.

Fig 4.15 A good look at anchored vessels, buoys, etc., will enable you to estimate the speed and direction of the tidal stream.

41

A tidal stream flowing over a shallow bank often produces a standing wave just downstream of the bank. You should keep well clear of any such standing waves.

Wind and tidal stream directions

It is important to be aware of the fact that wind direction is given *from* the direction the wind is blowing whereas tidal stream direction is shown as the direction *towards* which the tidal stream is setting.

QUESTIONS

Use extracts 1 to 7.
Use tidal curves extracts A to D for plotting.

4.1 Where can information be obtained on times and heights of tides?

4.2 A boat with a draught of 1.5m needs a clearance of 0.5m to cross a sandbar, which dries 1.0m. What is the height of tide required?

4.3 At Dover at what time (BST) in the afternoon of 4 August will the tide rise to a height of 3.0m?

4.4 At Dover what is the height of tide on 17 July at 0930 (BST)?

4.5 At Ramsgate when does the tide first fall to a height of 2.7m on 20 May?

4.6 A boat has a berth in the River Medina at Cowes that has a drying height of 0.5m. She draws 0.5m and she likes to have a clearance of 0.5m before entering or leaving the berth. On the morning of 16 May, between what times is she unable to enter her berth?

4.7 At Yarmouth on the morning of 5 May a yacht goes aground on a sandbank with a drying height of 0.7m. She draws 1.3m. At what time (BST) will she refloat?

4.8 In a position 50° 33'.7N 2° 00'.1W on 12 August between what times will the tidal stream be west-going? For 11 August, HW Plymouth is at 2050 (BST). For 12 August, HW Plymouth is at 0921 (BST) and 2134 (BST).

4.9 It is 1530 (BST) on 3 June. There is little wind. In Studland Bay at the entrance to Poole the boats at anchor are lying with their bows pointing west. What comments would you have?

4.10 Approaching Bar Buoy No 1 in the approaches to Poole Harbour, how can you check on the direction of the tidal stream?

5 ▪ PILOTAGE

Pilotage: finding the way without plotting

When making a short passage relatively close to the shore in good visibility, the navigator relies upon what he can see to establish his position and to work out the direction to go. There is often little time for regular chart work. There are many landmarks such as headlands, lighthouses, churches, water towers. There are also buoys and beacons. Using these as signposts to establish the boat's present position and where to go next is *pilotage*. Should the visibility deteriorate and these signposts disappear, then it will be necessary to start plotting on the chart; and pilotage becomes *navigation*.

Referring to chart 15, chartlet 3, Poole Bay, let us imagine that we are in a yacht about to enter Poole Harbour from a position 50° 39′.2N 1° 54′.8W. It is a sunny day, the visibility is good, there is a following breeze and there is a flood tide; so both the wind and tide are fair. The boat's speed is 4 knots. Looking to the northwest in the distance, we can see the harbour entrance by the Haven Hotel and the Training Bank marked by beacons off to port. The chart shows the lines of green (starboard hand) and red (port hand) buoys leading towards the entrance.

Looking at the chart, we see that there is a small boat channel to the left of the port hand markers. Referring to the notes at the top of the chart we see that small boats of less than 3m draught must use this channel wherever possible.

With a following wind It is quite easy to sail from one buoy to the next. The distance is about 2.4M which, at 4 knots, will take just over 30 minutes. We can enter the harbour; but watch out for the chain ferry!

Fig 5.1 The conventional direction of buoyage around the British Isles follows the arrows shown.

Lights and lighthouses

Lights used for navigational purposes are indicated on the chart with a magenta blob. They may be magnificent lighthouses or they may be sited in the windows of buildings. Often the light can be seen easily at night, but the structure cannot be identified by day. Two lights in transit (leading lights) offer an ideal method of keeping within a channel, particularly if some of the buoys are unlit.

Sometimes a single light will have an intensified sector on a certain bearing that marks the centre of a channel. Lights may be sectored (White, Red, Green) to indicate potential hazards, Fig 5.2.

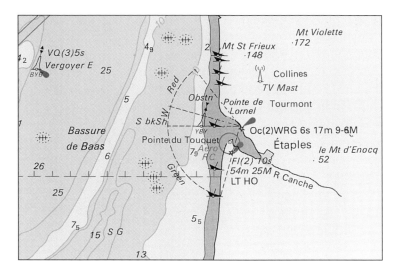

Fig 5.2 Sectored lights. Many lights have sectors of different colour: here a vessel must keep in the white sector until she can identify the harbour entrance.

Buoyage plan

For an unfamiliar passage, where a buoyed channel is to be followed, it is a good idea to draw up a list of the marks in the order that they will be seen, with sufficient characteristics so that it will not be necessary to keep returning to the chart table. The direction and distance between marks should be included so that in poor visibility you know where to look.

Buoys and beacons

Buoys are plentiful in the approaches to commercial ports. For small harbours and secondary channels beacons are used extensively. Occasionally, down infrequently used channels, tree branches (called withies) are stuck in the mud to indicate the edges of deep water channels.

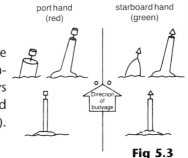

Lateral marks

These show the port and starboard side of the channel. When a vessel is proceeding in the general direction of buoyage or into harbour, buoys marking the channel will be green conical shaped to starboard and red can-shaped to port (Fig 5.3).

Fig 5.3

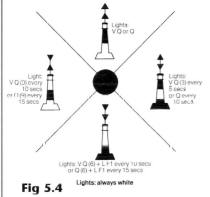

Fig 5.4

Cardinal marks

These warn of a danger or hazard and are placed around it in relation to the four cardinal points of the compass. They are pillar-shaped yellow and black with distinctive topmarks (Fig 5.4). The colours are yellow and black in various sequences. You will need to memorise the shapes: **N**orth and **S**outh are easy as they have double 'arrows' pointing up and down. **E**ast looks a bit **E**gg shaped and **W**est looks like a **W**ine glass.

Fig 5.5

Isolated danger mark

This marks a danger such as a wreck or lone rock and is placed over the danger. It is pillar-shaped black and red (Fig 5.5).

Fig 5.6

Safe water mark

This is used to indicate navigable water around the mark. It may mark the middle of a channel or be used as a landfall mark. Safe water marks can be spherical or pillar-shaped red and white (Fig 5.6).

Special marks

Non-navigational marks of special significance such as sewer outfalls, firing range, or racing marks. They vary in shape and are coloured yellow (Fig. 5.7).

Fig 5.7

This sequence of photos shows the approach and entrance into Poole Harbour.

▲ **1** Heading up from the south, the very distinctive rock formation of Old Harry marks Handfast Point.

▼ **2** No 1 Bar starboard buoy is positioned at the entrance to the Swash Channel; beyond you can see the conspicuous Haven Hotel and No 4 buoy. To the west of the Swash is a subsidiary channel which should be used by recreational craft with a draft of less than 3m.

3 *No 4 buoy with ▶ the Training Bank just to the left. This buoy is left to port to remain in the Swash Channel but the subsidiary channel for recreational craft leads between the beacon and the buoy.*

◀ **4** *This beacon marks the start of the Training Bank. In the distance you can see, from right to left, the Haven Hotel, the chain ferry and Brownsea Island.*

5 *Brownsea east ▶ cardinal buoy looking north towards Middle Ship Channel.*

◄ **6** Looking north with Brownsea Roads south cardinal buoy, 20 Bell in the foreground.

▼ **7** The approach towards Town Quay leaving the Ro-ro ferry terminal to port and south cardinal buoy 55 Stakes to starboard.

◄ **8** Destination in sight: Poole Quay (far left) with Dolphin Boat Haven behind 55 Stakes buoy. PHOTOS: PHOTO-LINK.

Lights

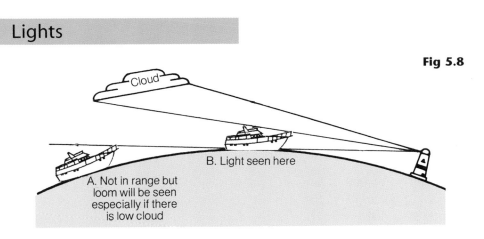

Fig 5.8

A. Not in range but loom will be seen especially if there is low cloud

B. Light seen here

The distance over which you can see a light is called its *range*. Ignoring the curvature of the earth, this distance would be dependent on the luminous intensity of the light and is known as the *luminous range*. The *nominal range* of a light is the distance at which it would be seen if the standard visibility, as announced by the Meteorological Office, is 10 nautical miles (see page 38).

Taking into account the curvature of the earth, however, the light will not be seen until well within its luminous range. The point at which the light appears on the horizon is the geographical range. It is said to rise or dip according to whether you are moving towards or away from it. The geographical range is dependent on the height of the light above sea level and the height of the observer's eye above sea level. Sets of tables are available which give the 'distance off' for different respective heights. Obviously, as the height of the light and the height of the observer's eye increase, the distance at which it can be seen increases.

Light characteristics

Fig 5.9 Shows the different characteristics.

Leading lines

One of the most helpful guides to entering or leaving an unfamiliar harbour are leading lines. They consist of two readily identifiable marks (or lights at night) which, when

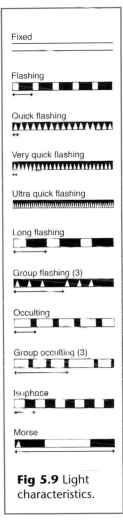

Fixed

Flashing

Quick flashing

Very quick flashing

Ultra quick flashing

Long flashing

Group flashing (3)

Occulting

Group occulting (3)

Isophase

Morse

Fig 5.9 Light characteristics.

kept in line or in transit, indicate the direction of the safe water channel or harbour entrance. It is useful to note from the chart the direction (or bearing) of the transit as sometimes it is difficult to identify one of the transit marks or lights, so knowing where to look for one relative to the other is important.

Transits

To keep two objects in line or in transit, you don't need them to be designated as a leading line. You can use any two objects identifiable on a chart to indicate a desired direction or bearing. In open water a good way to compensate for a cross tidal stream is to keep the destination, which may well be a buoy, in transit with a fixed point on the coastline. The use of a transit on the approach to an anchorage is recommended (Fig 5.10).

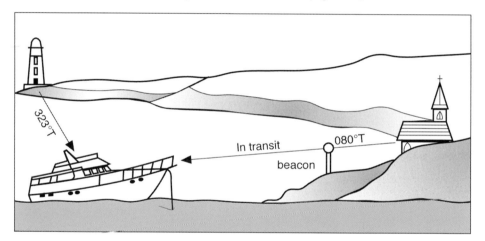

Fig 5.10 Boat anchors when the beacon and the church are in transit and the lighthouse bears 323°T.

Clearing bearings

Underwater hazards or dangers are not always marked. In the approaches to a harbour there is usually an identifiable landmark in the locality. From the chart a line from this landmark passing clear of the hazard is determined. The direction of this line, represented as a bearing of the landmark, is known as a *clearing bearing*. From safe water, if this bearing line is not crossed, then the boat will not be in danger from the hazard (Fig 5.11).

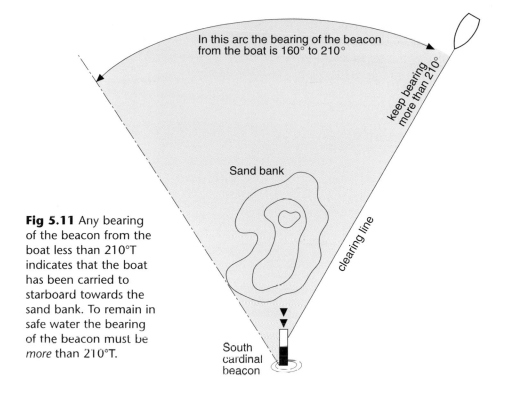

In this arc the bearing of the beacon from the boat is 160° to 210°

keep bearing more than 210°

Sand bank

clearing line

Fig 5.11 Any bearing of the beacon from the boat less than 210°T indicates that the boat has been carried to starboard towards the sand bank. To remain in safe water the bearing of the beacon must be *more* than 210°T.

South cardinal beacon

Depth contours

The depth of water in the boat's present position can be measured using an instrument known as a depth sounder or echo sounder, or by using a lead line (a heavy weight on the end of a line knotted at 1 metre intervals, Fig 5.12).

A line joining points on the seabed of equal depth is known as a *depth contour*. In areas where these contours are fairly straight they can be used either as a position line or as an indication of the edge of a channel (Fig 5.13).

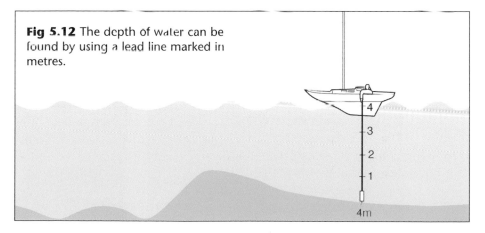

Fig 5.12 The depth of water can be found by using a lead line marked in metres.

4

3

2

1

4m

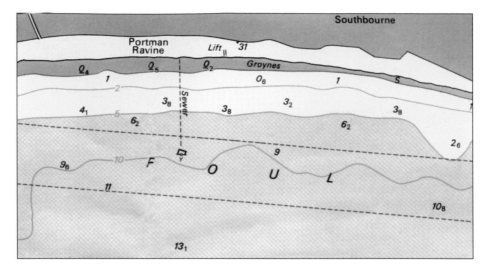

Fig 5.13 Depth contours at 2m, 5m and 10m.

QUESTIONS

Refer to chart 15, chartlet 3, Poole Bay.

5.1 For pilotage and passage planning which up-to-date nautical publications are necessary?

5.2 What are the characteristics of the lights on the end of Boscombe Pier?

5.3 Is Anvil Point light visible in Swanage Bay?

5.4 Approaching Poole Harbour entrance a boat sees a black ball hoisted on the seaward end of the chain ferry. What does it signify?

5.5 At night a boat is in position 50° 35'.5N 1° 57'0W heading for the anchorage in Swanage Bay. The visibility is good and the tidal stream is north-going.

    a) How can she identify Swanage Pier?

    b) What action is necessary to keep clear of Peveril Ledge?

6 ■ WHERE HAVE WE BEEN?

Symbols

There are a number of symbols used in chartwork which you will need to be able to identify and use:

+	Dead reckoning position (DR). Position derived only from course steered and distance travelled.
△	Estimated position (EP). Position derived from course steered, distance travelled, leeway and tidal stream.
⊙	Fix. Position derived from direct reference to terrestrial landmarks.
⌀	Waypoint.
→	Water track.
→→	Ground track.
→→→	Tidal stream.
⟶	Position line.
	Position obtained from a bearing and a position circle.
	Position obtained from two position circles.
≪⟶≫	Transferred position line.
⊕	GPS fix.

Estimated Position

We have until now been using the chart for pilotage, where we have known our position in relation to the navigational marks. However, we will not always be in sight of such marks so, to keep a record of our progress, we estimate our position by recording the boat's course and distance run together with estimated *tidal stream* and *leeway* (the sideways movement caused by the wind).

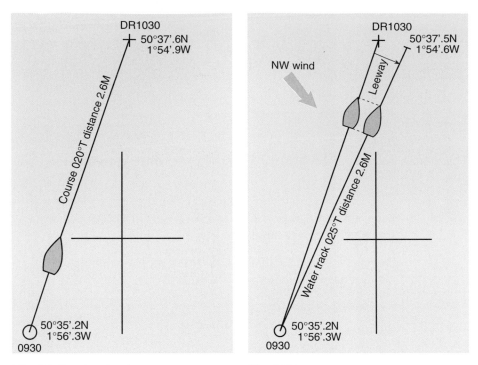

Fig 6.1 Dead reckoning.   **Fig 6.2** Leeway.

Let us assume that it is 0930 and we are in a position 50° 35'.2N 1° 56'.3W. From this position we steer a course of 020°T for a distance of 2.6M over a period of one hour. With no allowance for tidal stream or leeway, our 1030 position would be 50° 37'.6N 1° 54'.9W. This is a *dead reckoning (DR)* position (Fig 6.1), and is shown on the chart by using the symbol +.

(*Note*: Normally distances and speeds are rounded up to the nearest tenth of a mile or tenth of a knot. The large scale of chart 15 sometimes makes this difficult.)

However, a northwest wind has pushed the boat off course through an angle of 5° so that the track of the boat through the water is 025°T. This sideways displacement is known as *leeway*. The track of the boat through the water is known as the *water track*. Allowing for this leeway, the 1030 position is 50° 37'.5N 1° 54'.6W. In practice it is the water track which is plotted on the chart, not the true course (Fig 6.2).

There is also a tidal stream setting towards the direction 053°T at a rate of 0.6 knots. A *knot* is the equivalent of one nautical mile per hour, and is usually indicated by the suffix 'k' or 'kn'. We must allow for this tidal stream. We plot it from the end of the water track (Fig 6.3).

The resultant position at 1030 now takes into account both leeway and

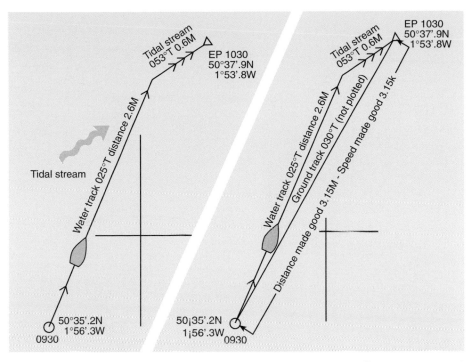

Fig 6.3 Tidal stream and estimated position.

Fig 6.4 Ground track, distance and speed made good.

tidal stream. It is known as an *estimated position (EP)* and is marked on the chart with the symbol △. The EP is 50° 37'.9N 1° 53'.8W.

In the example the boat's speed was 2.6k (2.6M in one hour). The line drawn from the 0930 fix to the 1030 EP is known as the *ground track* and represents the effective track of the boat over the land (as opposed to through the water), Fig 6.4. The distance along the ground track from the 0930 fix to the 1030 EP is the *distance made good over the ground* or just *distance made good (DMG)*. In this example we can see that the distance made good is 3.15M (rounded to 3.2M). The *speed made good (SMG)* is the distance made good over a period of one hour; which, in this example, is 3.15k (rounded to 3.2k). Do not confuse the boat's speed through the water (2.6k) with her speed made good over the ground (3.2k). (*Note:* The ground track is not normally plotted.)

Estimated positions are usually plotted at hourly intervals, but you can plot them for any period of time. In the above example let us find the EP at 1000, which represents a time period of 30 minutes. The water track is still 025° but the distance run is 1.3M (which is the distance travelled at a speed of 2.6k for 30 minutes). The tidal stream is still 053° but the drift (distance that the water moves relative to the ground) is 0.3M (0.6k for 30 minutes). We now have the 1000 estimated position and can measure the distance made good

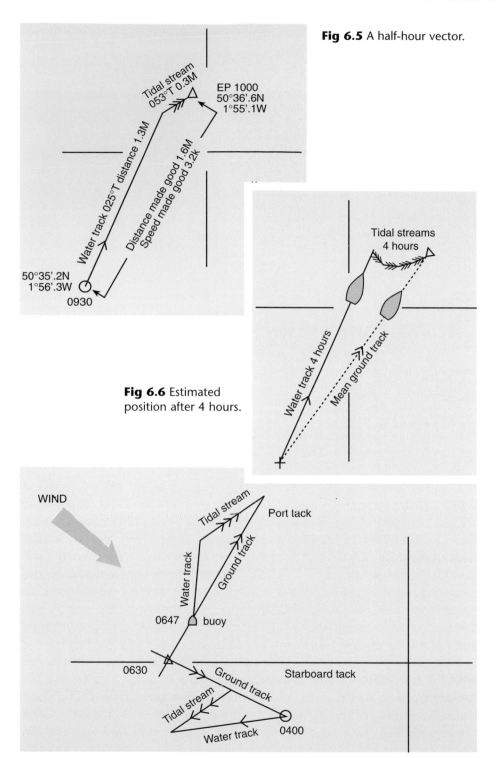

Fig 6.5 A half-hour vector.

Tidal stream
053°T 0.3M

EP 1000
50°36'.6N
1°55'.1W

Water track 025°T distance 1.3M

Distance made good 1.6M
Speed made good 3.2k

50°35'.2N
1°56'.3W

0930

Fig 6.6 Estimated position after 4 hours.

Tidal streams
4 hours

Water track 4 hours

Mean ground track

WIND

Tidal stream

Port tack

Water track

Ground track

0647   buoy

0630

Starboard tack

Ground track

Tidal stream

Water track   0400

Fig 6.7 Time to tack.

◀ *A sound knowledge of chartwork is the key element of the RYA Day Skipper theory syllabus.* PHOTO: DAVID WILLIAMS.

between 0930 and 1000, which is 1.6M, Fig 6.5. Note that the speed made good is equivalent to the distance made good divided by the time in hours: in this example it is still 3.2k.

The triangle formed by the water track, the tidal stream, and the ground track is known as a *vector triangle* or *vector diagram*. For a passage of several hours we can derive the estimated position by plotting the DR position for the passage then including all the tidal streams consecutively (Fig 6.6). Note that the resultant ground track only represents the mean of the course and tidal streams over the *duration* of the passage.

Time to tack

If a sailing boat is beating to windward, she may wish to know the time at which to tack in order to reach her destination. Firstly determine the best course that the helmsman can steer on each tack, and then convert these two courses to water tracks. The better tack with which to start is that which keeps the boat's ground track nearest to the direct course to the destination. From the starting point draw on the chart the ground track for the next hour, or half hour if the distance to go is small (Fig 6.7). Estimate roughly the time to tack and the approximate duration of the passage on the second tack. For this period (rounded to the nearest hour or half hour) you then draw on the chart *from the destination* the ground track for the second tack. (Note that this is only a construction so it does not matter where the lines go.) Project this ground track backwards to intersect the ground track of the first tack. The point of intersection of the two ground tracks is where you must change tack. Measure the distance and speed made good along each track and work out the *time to tack* and the *ETA* (estimated time of arrival) at the destination.

QUESTIONS

Use chart 15 and variation 3°W.   All times BST.

6.1   At 1515 (log 7.1) a boat is in position 50° 41'.0N 1° 41'.7W on a course of 308°M travelling at a speed of 6.3k. What is the EP at 1535? With a draught of 2.0m, could she continue on the same course for a further 7 minutes?

6.2   At 1410 (log 23.1) a boat is in position 50° 41'.8N 1° 45'.0W on a course of 287°M. At 1440 the log reads 25.8. The tidal stream is estimated as 293°T 1.0k. What is the EP at 1440? What is the speed made good?

6.3   At 1000 (log 17.6) a boat is in a position 50° 40'.7N 1° 41'.0W on a course to Poole of 275°M. At 1048 (log 20.8) she alters course to 287°M to avoid a fishing boat. What is her EP at 1102 (log 21.7)? Tidal stream 290°T 0.8k.

6.4   At 1845 (log 16.6) a boat is in position 50° 37'.4N 1° 54'.7W. She is on a course 034°M beating against a northerly wind, which causes a leeway of 10°. Her speed is estimated as 3k. At 1918 (log 18.4) she tacks onto a course of 299°M. What is her estimated position and log reading at 1945? Use tidal diamond H (HW Portsmouth 1915, neap tides).

6.5   At 0640 (log 4.4) a boat passes Poole Bar Buoy No 1 making for Christchurch. Her initial course is 068°M and her speed is 5.4k. She is making no leeway. Use tidal diamond H (HW Portsmouth 0100 spring tides). What is her EP at 0710? At what time will the yellow buoy (Dorset Yacht Mark) be abeam?

7 ■ FINDING OUR POSITION

Position lines

In the last chapter we found out how to estimate our position in the absence of suitable navigational marks. Whereas it is essential to keep a record throughout a passage of the estimated position, accurate positions (*fixes*) should be plotted where possible using bearings of suitable land and seamarks that can be identified both visually and on the chart.

We normally use the hand-bearing compass to take the bearings to fix our position. Referring to chart 15, chartlet 2, St Alban's Ledge, and assuming we are in a DR position (approximate) of 50° 35'.2N 1° 55'.4W, we take these bearings:

Anvil Point lighthouse	297°M
Durlston Head	319°M
Peveril Point	356°M

Then we plot these bearings using the course plotter, first converting the magnetic bearings to true bearings allowing for the local variation, which is 3°W:

Anvil Point lighthouse	294°T
Durlston Head	316°T
Peveril Point	353°T

Plot a line from the lighthouse in the opposite direction to the bearing: this line is called a *position line* and will have an arrowhead on the end furthest from the lighthouse. In practice only that part of the position line in the vicinity of the DR position is drawn. We know that our position is somewhere along this position line. A second position line which crosses the first will give our exact position at the point of intersection. To verify the accuracy a third position line (from a third bearing taken at the same time) should pass through the same point.

But looking at Fig 7.1 you can see that the three position lines do not intersect at a common point but form a triangle known as a *cocked hat*. The variation has been correctly applied. The error is due to incorrect identification of Durlston Head because of its 'end on' aspect. There is a prominent castle on Durlston Head which makes a better landmark. The bearing of the castle is 318°M or 315°T which gives a much better fix (Fig 7.2).

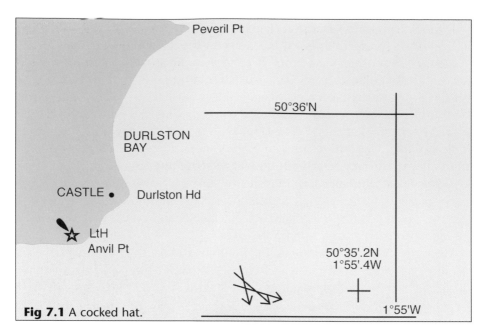

Fig 7.1 A cocked hat.

In practice if three bearings are taken to give three position lines, it is quite likely that a small cocked hat will result particularly if the boat is moving fast or if there is a rough sea. Provided there are no immediate hazards, the centre of a small cocked hat is acceptable as the boat's position. If there is a hazard on the course ahead, you should assume a position at the corner of the cocked hat nearest the hazard.

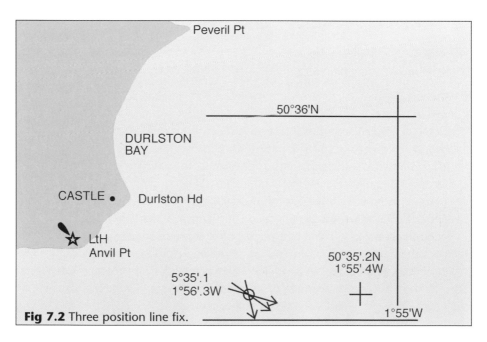

Fig 7.2 Three position line fix.

If you find you have a large cocked hat, you may have applied the variation in the wrong sense; if this is not the case you should take the bearings again.

Ideally two position lines should cross at right angles and three should have a relative difference of 60°. Avoid the temptation to take bearings of objects at greater distances, particularly if there are others nearby. Buoys can be out of position so land-based objects are preferred. A position obtained from two or more bearings of landmarks (or buoys) is known as a fix and is indicated on a chart using the symbol ⊙. Any position on a chart must have the time marked beside it; and it is also a good idea to make a note of the log reading (in the form of distance travelled).

Anvil Point and the distinctive Durlston castle. PHOTO: PHOTO-LINK.

Considerations when taking bearings are:

- Nearer objects are preferred to distant ones as angular differences will cause smaller errors.
- Bearings ahead and astern should be taken first as bearings abeam alter more rapidly.
- The use of left or right hand edges of headlands is acceptable provided they are steep.
- Off-lying features may merge with the background and be difficult to locate.
- Spot heights are useful for identifying sections of a coastline but they are no good for bearings as the highest point on the chart may not in fact be visible from the boat.
- At night, lights must be positively identified from their characteristics. Car headlights or fishing boats bobbing up and down on the waves sometimes give the appearance of the lights of a lighthouse or a buoy.

Transferred position line or running fix

If at any moment we obtain a bearing of a single landmark and sometime later we obtain another single bearing, provided these bearings are different by around 90° we can determine our position.

For example, refer to Fig 7.3. At 1145 Peveril Point bears 352°T. The boat continues on a course of 020°T at a speed of 2.6k with a northwest wind causing 5° of leeway. The tidal stream is 053°T 0.6k. At 1215 Peveril Point bears 265°T.

Plot the 1145 position line on the chart. From any point on this line, normally the closest point to the 1145 DR position, plot the water track (025°T) for the distance travelled between 1145 and 1215 (1.3M). Then add the tidal stream (053°T 0.3M) for the same period. The point obtained is an EP relative to the starting point on the 1145 position line. Then plot the second position line taken at 1215, and transfer the first position line to pass through the EP and to cross the second position line. The point of intersection is the 1215 position. This method of obtaining a fix is known as a *running fix* or a *transferred position line*. The accuracy of a running fix depends on the assessment of the boat's course and speed, the leeway, and the tidal stream. It is not as good a fix as one obtained from two or more bearings taken at the same time.

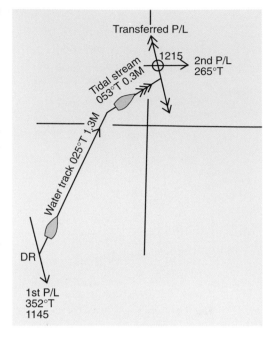

Fig 7.3 Transferred position line.

Line of soundings

An *echo sounder* is an instrument for measuring the depth of water. (The depth measured is actually between the seabed and the sensor or transducer mounted on the boat's hull.) The depth of water when corrected for the height of tide corresponds with the depths shown on the chart (called *soundings*). If your boat is crossing a shelving seabed and you record corrected depths at regular time intervals or regular distances from the log readings, you will have a line of soundings (Fig 7.4).

If you mark this line of soundings on a strip of paper, it can be placed alongside the ground track on the chart and moved forwards or backwards to give you a correlation with the depths shown on the chart.

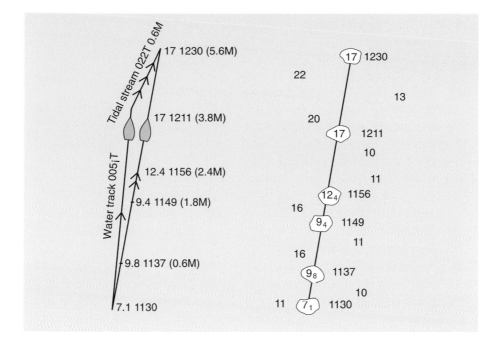

Fig 7.4 Running a line of soundings.

If the depth contours (usually 5m, 10m, 15m) on the chart are regular (fairly straight lines), they can be used as underwater position lines. By following a depth contour (altering course to remain in a constant depth of water) you can often skirt round an underwater hazard in conditions of poor visibility.

Methods used to determine position

- *Two or more visual bearings*: very accurate provided that there is a good angle of cut between the position lines.
- *Transferred position line*: only as accurate as the assessment of water track, distance run and tidal stream.
- *Line of soundings*: the approximate position of the boat must be known and there must be distinguishable features on the seabed.
- *Estimated position*: the best estimate of the boat's position, taking into account the accuracies of the course steered, the distance run, the leeway and the direction and rate of the tidal stream.
- *Dead reckoning*: position obtained only from the course steered and distance run.
- *Satellite navigation using Global Positioning System (GPS)* is very accurate.
- Close inshore, there may not be time to fix the boat's position. A *leading line* allows a rapid appreciation of any tendency for the boat to be set off track. *Clearing bearings* help ensure that navigational hazards are avoided. An *echo sounder* should always be used for verification of position.

QUESTIONS

Use chart 15 and variation 3°W.

7.1 At 1430, log 8.2, a boat on a westerly course is passing south of Hengistbury Head south of Christchurch. The beacon at the end of the groyne bears 059°M and the Coastguard lookout bears 339°M. Plot the position at 1430. What is the latitude and longitude of this position? Comment on the fix.

7.2 At 0800 a boat leaves Swanage on a southerly course. At 0845, log 12.1, she takes bearings of the Castle on Durlston Head of 283°M and the right hand edge of Peveril Point of 333°M. Plot her position at 0845. What is her bearing and range from Anvil Point lighthouse?

7.3 At 1800 a boat on passage from Portland to Poole passes south of St Alban's Head. At 1805, log 23.2, she takes bearings of the left hand edge of St Alban's Head of 272°M, the church spire at Worth Matravers of 314°M and Anvil Point lighthouse of 063°M. Plot her position at 1805. What is the latitude and longitude of this position? Do you consider this fix is satisfactory?

7.4 A boat is on passage from Swanage to Weymouth. At 0645 she rounds Peveril Point. At 0710, log 3.2, the two church spires in Swanage are on a transit of 305°M. At the same time the echo sounder shows a depth of 10 metres. Plot her position at 0710. What is the latitude and longitude of this position? Comment on the accuracy of this fix. Is the hand-bearing compass accurate?

7.5 At 1610, log reading 2.4, a boat in DR position 50° 42'N 1° 46'W takes a bearing of the water tower at Southbourne of 325°M. She then continues on her course of 268°M speed 3.0 knots. At 1640, log 3.9, she takes a second bearing of the water tower of 026°M. The tidal stream was 300°T 1.1k. Plot the position at 1640. What is the latitude and longitude of this position? What is the accuracy of this fix?

8 ▪ HOW DO WE GET THERE?

Course to steer

We need to know our present position both to be sure that we are clear of any hazards and to determine the direction and distance to the next point on our way or passage (a *waypoint*). On a large-scale chart (such as chart 15) we can draw in the desired ground track from waypoint to waypoint and then check our position at regular intervals to ensure that we are close enough to the track and clear of any potential dangers. For longer passages and in poor visibility we must be able to work out the course to steer to the next waypoint compensating for the tidal stream, leeway, variation and deviation with the same degree of accuracy that we required for working out our estimated position.

Referring to chart 15 and chartlet 2, St Alban's Ledge, and chartlet 3, Poole Bay, let us assume that at 0900 we are in position 50° 35'.9N 1° 52'.5W and we want to know the course to steer to a destination position 50° 39'.0N 1° 54'.8W. We first draw a line from our 0900 position to the destination position. This line represents our desired ground track (Fig 8.1).

The distance along the ground track is 3.4M. If we were able to sail directly along the ground track with no leeway or tidal stream at a speed of 4k, we would reach the buoy in 51 minutes at 0951.

$$\frac{3.4 \times 60}{4} = 51 \text{ minutes: that is 0951.}$$

For a tidal stream setting towards 046°T at 1.3k we make allowances in the following manner. The time to reach the buoy will be (as an initial rough estimate) about one hour, so we will use one hour's worth of tidal stream: 046°T 1.3M. The tidal stream is drawn from the 0900 position (Fig 8.2).

In one hour the boat will have travelled through the water a distance of 4.0M. Using the dividers measure a distance of 4.0M on the latitude scale. With one point of the dividers on the end of the tidal stream vector, place the other point of the dividers on the ground track (extending it if necessary) and mark this position. The line from the end of the tidal stream vector to this position is the water track. The position marked will be the estimated position after one hour, that is at 1000, Fig 8.3. We now measure the direction of the water track: 317°T.

In order to convert water track to the correct course to steer to get the ground track we want, we have to compensate for any leeway by steering into the wind: towards the direction from which the wind is blowing. If there were a wind from the northeast causing 10° of leeway, we would need to steer a course of 327°T (Fig 8.4).

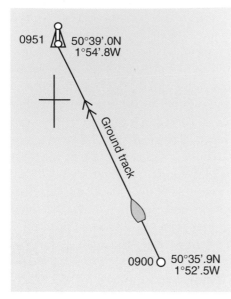

Fig 8.1 Ground track.

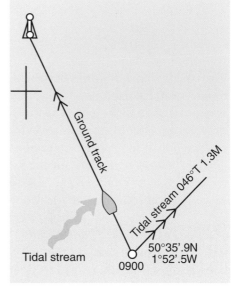

Fig 8.2 Tidal stream.

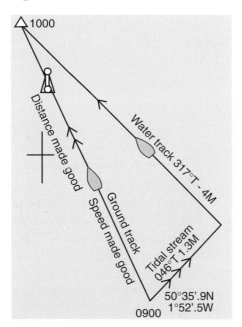

Fig 8.3 Water track, distance and speed made good.

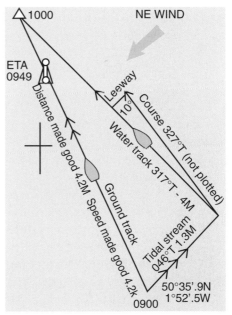

Fig 8.4 Leeway and true course.

The *course to steer*, ie the course given to the helmsman, must include corrections for compass variation and (if necessary) deviation. With a variation of 5°W and zero deviation, our course to steer is 332°C.

The *speed made good* is the distance made good for a period of one hour as measured along the ground track between the positions at 0900 and 1000. It is 4.2k (Fig 8.4).

We may need to know our *estimated time of arrival* or *ETA* at the destination position. The 1000 estimated position is beyond our destination so we will take less than one hour to reach it. From the 0900 position the distance to the destination position, measured along the ground track, is 3.4M. The speed made good is 4.2k. The time taken to reach the buoy is 49 minutes.

$$\frac{3.4}{4.2} \times 60 = 49 \text{ minutes.}$$

So the ETA at our destination is 0949.

Appearances can be deceptive – make sure you really know what headland you are looking at by carefully checking your position. PHOTO: DAVID WILLIAMS.

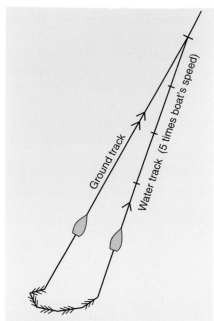

5 hours of tidal stream

Fig 8.5 Plotting a 5-hour vector.

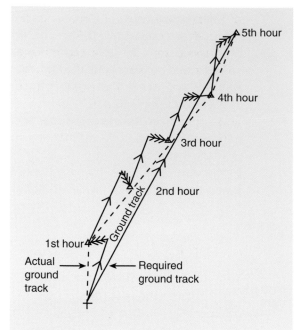

Fig 8.6 Plotting the estimated position hourly shows that the boat is near the required ground track but not on it until the fifth hour.

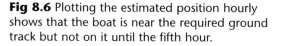

Fig 8.7 Plotting a one-hour vector ▶ using the mean tidal stream for 5 hours.

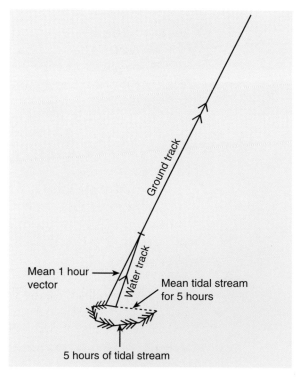

You do not need to use a period of one hour. For instance on a large-scale chart a half-hour period may be more suitable. The distances drawn would correspond to half an hour of tidal stream and half an hour of boat speed giving the distance made good in half an hour (so speed made good would be twice the distance made good).

For a long passage of 5 hours the tidal streams over that period are aggregated together from the starting point; you would draw a distance of 5 times the boat's speed from the tidal stream vectors to the ground track; this line is then the water track, and the point of intersection with the ground track is the estimated position for a time 5 hours after the start (Fig 8.5).

In this case, whilst we can make a reasonable estimate of the course to steer (from the water track), the boat may well not be on the ground track until the end of the passage (Fig 8.6).

An alternative is to determine the mean tidal stream over a period of time and apply it on an hourly basis (Fig 8.7).

QUESTIONS

Use chart 15 and variation 3°W.   All times BST.

8.1 At 1045 (log 11.2) a boat is in position 50° 33'.1N 2° 19'.2W. At a speed of 4.5k, what is the course to steer and the estimated time of arrival (ETA) at Lulworth Cove? The tidal stream is negligible and the wind is SW force 3.

8.2 At 1430 (log 17.3) a boat is in position 50° 29'.0N 2° 11'.0W. At a speed of 5.0k, what is the course to steer for and the ETA at E Shambles East Cardinal buoy? Use tidal diamond F (HW Plymouth is at 1600 and it is a spring tide). Wind is south force 4; there is no leeway.

8.3 At 1015 (log 18.1) a boat is in position 50° 30'.0N 1° 53'.0W making good a speed of 4.0k. To pass south of St Alhan's Ledge, she heads for a position 0.6M south of the yellow danger zone buoy (DZ 'B'). What is her course to steer and ETA at this position? Wind is SW3 and she is making 5° of leeway. Use tidal diamond G (HW Plymouth is at 0415 and it is a spring tide).

8.4 a) At 1230 (log 7.2) a boat leaves Lulworth Cove heading for Poole at a speed of 5k. What is the course to steer for and the ETA at the FlY 5s buoy in the Firing Practice Area (50° 35'.0N 2° 11'.6W)? Use tidal diamond E with HW Plymouth at 1800, neap tides. Wind NW5. No leeway.

b) On arrival at the buoy it is found that the wind blowing against the tidal stream causes an uncomfortable rough sea. It is decided to head for the anchorage at the eastern end of Worbarrow Bay (50° 37'.1N 2° 11'.7W). What is the course to steer for and the ETA at the anchorage? Leeway is 10°.

8.5 At 0705 (log 22.8) a boat is in a position 120°T danger zone buoy (DZ 'B') south of St Alban's Ledge 1.0M. She is making for position 50° 31'.6N 1° 53'.3W. Her speed is 2.5k in a light southerly wind. There is no leeway. Use tidal diamond G (HW Plymouth is at 0835 and it is a spring tide). What is her course to steer and what is her ETA?

9 ■ WEATHER

Before embarking upon any voyage it is essential to have a good look at the weather situation; not just the existing weather, but expected weather for the duration of the whole trip.

Fortunately, there are many excellent sources available to the small craft user, such as weather reports, shipping forecasts, surface analysis charts and satellite pictures to name but a few. You can also derive much valuable information from your own personal observation.

Any sailor needs an elementary understanding of weather systems, with its associated wind and cloud, in order to take full advantage of the services offered. Try and understand the significant features on a surface analysis chart. A visual picture can often explain a situation better than words.

The isobars (lines joining points at the same barometric pressure) are a key feature. The wind follows the direction of the isobars flowing in the northern hemisphere anti-clockwise around a low pressure area. The closer together the isobars, the stronger the wind. The fronts shown on a surface analysis chart are indications of rain and reduced visibility.

Weather systems

Fig 9.1 shows a surface analysis chart that includes high and low pressure systems. Look at the deep low-pressure system with its centre near the Faeroes, surrounded by isobars, giving rise to strong winds over the UK.

In a high pressure system in the northern hemisphere the wind circulates in a clockwise direction at a slight outwards angle across the isobars, whereas in a low pressure system it circulates in an anti-clockwise direction at a slightly inwards angle (Fig 9.2).

So by looking at the chart we can see the different wind directions in the areas covered by the system. The spacing of the isobars also has a relationship to wind strength. The closer together the isobars on the same scale, the stronger the wind.

Low pressure system

When two air masses with very different characteristics meet they do not mix readily. The boundary between them is called a front. Typically, where the warm humid air mass from the tropical regions meets the cold damp air mass

Fig 9.1 Surface pressure charts and forecasts from MetWEB.

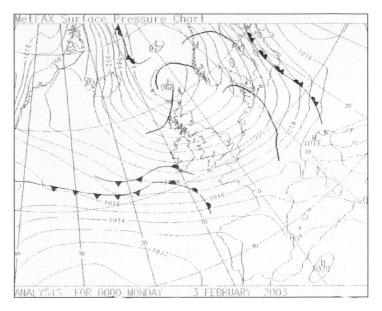

from the polar regions the boundary is called the polar front. Sometimes, however, a wedge shaped portion of rising warm air extends into the colder polar air, and a low-pressure system develops on the earth's surface. The section of the polar front before the warm air is called the *warm front* and the section in front of the cold air is called the *cold front*. Knowing the position of these fronts and their forecast location is useful to the mariner as they exhibit specific weather conditions.

Cumulus clouds are indicators of a cold front approaching. These seem to be developing into cumulonimbus bringing possible squalls.

Weather indications

Visual signs are very important. As well as listening to and studying the weather reports, you should be aware of and able to make use of the changes occurring around you. Cloud observations are of prime importance because they often warn of approaching weather systems, especially depressions. Make a series of observations over several days and use this information alongside other indications such as the barometric trend.

The order in which cloud formations occur during the approach and passage of a typical depression is as follows:

Warm front

Cirrus (Ci) Thread-like delicate clouds high up in the sky, still fine, visibility good.
Cirrostratus (Cs) A veil-like covering lower than cirrus, giving the sky a misty appearance, visibility still good.
Altostratus (As) A layer of cloud thicker and lower than cirrostratus giving a dull effect. Visibility starts to deteriorate with possibly frontal rain or fog.
Nimbostratus (Ns) Very thick and sombre looking layer cloud low in the sky. Visibility deteriorates further in heavier rain.
Fractostratus (Fs) Detached pieces of cloud flying along under the nimbostratus.

During the passage of a warm front, layer cloud (stratus) is often present, whilst at the end nearest the cold front, cumulus appears. There may be rain or snow.

Cold front

Cumulus (Cu) Large cauliflower shaped clouds of great vertical height.
Cumulonimbus (Cb) Cumulus rain cloud of great vertical height spreading out into an anvil shape. This can reach an altitude of 12,000m and bring heavy rain, snow, hail or sleet. There may also be thunder and lightning. Visibility deteriorates during precipitation and frontal fog can occur.

After the passage of a cold front there is a dramatic improvement in visibility, rain stops and skies clear, although there may be showers later.

Temperature
The temperature rises slightly before the warm front, rises on the passage of the front, remains constant in the warm sector and falls as the cold front passes.

Barometric trend
The barometer falls at the approach of the warm front, stays steady in the warm sector, unless the depression is deepening when it will fall further, and rises on the passage of the cold front.

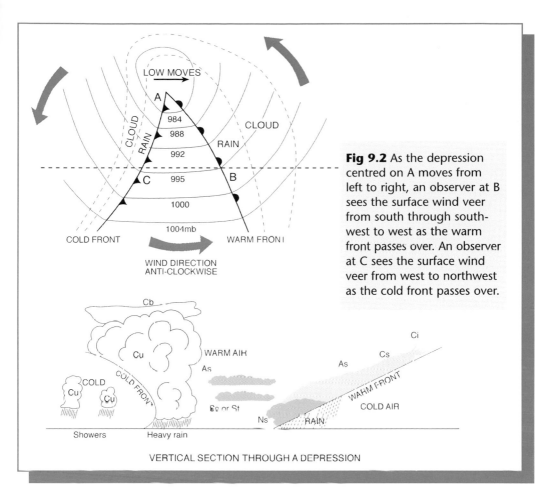

Fig 9.2 As the depression centred on A moves from left to right, an observer at B sees the surface wind veer from south through south-west to west as the warm front passes over. An observer at C sees the surface wind veer from west to northwest as the cold front passes over.

VERTICAL SECTION THROUGH A DEPRESSION

	Warm front		Warm sector	Cold front	
	Approach	*Passage*		*Passage*	*Rear*
Pressure	Steady fall	Stops	Little change	Sudden rise	Rising rapidly at first becoming slower
Wind	Increases	Veers	Little change	Sudden veer	Decreases slowly
Cloud	High cloud becoming lower: Ci, Cs, As, Ns, Fs	Low: Ns, Fs	Overcast: St, Sc	Clouds with great vertical height: Cu, Cb	At first As, Ac. Later Cu, Cb. Blue sky increasing

	Warm front		Warm sector	Cold front	
	Approach	Passage		Passage	Rear
Precipitation	Continuous rain – light becoming medium	Rain turns to drizzle or stops	Intermittent slight rain, drizzle or fog	Heavy rain thunder, maybe hail	Heavy rain clears followed by isolated showers dying out later
Visibility	Good at first, deteriorating in precipitation	Poor, maybe mist or fog	Moderate or poor, mist or fog	Poor in heavy rain	Improves rapidly to good except in showers
Temperature	Slow rise	Rises	Little change	Falls suddenly	Perhaps a slow fall

Wind

The wind backs and increases as the warm front approaches, veers on the passage of the front and remains fairly constant in the warm sector, usually backs a little as the cold front approaches and veers as the front passes.

An occlusion

Because of strong winds behind the cold front, it travels faster than the warm front, eventually catching it up and lifting the air in the warm sector upwards. When this happens the system has occluded and will die out and disappear. The isobars at an occluded front develop a sharp angle and squally conditions can be present.

Trough

A trough occurs in a low-pressure system when the isobars are drawn out into a U or V shape. When this happens on the passage of the cold front it is called a frontal trough. The isobars in a non-frontal trough are more rounded.

High-pressure system (anticyclone)

An anticyclone is usually associated with stable conditions and fine weather. In a high-pressure system, isobars form a round or oval shape. Winds are light and variable near the centre. In the northern hemisphere wind flows out from the centre in a clockwise circulation. If the isobars at the outer edge are squeezed by an approaching low-pressure system, strong winds and gales can occur; a good example of this can be seen in Fig 9.1. In summer the weather is usually dry with clear skies, though there may be cloud and rain at the outer part of the system. Because of the absence of cloud the earth's surface radiates a great deal of heat at night and radiation fog can form which may persist during winter days. Land and sea breezes are more noticeable in this system. Dust or smoke haze often occurs in areas of high pressure.

Ridge of high pressure
This is a tongue-shaped portion of a high-pressure system, which often occurs between two depressions and generally brings fine weather.

Col
This is an area of intermediate pressure and light variable winds occurring between two low- and two high-pressure systems.

Visibility

Conditions affecting visibility include haze caused by smoke or dust particles, heavy rain, hail, snow, mist and fog. Poor visibility is a major hazard, the main dangers of which are being run down by larger shipping, hitting an obstruction or going aground.

Fog
Air holds water as water vapour. The temperature of air determines the amount of water vapour it can hold; the higher the temperature, the more it can hold.

Saturation level When air is holding all the water vapour it possibly can for a given temperature, it is at saturation level and is said to have reached its dew point. If it is then cooled, condensation occurs, and fog will form.

This cooling can be caused by a fall in land temperature, by warm air passing over a cold sea area, or, at a polar front, by the mixing of the warm and cold air masses.

Radiation fog This forms as land cools at night after a relatively warm day, especially if there is a clear sky when a great deal of heat is lost through radiation (see Fig 9.3). If the layer of air in contact with the ground is cooled below its dew point, fog can form.

In summer, temperatures are often high during the day, and nights are short so fog occurs infrequently; in winter the air may be near its dew point during the day, and as the nights are also long and cold fog occurs more often.

Radiation fog forms over land but can drift out to sea for several miles. It is most dense shortly after sunrise when the sun has warmed the land

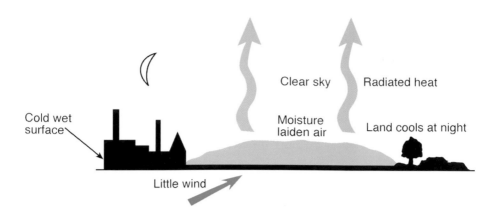

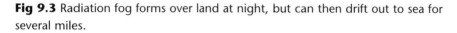

Fig 9.3 Radiation fog forms over land at night, but can then drift out to sea for several miles.

sufficiently to create turbulence, and usually lifts off around midday when the land is warmer.

Favourable conditions for radiation fog include:
- Air which is near its dew point
- A clear sky
- A long, cold night
- A little wind at surface level to create turbulence. Too little wind, and marsh mist, dew or frost will form, too much, and low cloud will develop.

Advection fog When an air mass passes over land or sea which is colder than the air mass dew point, advection fog forms (Fig 9.4). It can persist at sea in winds of up to force 6, as friction, and therefore turbulence, is less over sea than over land. Over land advection fog usually lifts off and becomes stratus cloud in winds greater than force 3.

Advection fog is most likely to occur in spring and early summer when the sea is at its coldest. Tropical maritime air moving along the English Channel over a progressively colder sea surface is a good example of this.

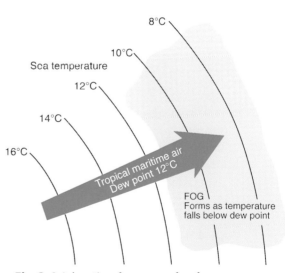

Fig 9.4 Advection fog or sea fog forms when an air mass passes over sea, which is colder than the dew point of the air mass. It can occur in winds up to force 6.

Frontal fog Frontal fog occurs along the boundary of two air masses with very different characteristics when both are near saturation point, such as the warm and cold fronts in a depression.

Land and sea breezes

Land and sea breezes are local winds caused by differential heating between the sea and the land. They occur near the shore and can be felt for several miles either side of the shore, but rarely exceed force 3. More noticeable in calm, windless conditions such as those found in a high-pressure system, they are completely masked in strong winds. These breezes can be very useful for making a coastal passage on an otherwise calm day.

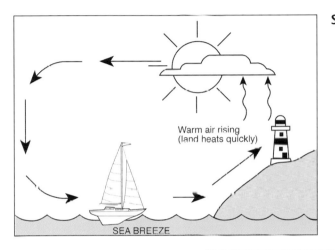

Sea breeze During late morning on a warm sunny day, air in contact with the land warms and rises and is replaced by air drawn in from over the sea. At a higher altitude the rising air cools and flows back out over the sea, eventually sinking to the sea surface and joining the sea breeze circulation. The breeze is strongest during the afternoon.

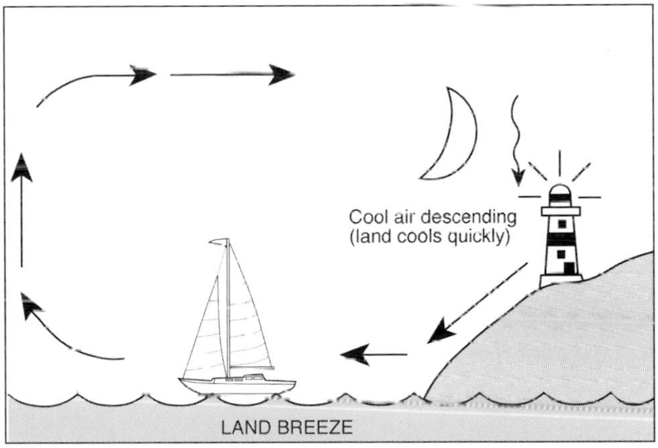

▲ **Fig 9.5** A sea breeze by day is usually fresher than the land breeze at night, but neither normally exceeds force 3.

Fig 9.6 Land breeze. ▶

Land breeze As land temperature falls after sunset, the air in contact with it cools, becomes heavier, sinks, and flows out to sea. The warmer air over the sea rises and, at a higher altitude, flows back towards the land, setting up the land breeze circulation.

77

Anabatic and katabatic winds

Wind can also develop through surface heating and cooling up or down a slope such as a mountainside.

Anabatic wind During the day the sloping surface heats, warming air in contact with it, which rises up the mountainside. This is known as anabatic wind.

Katabatic wind Towards evening the surface temperature of the mountain falls, and the air in contact with it cools, becomes heavier and rolls down the mountainside. This is known as katabatic wind. The steeper the slope, the stronger the wind, which can increase further in strength if funnelled through a valley. If your boat is anchored in the shelter of a bay in a mountainous area you could have a very uncomfortable night in these conditions.

The effect of wind on wave height

In addition to wind strength, we should note that wave height is affected by the following factors.

Fetch The distance the wind has travelled over the sea is called fetch. Wave height tends to increase the further the wind has travelled, particularly if it is blowing off the shore. The further a boat is offshore, the greater the wave height.

Duration The length of time the wind has been blowing in the same direction is also important. Initially waves may be short and steep, but as the wind continues they lengthen and increase in height. If the wind suddenly changes direction, say through 90°, a cross-wave pattern is established. The existing pattern does not stop immediately and this results in very confused seas. An example of this is a wind shift as a cold front passes.

Shallow water effect Wind blowing towards the shore over a shoaling seabed causes waves to shorten and increase in height, eventually toppling and causing surf. In strong winds it is dangerous to approach a lee shore.

Tidal stream The sea will be much flatter when the wind is blowing in the same direction as the tidal stream. Conversely, the sea can be rough when the wind is blowing in the opposite direction to the tidal stream. Particular areas to avoid in strong winds are tide races or overfalls. These are marked on large-scale charts.

Reflected waves Waves hitting a harbour wall or breakwater in relatively deep water are reflected back and interact with further incoming waves causing a steep confused sea which may make entry to the harbour difficult or dangerous.

This dinghy is powering along nicely under a stiff breeze.

Forecasts

As well as keeping up-to-date with the immediate weather prospects, it is important that you know the position of weather systems and their possible movement. This not only helps you to assess the likely weather in the area in which you plan to sail, it also shows you what to expect in the adjacent areas through which you may sail. In addition it helps to determine probable wind shifts and strengths.

The information comes in the form of a weather map known as a *surface analysis chart* or a *surface pressure chart*, which can be obtained by fax from the Meteorological Office. The British Broadcasting Corporation (BBC) also broadcast a shipping forecast that contains sufficient information to plot a simple version of such a chart.

It is difficult to forecast exactly the speed and direction of approaching weather systems, and weather patterns often change more quickly than expected so that different conditions are experienced from those forecast. This is why it is important to check all available sources throughout the day, and if possible obtain the local forecast.

Shorthand for recording forecasts

A form of shorthand is needed to record forecast information because the detail is only given once, and often faster than can be written normally. It is also helpful to have a prepared form if available. It is useful if all crew members use the same notation so that anybody referring to the form later will understand it. It is therefore a good idea to use standard abbreviations such as the Beaufort notation, an extract of which is shown below.

d =	drizzle	z	= dust haze
f =	fog	G	= good visibility
g =	gale	M	= moderate visibility
jp =	precipitation within sight	P	= poor visibility
m =	mist	o	= slight
q =	squalls	i	= intermittent
r =	rain	/	= after conditions in the last hour
s =	snow	double letters	= continuous
w =	dew	capital letters	= intense

falling

falling quickly

falling slowly

falling more slowly

steady

rising

Shipping forecast

The BBC broadcast a shipping forecast four times a day on Radio 4 (LW, MW or FM). These are at 0048 LW, MW and FM; 0535 LW, MW and FM; 1201 LW only; and 1754 LW only.

Extract from a shipping forecast broadcast at 0535 BST

> Here is the shipping forecast issued by the Meteorological Office at 0500 BST: There are warnings of gales in: **Cromarty, Forth, Tyne, Irish Sea, Malin, Hebrides.** The general synopsis at midnight: Low southeast Rockall 984 moving rather quickly northeast and filling. Associated trough **Fastnet, Sole** and **Fitzroy.**

The sea area forecasts for the next 24 hours:

> **Dover, Wight, Portland, Plymouth:** Southwest 5 to 6 veering north later, poor in fog patches.

Reports from coastal stations at 0400:

> **Jersey:** WSW 5, drizzle, 1 mile, 1013, steady.
>
> **Channel auto:** WSW 5, drizzle, 1 mile, 1011, steady.
>
> **Scilly auto:** WSW 6, heavy rain, 1 mile, 1008, steady.

With the introduction of facsimile machines small enough to be carried onboard, and the excellent information obtainable from the Meteorological Office, there are few occasions when you will find it necessary to plot a chart from the shipping forecast. It is usually sufficient to be aware of the position and movement of the pressure systems which are given in the general synopsis and to make a note of the present and forecast weather in the sea area concerned together with the reports from the relevant coastal stations. In unsettled weather, conditions can change unexpectedly, and it is wise to carefully monitor relevant sources of information, including direct observations.

Reports from coastal stations

Reports from Coastal Weather Stations are included after the 0048 and the 0535 shipping forecasts.

Inshore waters forecast

The forecast for all UK inshore waters up to 12 miles offshore covering a period up to 1800 is broadcast after the 0048 and 0535 shipping forecasts.

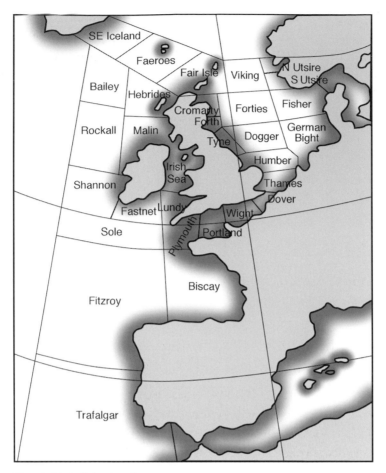

Fig 9.7 UK Shipping forecast areas

It includes a general synopsis, forecasts of wind direction and force, visibility and weather. After the 0048 broadcast, latest reports from additional coastal weather stations are given, including wind direction and force, visibility, barometric pressure and tendency.

Gale warnings
Gale warnings for UK shipping forecast areas are broadcast on BBC Radio 4 LW and FM at the first available programme juncture after receipt. If this does not coincide with a news bulletin, it will be repeated after the next news bulletin.

Land forecasts
Land area forecasts are broadcast at various times on Radio 4. They are extremely useful in conjunction with the shipping forecast especially when the centre of a weather system is over land. Details in daily newspapers and TV/Radio guides.

Leisure users forecast

On Sunday only, at 0542, a seven day planning outlook is broadcast on FM 92.4–94.6 MHz and LW 198 kHz (1515m), which includes weather patterns likely to affect UK waters. On Saturdays only at 0556 a leisure users forecast is broadcast.

Local radio stations

Both the BBC and local independent radio stations often repeat the portion of the shipping forecast covering their own area. Some stations also broadcast Small Craft Warnings (winds of more than force 6 expected within the next 12 hours up to 5 miles offshore). Details in most nautical almanacs.

HM Coastguard

The Coastguard broadcast weather forecasts at regular intervals. These include gale and strong wind warnings. Some Coastguards may also give local weather conditions and repeat the local forecasts on request. Details of times and operating channels are given in nautical almanacs.

Internet (MetWEB)

A range of meteorological information is available over the Internet including MetFAX marine services. The Meteorological website is: www.metoffice.com.

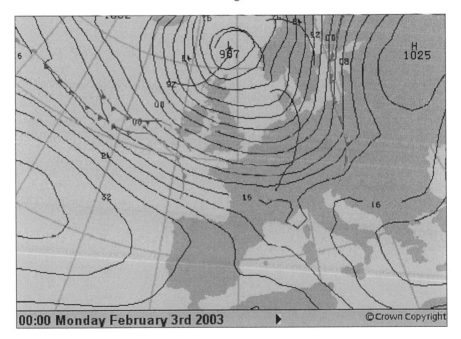

This is one of three animated charts, produced by the Met Office, showing surface pressure analysis for Europe for three days and which is available to view on the internet. CROWN COPYRIGHT.

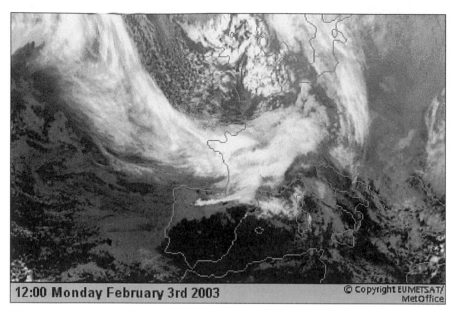

12:00 Monday February 3rd 2003 © Copyright EUMETSAT/ MetOffice

This infrared image of Europe shows the cooler cloud tops as white against the darker, warmer land and sea. CROWN COPYRIGHT.

Marinecall SELECT
Marinecall SELECT is an independently operated telephone weather information service. Most reports are updated hourly and give the following information: wind/gusts, visibility, weather, cloud, temperature, barometric pressure. After these reports, a 2 to 5 day forecast is available. Details in nautical almanacs.

MetCALL Direct
This is a telephone consultancy service allowing direct access to a forecaster. The call can be made from the United Kingdom or the Continent. Details in telephone directory. Payment by credit card.

Newspapers
Some newspapers print weather information that may include a synoptic chart. Because of the time interval between the initial forecast and publication, they are of limited value but they can be used in conjunction with other sources.

Television
Television forecasts often show a synoptic chart and satellite picture, which provide a useful guide to the general weather pattern.

Local sources
In addition to the services provided by the Met Office for a local area, it is often useful to ask advice from local services such as fishermen, yacht clubs, harbour-masters, marina staff, as these people will be aware of any local peculiarities.

Meteorological terms

Anabatic wind A wind blowing up a mountainside, caused by warm air rising.

Backing An anticlockwise change in wind direction.

Col An area of intermediate pressure and variable winds between two adjacent highs and two adjacent lows.

Forecast Details of the expected weather.

Imminent A situation which is expected within six hours.

Isobar Lines on a weather chart joining points of equal pressure.

Katabatic wind A wind blowing down a mountainside caused by cool air descending.

Later A situation which is expected after 12 hours.

Millibar A unit used to measure pressure on a barometer (barometers can also be scaled in inches).

Movement of Systems:

Slowly	=	< 15 knots
Steadily	=	15–25 knots
Rather quickly	=	25–35 knots
Rapidly	=	35–45 knots
Very rapidly	=	> 45 knots

Precipitation Deposits of water such as rain, hail, snow, frost and dew (not mist, fog or cloud).

Pressure Tendency:

Rising or falling slowly	=	0.1 mb–1.5 mb in the preceding 3 hours
Rising or falling	=	1.6 mb–3.5 mb in the preceding 3 hours
Rising or falling quickly	=	3.6 mb–6.0 mb in the preceding 3 hours
Rising or falling rapidly	=	more than 6.0 mb in the preceding 3 hours

'Now rising/now falling' pressure has been falling, rising or steady in the preceding 3 hours but at the time of the observation was definitely rising or falling.

Report Details of the existing weather.

Ridge Usually an elongated portion of an anticyclone.

Soon A situation which is expected between 6–12 hours.

Trough An elongated portion of a depression with V-shaped isobars (all fronts are troughs).

Veering A clockwise change in wind direction.

Visibility:

Fog	Less than 1000 metres
Poor	Between 1000 metres and 2 nautical miles
Moderate	Between 2 and 5 nautical miles
Good	More than 12 nautical miles.

Beaufort wind scale

No	Description	Limit of mean wind speed (knots)	Appearance	Approximate wave height (metres)
0	Calm	less than 1	Like a mirror	0
1	Light air	1 to 5	Ripples like scales	less than 0.1
2	Light breeze	4 to 6	Small wavelets	0.1 to 0.3
3	Gentle breeze	7 to 10	Large wavelets: a few white horses	0.3 to 0.9
4	Moderate breeze	11 to 16	Small waves: frequent white horses	0.9 to 1.5
5	Fresh breeze	17 to 21	Moderate waves: many white horses	1.5 to 2.5
6	Strong breeze	22 to 27	Large waves: white foam crests	2.5 to 4
7	Near gale	28 to 33	Sea heaps up: waves break	4 to 6
8	Gale	34 to 40	Moderately high waves of greater length beginning to break	6 to 8
9	Severe gale	41 to 47	High waves: breaking, spray	8 to 10
10	Storm	48 to 55	Very high waves	10 to 12
11	Violent storm	56 to 63	Extremely high waves	12 to 16
12	Hurricane	64 to 71	Heaped up white sea, visibility affected	

QUESTIONS

9.1 A boat is berthed in Poole Harbour and planning to sail to Plymouth after the early morning shipping forecast. The relevant extract from the shipping forecast was as follows:

Shipping Forecast issued at 0500 BST.
Warnings of gales Cromarty, Forth, Tyne, Irish Sea, Malin, Hebrides
General synopsis at midnight: Low Northern Ireland moving rapidly NE and filling associated trough Irish Sea Lundy Fastnet Sole
Area Forecast Dover Wight Portland Plymouth SW 5–6 veering NW 7 later poor fog patches
Reports from coastal stations at 0400 Channel Light Vessel Auto WSW 5 drizzle 1 mile 1009 steady Scilly Auto WSW 6 heavy showers 10 miles 1006 rising rapidly

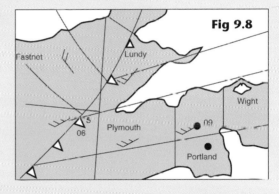

Fig 9.8 is an extract from the surface analysis chart for time of shipping forecast. After studying this extract comment on the viability of the passage.

9.2 The day has been warm and the sky is clear during the early part of the night. A boat anchors overnight in a bay intending to continue her passage along the coastline the next morning. About an hour after dawn she finds the coastline obscured by fog. What action should she take?

9.3 An anticyclone is predominant and the conditions have been calm and generally windless over the past few days. A boat is considering a passage close inshore along the coast. Throughout the day, what are the wind conditions likely to be?

9.4 Of what use is a surface analysis chart?

9.5 A boat enters an anchorage close to a mountain range. The day has been sunny with light winds blowing onshore. As evening approaches an offshore wind develops and steadily increases throughout the night making the anchorage very uncomfortable. What is the reason?

10 ■ PLANNING AHEAD

Before embarking on any sea passage, whether it is just a trip out of the harbour or a voyage across the English Channel, it is necessary to plan things well beforehand. Here are some of the things to do:

■ You should check all your charts to see whether they need updating; obtain the latest Notices to Mariners to see that no corrections have been missed. A visit to the harbourmaster's office usually pays dividends as he will have details of any activities or changes within the harbour limits such as dredging or maintenance of navigational marks.

■ You will need a small-scale chart initially to plan the voyage with larger-scale charts for coastal passages. The largest-scale charts will be required for harbours or anchorages.

■ Read the relevant sailing directions.

■ Look over the sails; check standing and running rigging, safety equipment, wet weather gear, cooking facilities and engine. Check the batteries. Check the dinghy and outboard motor. Make sure that the crew are familiar with the location of safety equipment and emergency procedures.

■ Start a record of the general weather pattern.

■ Work out the starting time for the voyage, taking into consideration tides and daylight hours. Check the tides at the destination, bearing in mind the opening times of locks and basins. Measure the mileage, inspect the tidal streams and make a rough estimate of the time to complete the passage allowing for the boat's normal cruising speed. Check times of sunrise and sunset. Fill in the tidal stream atlas. Draw in the proposed track and check for any hazards on the way. If you are using an electronic position fixing system, mark in the waypoints. Highlight any conspicuous landmarks. For a night passage, list the characteristics together with the visibility range and bearing of all lights likely to be encountered (remembering that buoys are not generally visible at a range greater than 2M). Establish alternative destinations in case of unforeseen circumstances.

■ Before the passage, fill up with water and fuel and check that a spare gas bottle (for the cooker) is on board. Stow all gear below and secure all items on deck. Get the latest weather forecast. Ensure that a responsible person ashore knows both the details of your passage and who will be on board. As soon as departure time is confirmed, work out the DR positions (and estimated positions if time) for the first leg of the passage.

■ As the harbour entrance is cleared, set the log to zero and give the helms-

Before leaving harbour, you need to brief your crew on the passage ahead and do a series of checks; make up your own checklist and delegate tasks. PHOTO: DAVID WILLIAMS.

man the course to steer (assuming if under sail that the course to steer is not into the wind). As soon as the boat's speed can be established, check the estimated positions for the first part of the passage

■ If the course to steer is into the wind, it is important to establish from the helmsman the best course he can steer on each tack. When beating to windward (making a series of tacks into the wind) the navigator will need to decide when to tack to make best use of any tidal streams and to keep clear of any navigational hazards. In anticipation of any shift in wind direction, keep within 5M of the desired track, reducing this distance progressively as the destination or waypoint is approached. (Keep within a cone of 20° from the desired track as measured from the destination.)

■ Fix the boat's position regularly: at least every 30 minutes if within sight of land. Compare the estimated positions and fixes to make allowance for any deviation from the desired track. Record the log reading every hour; and the barometric pressure and wind direction and speed at least every four hours. The deck log should contain sufficient navigational information so that the broad details of the passage could be re-created at a later date.

■ If the weather conditions are deteriorating, be prepared to make for an alternative destination or to turn back.

■ When the ETA (estimated time of arrival) at the destination is established, re-check any restrictions due to tidal stream or height of tide. Be prepared to anchor or pick up a mooring near the entrance. Check for local signals restricting entry to the harbour or any tidal basins.

Tell the Coastguard your passage plan before leaving. PHOTO: COURTESY OF HM COASTGUARD *(DOVER).*

- Frequently when entering an unfamiliar harbour, it is not clear where a visitor should go initially. Use of a VHF radio (if available) to call up the local marina or harbourmaster is ideal. If visitors' moorings or berths can be identified, they should be used. Otherwise it may be necessary to secure to a vacant buoy or pontoon whilst seeking advice on berthing. Should the owner return meanwhile, at least he will be able to give guidance on an alternative berth; but be prepared to move at short notice.
- All seagoing boats should register with HM Coastguard using Form CG66. This means that, in the event of emergency, the Coastguard have on file details of the boat and owner. The Coastguard recommend nomination of a shore contact who will normally have details of any passages planned.

What part does the weather play?

Mist and fog
One of the worst hazards at sea is poor visibility. All visual landmarks disappear. Consequently electronic aids to navigation become most desirable and should be constantly monitored. It is also essential to plot the DR or EP regularly. If fog is forecast, frequent fixes must be taken until landmarks are no longer visible. A steady course should be steered and distance run recorded.

Be prepared to change the passage destination for one which can be safely reached before visibility deteriorates. It is relatively straightforward to avoid underwater hazards; the main problem is collision with other vessels. Always travel at a safe speed.

However, suppose we set out on a clear sunny day not expecting a change. The horizon has become indistinct; the fishing boats that have passed are becoming blurred; the sun's rays seem less warming – definite signs of an approaching fog bank. What actions should we take?

1 **Get a fix.** Try to get a fix of the boat's position by any means available. Record the time and log reading. If this is not possible, work out the estimated position from the last known position. Draw on the chart the anticipated course and DR positions for the next few hours. Use all available navigational aids. Switch on the echo sounder and navigation lights.

2 **Note positions and direction of travel** of any other shipping, particularly any vessels that might pass close by.

3 **Take safety precautions.** Hoist radar reflector; check fog-signalling apparatus; put on lifejackets; check that the liferaft is ready to launch, inflate the dinghy and tow it astern; if under sail, check that the engine is ready to start immediately; post a look-out in the bows; maintain silence; brief all crew on deck to listen for fog signals from other vessels.

4 **Review the passage plan.** Decide whether to maintain the present course and destination, go out to sea, or anchor in shallow water. If following a buoyed channel, *list the buoys and their characteristics, with distances and directions from one buoy to the next.* Tick each buoy as it is passed and compare elapsed time with distance run. Use an echo sounder to keep within the channel and be aware which side of the boat the deeper water lies.

5 **Approaching a harbour** clear of any outlying dangers, *set a course towards one side of the entrance.* When the shoreline is sighted or a particular depth contour reached, there is no doubt which way to alter course for the harbour entrance. With a strong tidal stream across the entrance, set a course well upstream so that the tidal stream will be fair when the shoreline is sighted.

6 **Listen for the fog signals of lighthouses.** It is not easy to determine the direction of sound in fog but try to keep it on a constant bearing.

Strong winds

Slow-moving zones of high pressure give settled and stable weather. There can be strong winds but they are usually steady in strength and direction. Areas of low pressure cause unsettled weather with much cloud, poor visibility, rain, and winds which vary in strength and direction. In the northern hemisphere, air circulates in a clockwise direction in a high pressure system and in an anticlockwise direction around a low pressure system.

It is important to record regularly barometric pressure, wind strength and direction and to observe cloud formation. For a small boat of length less than 9 metres, a wind of strength less than force 6, which is a wind speed of 25 knots, is normally the limit of comfortable sailing. A larger boat may be able to cope with gale force 8 (35 knots).

Running downwind is more comfortable than beating to windward; however, it is the combination of wind and sea-state which affect the ability of a sailing boat to make a safe passage in strong winds. If the wind is blowing in the opposite direction to the tidal stream, the sea may become very rough, particularly at spring tides. Under these conditions shoal water, tide races and overfalls can become dangerous even though charted depth may be adequate. In open seas a wave pattern can build up which is not particularly hazardous in itself, but if the wind changes another wave pattern can be superimposed on the original which causes very rough seas. This effect can also occur near (within a half mile of) a sea wall where the reflected wave is superimposed on the original.

Provided a boat is well constructed and equipped, the sails are reefed, and the crew are not prone to seasickness, then strong winds need be no deterrent to the completion of a passage, provided sensible precautions are observed. More prudence may be required before setting off on a long passage with a forecast of strong winds and the following precautions should be observed:

- Most emergencies in rough weather are caused by the failure of the crew rather than the boat. Tiredness, cold and hunger increase the likelihood of seasickness. If you anticipate an extended sea passage, let any crew not required on deck go below to rest. Wind chill cools quicker than most people realise, so extra warm clothes must be put on early before shivering starts. Encourage everyone to have a substantial hot meal before a night passage and at breakfast time. Make sure that there is a good supply of snack foods and drinks readily available. If necessary make a large box of sandwiches. Above all, issue seasickness tablets well in advance, not just as the motion starts to deteriorate.
- In a small boat it is very difficult to navigate in rough weather. Often the deck log is not kept up to date: with no log readings and course alterations recorded, it is impossible to estimate a position. Usually it is not easy to remain at the chart table for prolonged periods without feeling queasy. The solution is careful preparation. The charts should be stowed accessibly in the order that they will be required. All tidal information should be extracted from the almanac and recorded in a 'navigator's notebook'. Fill in the time of high water and the hours before and after high water on the tidal stream diagrams. For all harbours along the route of the passage, key information should be noted: direction of tidal streams in the approach; conspicuous landmarks; characteristics of lights and buoys; details of clearing bearings and transits. Each chart should be marked up with the route including the compass course for each change of direction; together with highlighting of all hazards and conspicuous landmarks, clearing bearings, and change-over positions from one chart to the next.
- Secure the boat for sea. In a rough sea everything that can move will move. Keeping accessible those items that may be required, lash down or secure

Beating to windward in a fresh breeze –
for some this is what sailing is all about.
PHOTO DAVID WILLIAMS.

everything else so that it cannot shift about. Check all hatches are secure. The anchor may be better lashed inboard rather than over the bow.

- Reef the sails early; you will find it much easier to increase sail if the wind drops than to shorten sail if the wind increases. When the wind increases enough for sails to be reefed, make sure that all your crew on deck and in the cockpit are wearing safety harnesses and have clipped them on to the safety lines or strong points. Do not use guardrails for securing safety harnesses: they are not strong enough to take the snatch load of a person falling overboard.

- If you decide to anchor or remain in an anchorage, you will need more anchor cable in strong winds. In fair weather if the anchor cable is all chain, then the simple rule is 4 × maximum depth of water; if the cable is a short length (6m) of chain backed by a nylon warp, then let out 6 × *maximum depth of water*. In strong winds let out 8 x *maximum depth of water*; and, if possible, let go a second anchor.

Lee shore

For hundreds of years seafaring yarns have recounted the hazards of a lee shore. If there is a shoreline on the leeward side of the boat, it is called a lee shore. It is a shoreline on to which the wind is blowing. A powerless vessel will be blown by the wind on to a lee shore. If the seabed gradually shelves upwards to the shore, then in strong onshore winds the waves will build up into breakers which will crash down on the coastline. Any vessel caught up in these breakers has little chance of survival. Any harbour with its entrance or approach open to windward becomes extremely hazardous in strong winds. A small craft at sea should keep clear of a lee shore in heavy weather and should not contemplate entering such a harbour. Not a happy decision if you are the skipper of a small boat with nightfall approaching and your crew is tired, cold and seasick.

Weather forecasts

To avoid some of the problems of poor visibility and strong winds, careful attention should be paid to weather forecasts. The sources are given in Chapter 9.

QUESTIONS

10.1 Before planning a passage, what measures would you take to see that your charts are up to date?

10.2 What charts and other nautical publications will you need before a passage?

10.3 What action might you take up to five days before the proposed passage to determine the weather forecast?

10.4 How would you prepare the boat before a passage lasting several days?

10.5 What chart preparation can be done before a passage?

11 ■ PILOTAGE AND PASSAGE PLANS

Pilotage plan

It is 15 May. The weather forecast is not too good. You are in Salterns marina and you plan to spend the next day looking around Poole Harbour. You decide to go around Brownsea Island via South Deep returning later in the day to the Town Quay Boat Haven (Dolphin Boat Haven) at Poole.

Prepare a pilotage plan. Your boat draws 1.2m; assume clearance of 0.5m. Examine Stanfords chart 15: Poole Harbour plans.

There is sufficient depth of water round past Cleavel Point south of Green Island northwestward as far as Ramshorn Lake. To the west of Brownsea Island the least charted depths are 0.3m in Ramshorn Lake, 0.3m southwest of Pottery Pier and 0.7m northward in Wills Cut (crossing Middle Mud).

Tides
Use Extract 8 and Extract 9.

May 16 Poole	HW	LW		HW	LW	
GMT	2.0	0628	0.7	2.0	1848	0.8
BST	2.0	0728	0.7	2.0	1948	0.8

Range of tide 1.3m
Minimum depth required (boat's draught + clearance) = 1.7m
Least depth on passage = 0.3m
Minimum height of tide required = 1.4m

From tidal curves (Fig 11.1), there is sufficient depth of water for the passage from 0908 to 1758.

Tidal stream
Tidal stream east of Brownsea Island:
Below 1.0k except

S-going	LW − 2½ to LW − ½ (1718–1918)
N-going	LW + ½ to LW + 3½ (0758–1058)

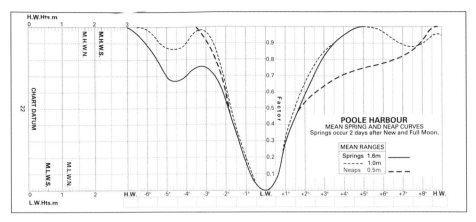

Fig 11.1 Poole tidal curves

Key times

- Boat speed 3k
- Get to Town Quay Boat Haven by 1800
- Leave Salterns Marina around 1030
- Distance Salterns Marina to Goathorn Point 2.0M – 40 minutes
- Distance Goathorn Point to Cleavel Point 1.0M – 20 minutes
- Distance Cleavel Point to Pottery Pier 1.0M – 20 minutes
- Pottery Pier to Town Quay 1½M – 30 minutes

Brownsea east cardinal buoy looking south towards South Deep. PHOTO: PHOTO-LINK.

Plan

Out of Salterns Marina turn to port and follow buoyed channel. Leave Brownsea Road Bell buoy (south cardinal mark) to starboard, North Haven Point to port, Brownsea east cardinal mark to starboard to enter South Deep. Follow beacons past Goathorn Point to port. On approaching Furzey Island, having passed beacons No 20 and No 19, turn to port on a course of 265ºM coming round to 215ºM, identifying edge of channel marked by stakes clear to starboard. Locate port and starboard beacons off Cleavel Point and follow South Deep channel round to the west of Green Island. Locate the green starboard hand beacon at the entrance to Ramshorn Lake. The water is very shallow here so proceed with utmost caution, carefully observing the echo sounder. Follow the line of stakes to starboard. Pass the west cardinal beacon to starboard and the south cardinal beacon to port. Continue following the staked channel to Pottery Pier (to starboard). (Note here that the buoyage system appears to change as you are now technically leaving harbour.) Locate and pass two red beacons to starboard and a green beacon to port. Locate the east cardinal beacon at the entrance to Wills Cut, leaving it to port, then follow a northerly course along the line of stakes leaving the second east cardinal beacon to port. From this beacon head north through the Little Channel to Poole Town Quay Boat Haven.

Passage plan:

Poole Town Quay Boat Haven to Dartmouth

You have a sailing yacht named STARLIGHT, which is currently berthed at Poole Town Quay Boat Haven. Her draught is 1.2m. She has a good engine, which enables you to maintain a passage speed of 4k if the wind is insufficient. Next weekend, 20/21 July, you are thinking about making a passage to Dartmouth, Devon. Prepare a passage plan.
[*Note: The extracts and chart 15 do not contain all the relevant data for planning purposes.*]

Charts

The first thing is to collect together the relevant charts, ensuring that they are corrected up-to-date, and the appropriate almanacs and pilots. Fortunately virtually all the relevant information (except the charts) is contained in *Macmillan Reeds Nautical Almanac*, which is reprinted annually so it does not become dated. The Stanfords charts required are 12 – *Needles to Start Point*, 15 – *Dorset Harbours and approaches* and 22 – *South Devon Harbours*.

Studying the charts and the pilotage information, the principal hazards are the tide races off St Alban's Ledge and Portland Bill and the Firing Practice Area off Lulworth Cove. The passage information, Extract 10, recommends that small craft should avoid the Portland Race by passing clear to seaward of it: between 3 and 5M south of the Bill. Shambles Bank, 3M east of Portland Bill, should be avoided by passing 2M south of East Shambles buoy. The St Alban's Ledge Race and the Firing Practice Area can be safely passed by going 1 mile south of DZ 'B' buoy on St Alban's Ledge. Peveril Ledge should be passed 1 mile to seaward on a west-going stream against a southwest wind. Handfast Point needs to be given a berth of half a mile.

Now make up a list of waypoints (Fig 11.2).

Waypoint	Location	Latitude	Longitude	Next waypoint	
				Course °M	Distance M
WYP 1	Poole Bar Buoy No 1	50° 39'.3N	1° 55'.2W	147	1.0
WYP 2	½M E of Handfast Pt	50° 38'.5N	1° 54'.3W	195	2.2
WYP 3	1M E of Peveril Pt	50° 36'.4N	1° 55'.0W	233	2.2
WYP 4	½M S of Anvil Pt	50° 35'.0N	1° 57'.6W	238	6.5
WYP 5	1M S of DZ 'B' buoy	50° 31'.3N	2° 05'.7W	258	9.7
WYP 6	2M S of E Shambles buoy	50° 28'.8N	2° 20'.1W	262	4.7
WYP 7	3M S of Portland Bill	50° 27'.9N	2° 27'.4W	262	41.4
WYP 8	Dartmouth – Castle Ledge buoy	50° 20'.0N	3° 33'.1W		

Fig 11.2 Waypoints – Poole to Dartmouth (variation 3°W)

Handfast Point and Old Harry Rocks from the north with Durlston Head in the background. PHOTO: PHOTO-LINK.

At this moment you receive a telephone call from a friend who says he is intending to make a passage from Lymington to Dartmouth during the same weekend. He proposes meeting for lunch in Lulworth Cove on Saturday, cruising in company that afternoon to Weymouth, and continuing to Dartmouth on Sunday. This seems reasonable to you as the weather and tidal streams are all favourable. It is necessary, however, to amend the waypoint list (Fig 11.3).

Waypoint	Location	Latitude	Longitude	Next waypoint	
				Course °M	Distance M
WYP 1	Poole Bar Buoy No 1	50° 39'.3N	1° 55'.2W	147	1.0
WYP 2	½M E of Handfast Pt	50° 38'.5N	1° 54'.3W	195	2.2
WYP 3	1M E of Peveril Pt	50° 36'.4N	1° 55'.0W	233	2.2
WYP 4	½M S of Anvil Pt	50° 35'.0N	1° 57'.6W	261	3.8
WYP 5	½M S of St Alban's Head	50° 34'.2N	2° 03'.5W	294	7.8
WYP 6	Entrance to Lulworth Cove	50° 37'.0N	2° 14'.8W		

Fig 11.3 Waypoints – Poole to Lulworth Cove (variation 3°W)

These waypoints can now be entered, where appropriate, into the Global Positioning System (GPS) receiver and Yeoman Plotter.

Weather

The *Reeds and Marinecall* weather summary for the weekend 20/21 July was:

General An anticyclone over the British Isles will slowly decline as a shallow low moves E across Scotland on Friday. This low will move into the central North Sea on Saturday, deepening on Sunday while the anticyclone shifts into the E Atlantic at the same time.

Saturday All areas. Light or moderate winds mainly N to NW. The weather will be a mixture of sunny or clear periods and scattered showers. Visibility will be good, falling to moderate in scattered showers.

Sunday Winds will be light to moderate N to NW. The weather will be a mixture of sunny or clear periods and scattered showers. Visibility good.

The forecast surface analysis chart and satellite image for 20 July are shown in Figs 11.4 and 11.5.

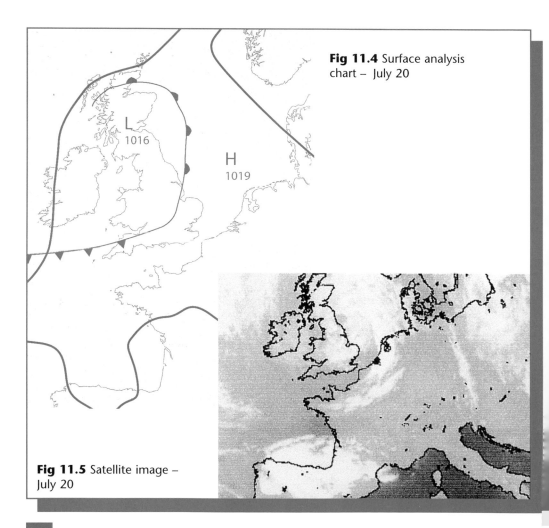

Fig 11.4 Surface analysis chart – July 20

Fig 11.5 Satellite image – July 20

Tides
Use Extracts 1, 4 and 8.

	LW		HW		LW		HW		Range
	Time	Height	Time	Height	Time	Height	Time	Height	
Dover									
20 July GMT	0152	1.6	0731	5.6	1414	1.8	1957	5.8	4.0
Dover									
20 July BST	0252		0831		1514		2057		
Dover									
21 July GMT	0301	1.6	0837	5.7	1536	1.7	2105	5.9	4.2
Dover									
21 July BST	0401		0937		1636		2205		

	HW	HW
	Time	Time
Portsmouth		
20 July GMT	0727	2001
Portsmouth		
20 July BST	0827	2101
Portsmouth		
21 July GMT	0839	2107
Portsmouth		
21 July BST	0939	2207

	LW	LW
	Time	Time
Poole		
20 July GMT	0023	1253
Poole		
20 July BST	0123	1353

Tidal streams (see chart 15)

	Off St Alban's	Off Portland
West-going	HW to HW + 5	HW to HW + 5
East-going	HW − 6 to HW − 1	HW − 6 to HW − 1

High Water at Dover

	Off Poole approaches
South-going	HW − 1 to HW + 4
North-going	HW + 5 to HW − 2

High Water at Portsmouth

Off Brownsea Island	
South-going (ebb)	LW + 5 to LW
Slack	LW + 3 to LW + 5

Low Water at Poole

Departure

There are no problems with the weather as forecast. For a long passage it is important to make the most of the favourable tidal stream. The west-going stream off St Alban's Ledge starts at HW Dover, which, on 20 July, is 0831 BST. The distance from Poole Town Quay Boat Haven to St Alban's Ledge is about 12M, which, at a boat speed of 4k, will take 3 hours. Departure from the Boat Haven at 0530 BST would be ideal and the tidal streams would be negligible or favourable. The timings are equally valid for the shorter passage to Lulworth Cove, which should be reached about 1030 BST. However, a 2-hour delay in the departure time (to 0730 BST) would not mean that foul tidal streams would be encountered and the estimated time of arrival (ETA) at Lulworth Cove would be 1230 BST.

Information on the firing times at Lulworth Firing Practice Area is passed to the local yacht clubs and harbourmasters, so a visit to these offices is recommended. They usually have the latest weather forecasts and details of any navigational warnings in the locality.

QUESTIONS

11.1 For a shallow-draught boat in Poole Harbour, where might you anchor overnight round South Deep and west of Brownsea Island?

11.2 List the yacht clubs or yacht harbours in Poole Harbour that welcome visitors.

11.3 You wish to leave Poole Harbour in daytime by the East Looe Channel. Describe your passage.

11.4 From Poole to Weymouth where might you expect to find tide races? How dangerous can they be?

11.5 Between Lulworth Cove and St Alban's Head list any possible anchorages, commenting on their suitability in various weather conditions.

12 ▪ ELECTRONIC AIDS

The most important aspect of navigation is safety. You need to know where you are and where you are going, but also be prepared for bad weather or equipment failure.

When you use a chart, whether it is paper or electronic, you need to be able to recognise features on land by identifying their symbols or representations on the chart. Then you take bearings of these land features in order to plot your current position on the chart.

Electronic aids to navigation use satellites and electronic beacons to determine a boat's position, which you can then plot on a chart. These electronic positions are usually given as latitude and longitude, which are rather cumbersome for plotting, particularly on a small chart table. An alternative is to give the position as a bearing and range from a selected point.

Using electronic nav aids involves a certain amount of pre-voyage preparation. If you spend some time studying the chart and pilotage information you can select key points such as harbour entrances, buoys, or positions for altering course. They could also be easily identifiable land features from which a range and bearing can be plotted. These various points are known as *waypoints*. Pre-voyage preparation requires the latitude and longitude of these waypoints to be measured and then entered into the memory of the electronic aids.

The nav aid will tell you where you are and the bearing and range of the next waypoint on your selected route. If it has been correctly programmed, then you could complete your passage without further reference to a chart. However, it is more sensible and safer to use your electronic aids to check visual navigation so that any discrepancies can be highlighted and investigated. You should mark on the chart at regular intervals (say every 30 minutes) the boat's position with the time and log reading if appropriate. So if you suddenly run into a fog bank, or the electronic aids fail, it is reasonably easy to estimate the current position.

The main current electronic nav aid is the Global Positioning System (GPS).

Global Positioning System

A network of 29 satellites orbits the earth at a height of 11 000M, with their orbital plane at 55° to the equator. These satellites transmit continuously to earth on two frequencies in the D band (1 to 2 GHz) and supply users with

A GPS set like this handheld Magellan 320 is standard equipment for most sailors these days, but it is essential to be able to find your position by conventional chartwork in case of electronic equipment loss or failure.

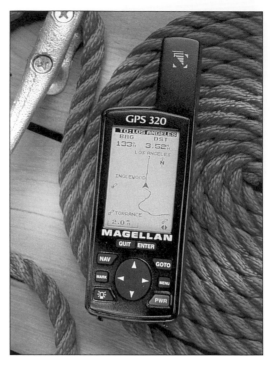

their position, velocity and time. Time is obtained from three atomic clocks, which are so accurate that they will gain or lose only one second in 50 000 years. The satellites have an elaborate control system. There are five ground control monitor stations located around the earth to receive technical telemetered data from the satellites. The master control station sifts all the information it receives and transmits to the satellites their own true position in space and the satellites in turn transmit their positions to the ground users.

Typically, a small craft will have a two-channel receiver. To use the receiver, you switch it on and enter DR position, course and speed, and ship's time. The receiver then searches for available satellites, selects the most suitable, and starts tracking them. From each of these satellites it receives its position, number and accurate time. The receiver then calculates the satellite's range by measuring the time of receipt of the signal and multiplying the time taken for the signal to come from the satellite by the speed of radio waves in air.

The receiver has thus located itself on a position sphere of known radius whose centre is the first transmitting satellite (Fig 12.1a). The receiver then measures the range of the second satellite to define a second position sphere (Fig 12.1b). When a third position sphere is added, the receiver's position is narrowed down to two points in space (Fig 12.1c). As one of these two points is either thousands of miles away from the surface of the earth or moving at a very high velocity, the computer can easily resolve which point is correct; or it could take a range measurement from a fourth satellite. The receiver can work out that point as a latitude and longitude. For non-maritime operations, height above sea level is an additional output.

This calculation assumes that the receiver's clock is perfectly synchronised with those in the satellites. If there is an error of as little as one millisecond,

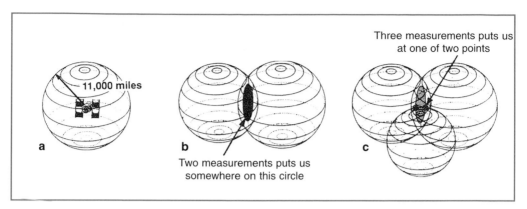

Fig 12.1 In order to provide an accurate position, a GPS receiver needs signals from three, preferably four satellites.

there will be a range error of 163 nautical miles, resulting in a huge three-dimensional version of a 'cocked hat' (see Fig 12.2). The computer will adjust the clock time, which affects all measured ranges by the same amount, until the position spheres meet in a perfect pinpoint fix.

More sophisticated receivers have four or five channels which enables satellites to be tracked simultaneously, giving improved accuracy and response and eliminating the need to enter DR position on start-up.

The accuracy of GPS will be better than 30m for horizontal position and 0.1k for velocity information. It operates for 24 hours per day, worldwide and in any weather conditions.

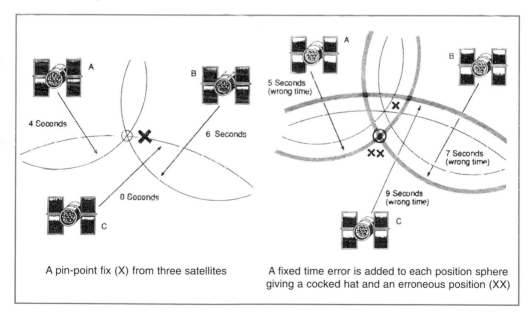

A pin-point fix (X) from three satellites

A fixed time error is added to each position sphere giving a cocked hat and an erroneous position (XX)

Fig 12.2 A time error can result in a large 'cocked hat'.

Satelllte derived positions

Satellite navigation systems use a slightly different datum reference, known as the World Geodetic System 1984 (or WGS84) to that used on some charts. Positions given by satellite navigation systems could differ by up to 200m from those shown on the chart.

Yeoman Navigator

In combination with the GPS, the Yeoman Plotter simplifies considerably the preparation of waypoints for a voyage and plotting on the chart whilst under-way. The key to the operation of the chart plotter is the mouse. As it is moved over the chart, it senses its position and identifies the boat's current location. It is particularly convenient in rough, dark or foggy conditions or when sailing shorthanded. It can also be used for regular pencil plotting on a paper chart.

The Yeoman navigator chart plotter uses a paper chart secured to an electronic backing pad. Shown here is the 'mouse' control which registers waypoints without dividers for course plotters.

Hyperbolic navigation

Before satellite navigators became universally available, electronic nav aids were based on terrestrial transmitters and special onboard receivers. Their accuracy was good but deteriorated as the distance from the transmitter increased. The Loran-C transmitters are still operational but can only be considered as a back up in case of failure of GPS.

Radiobeacons

Now obsolescent, radiobeacons were attached to buoys, lighthouses and at other key positions from which, using a radio direction finder, bearings could be taken to establish position.

Future systems

By 2013 the European Galileo network of satellites should be operational. They will provide an alternative to the American Global Positioning System.

Logs

Logs are used for measuring distance and speed.

Towed logs

The rotating impeller towed astern on a plaited log line (plaited because it thus has no inherent twist in it, as does conventional laid line), driving a simple distance counter, has been used in different forms for over 100 years. Most of those made by Walker Marine Instruments have an accuracy of plus or minus one per cent and are essential for long distance cruising. The rotator has to be streamed at the beginning and hauled in at the end of a passage, which is sometimes inconvenient. The rotator can also be fouled by seaweed (but is easily cleared) and can, in some parts of the world, be eaten by sharks. Some types have a speed indication as well, but speed is generally deduced by reading the log at regular intervals.

Electromagnetic logs

Modern electromagnetic logs use some variety of rotating impeller to send impulses to a display. The rotation of the impeller affects the magnetic field in the transducer, sending impulses to the instrument which converts them into a display of speed in knots and distance in nautical miles.

To be accurate, electromagnetic logs have to be set up and calibrated for every boat in which

This electronic log from Silva measures boat speed, total distance and average speed with elapsed time. PHOTO: SILVA.

they are installed. They can be fouled by seaweed and may be difficult to clear. However, they are convenient and can be switched on and off like a light. Over long distances, particularly if the boat is pitching, their accuracy may not be greater than ±6%. A towed electromagnetic log is on the market which may give improved accuracy. Most electronic logs can be withdrawn for examination while underway: some incorporate a seacock to prevent taking aboard even a jugful of water in the process.

Doppler logs

These logs have a detector inside the hull (ie no hull penetration), which measures ultrasonically the Doppler shift in the water passing within 3cm of the hull. They require careful and accurate calibration and can overread by up to 15 per cent, particularly in choppy conditions.

A different type of Doppler log actually measures speed over the ground (in depths less than 130m) which is a considerable advantage.

Pressure logs

These measure the difference between the static and impact pressure by means of a probe through the boat's hull, and are not normally used in small boats.

Sonic logs

By transmitting sound waves from transducers mounted on the hull and keel, these achieve an accurate measurement of water speed. With no moving parts, there is nothing to foul. Though more expensive, they are the most reliable of hull-mounted logs.

Echo sounders

Electronic echo sounders, used for measuring water depth, are generally very reliable and accurate. Their transducers (transmitter/receivers) do not have to penetrate the hull and can be mounted either singly or in pairs to give high accuracy at all angles of heel. The transducers are mounted somewhere between the waterline and the bottom of the keel, so that at low readings it is necessary to make an appropriate allowance for the depth of the transducer head below sea level. It is not a bad idea to check this by going aground gently and marking the depth scale at the precise point of grounding. In some echo

The depth range on this sounder is 0.6-100 metres; it has both shallow and deep alarms. PHOTO: SILVA.

sounders, the scale can be electronically zeroed to correspond with the bottom of the keel. There are two basic types of echo sounder:

Rotating dial
The ultrasonic transmission is reflected off the seabed and displayed on a rotating dial by either a flashing neon or a light emitting diode (LED). This gives a clear reading, except in direct sunlight, though at night it is not possible to read the printed scale. It can also indicate the type of bottom (hard or soft) and at the same time intermediate indications such as a shoal of fish. If the depth is beyond the full scale reading, it can appear as a second trace echo. For example: full scale reading 30m, depth 35m, reading 5m. To check this, you should select a range with a greater full scale reading.

Pointer
The pointer type of echo sounder shows only one depth indication, and the display, being a dial with a pointer or a digital readout, is much clearer to see and use without ambiguity. It is possible to have additional indicators.

Radar reflectors

See and be seen. Radar reflectors on small craft enhance the radar return of a radar operating in the vicinity. The degree of enhancement is partly due to the reflecting properties of the elements of the radar reflector but, to a greater extent, by its size. Whatever the design, a small reflector is unlikely to be as effective as a large one. To a radar set the level of reflection from an object is similar to the reflection of sunlight from a mirror: a concave or flat mirror gives a good reflection, provided the angle is right, but a convex mirror scatters the light and the reflection is poor.

The classic radar reflector is the octahedral type hoisted or fitted to the top of the mast in its catchwater position (Fig 12.3). On a small boat in a moderate sea the reflectability of this radar reflector is very poor. The photo on page 110 shows a Firdell 'Blipper' 210-7 reflector, which is designed to give a consistent response from a small craft in different weather conditions through 360° of azimuth to at least ±20°of heel.

A large vessel would expect to detect a small yacht or motorboat on his radar at a range of about 7 miles. Because his radar receiver is mounted high on the superstructure, if there are moderate or rough seas the radar may not be able to distinguish between the echo received from the boat and sea clutter at ranges less than 4 miles. It is therefore wise to assume that you have not been detected by a large vessel and to avoid crossing her bows.

Fig 12.3

FIRDELL
BLIPPER 210-7
RADAR
REFLECTOR

FIRDELL

The correct positioning of the radar reflector on the mast is essential if it is going to be effective. Inset left: classic octahedral reflector; inset right: The Firdell Blipper 210-7 radar reflector. PHOTOS: COURTESY OF FIRDELL RADAR REFLECTORS LTD.

Electronic charts

A chart can be displayed on an electronic screen as well as on paper. The UK Hydrographic Office have produced *raster* charts which are an electronic replication of their paper charts. The other form of electronic charts are *vector* charts in which various levels of detail can be selected independently. Ultimately the vector charts are more versatile but they take a long time to prepare

You will need a chartplotter such as the Raytheon RAYCHART 520 (photo above) to view electronic charts. The charts come on data cartridges about a quarter the size of a credit card. As well

This electronic chart plotter can store hundreds of waypoints and can give tide and port information. PHOTO: RAYTHEON.

as viewing electronic charts, the chartplotter can create, edit and navigate waypoints and routes. It can be used for route planning and for marking the man overboard position. The orientation of the display can be North Up, Head Up or Course Up. It can be linked to a Global Positioning System receiver or to an autopilot

QUESTIONS

12.1 Why is it always necessary to carry paper charts?

12.2 Which is more dangerous: an electronic log which over-reads or one that under-reads?

12.3 What are waypoints? How would you organise waypoints with an electronic position indicating system?

12.4 In a GPS system:
   a) What is cross track error?
   b) Does it calculate speed through the water?

12.5 What reservations would you have about the use in a tideway of the GPS man overboard facility?

The mobile phone has made possible almost unlimited instant communication from person to person. However, when at sea you might need to communicate with other ships or shore stations for which there may not be an individual number. Also, mobile phones do not operate further than a few miles from the coastline. To communicate, therefore, each ship has to have a marine radio. For short range operation (up to a range of 30 miles) we use the VHF radio telephone.

VHF radio telephone

Very High Frequency Radio Telephony (VHF R/T) is like a vast telephone party line. To avoid complete confusion it is necessary to impose a disciplined calling and operating procedure, and all potential operators are required either to pass a test to gain the European Conference of Postal and Telecommunications Administrations (CEPT) Short Range Certificate, or to be supervised by such a qualified operator. In an emergency, however, *all* crewmembers should be capable of initiating a distress call. The VHF R/T set itself must be licensed for marine use and for installation in a vessel.

A VHF set operates at frequencies between 156.00 and 174.00 Megahertz (MHz). There are nominally 57 channels in this frequency band, the allocation of which is divided between Intership, Port Operations, Ship Movement and Public Correspondence (including radio telephone)

A pair of robust hand-held VHF radios and a fixed unit. When buying a fixed unit, it is advisable to ensure that it is DSC compatible. PHOTO: ICOM.

with channel 16 (156.8 MHz) being used for Distress, Safety and Calling.

Operation can be either *Duplex*, in which separate antennae and frequencies are used for reception and transmission, or *Simplex*, in which a single frequency and antenna are used. Simplex requires a *press-to-speak* switch.

The range of VHF is limited to line of sight, so antennae should be mounted as high as possible. Another limitation is the 'capture' effect, in which a receiver will only pick up the strongest transmissions, all others being completely excluded.

The above may sound daunting, but with a little practice you will find that it becomes a simple routine and certainly opens up the capacity to communicate.

Distress (Mayday)

The distress call is used when the vessel and/or her crew are in grave and imminent danger requiring immediate assistance:

Select channel 16 and switch on. Check that no other transmissions are taking place. Operate the press-to-speak switch (usually on the handset), and use the *exact* broadcast procedure as outlined in the example below:

1	Distress call (3 times):	MAYDAY MAYDAY MAYDAY
2	Call sign of boat (3 times):	THIS IS YACHT JETTO YACHT JETTO YACHT JETTO
3	Distress call:	MAYDAY
4	Callsign of boat:	YACHT JETTO
5	Position:	MY POSITION IS ONE FIVE ZERO FROM BEACHY HEAD LIGHT ONE POINT FIVE MILES
6	Nature of distress:	STRUCK FLOATING OBJECT AND SINKING
7	Assistance required:	REQUIRE LIFEBOAT
8	Other information:	FOUR PERSONS ON BOARD
9	End of message:	OVER

You may receive an immediate reply or acknowledgement from the Coastguard or another ship. If no reply is received, check that the radio is correctly switched on and tuned, then repeat the entire message at regular intervals. Once a reply is received and communication established, pass on further information, preceding each message with 'Mayday'. The position of the vessel is of vital importance; do not give an apparently accurate position unless it is known to be so.

A vessel may initiate a distress call for another if the latter has no means of indicating her plight.

If you receive a distress message, listen for an acknowledgement by the Coastguard. If this acknowledgement is not forthcoming and assistance can be rendered, acknowledge receipt. If assistance cannot be rendered, then pass on the message to someone who can. The message must be preceded by the words 'Mayday Relay'.

Urgency (PAN PAN)

This is a very urgent message concerning the safety of a vessel or the safety of a person.

Select channel 16 and switch on. Check that no other transmissions are taking place. Operate the press-to-speak switch (usually on the handset).

Use the exact broadcast procedure as outlined in the example below:

1	Urgency call (3 times)	PAN PAN PAN PAN PAN PAN
2	Address (up to 3 times)	ALL STATIONS
		ALL STATIONS
		ALL STATIONS
3	Callsign of boat (up to 3 times)	THIS IS YACHT JETTO YACHT JETTO
4	Position	MY POSITION IS TWO SEVEN ZERO NEEDLES LIGHT SIX MILES
5	Nature of urgency	CREW MEMBER SUFFERED SEVERE INJURY
6	Assistance required	REQUIRE HELICOPTER LIFT TO HOSPITAL
7	End of message	OVER

Call Channel 16 to alert the emergency services for search and rescue.

Safety (securité – pronounced SAY CURE ETAY)

A call to give an important navigational or meteorological warning.

Securité warnings are normally transmitted by the Coastguard. A call is made on channel 16, but an alternative channel is used for the message itself:

> SECURITE SECURITE SECURITE
> ALL STATIONS ALL STATIONS
> THIS IS FALMOUTH COASTGUARD FALMOUTH COASTGUARD
>   FALMOUTH COASTGUARD
> NAVIGATIONAL WARNING
> CHANGE TO CHANNEL SIXTY SEVEN

On channel 67:

> SECURITE SECURITE SECURITE
> ALL STATIONS ALL STATIONS
> THIS IS FALMOUTH COASTGUARD FALMOUTH COASTGUARD FALMOUTH
>   COASTGUARD
> SHIPS ARE WARNED THAT DREDGING OPERATIONS ARE DUE TO START IN
>   SHIPPING CHANNEL EAST OF EDDYSTONE LIGHTHOUSE AT ONE
>   SEVEN THREE ZERO HOURS FOR A PERIOD OF SIX HOURS
> OUT

Intership and port operations working

Initial contact can be made on channel 16, but you must transfer to a working channel as soon as possible; intership operation is not for chatting or unnecessary messages. The transmitting boat should be identified on each transmission.

On channel 16:

> YACHT JETTO
> THIS IS YACHT MERMAIN
> CHANNEL SEVEN TWO
> OVER
>
> YACHT MERMAIN
> THIS IS YACHT JETTO
> CHANNEL SEVEN TWO
> OVER

On channel 72:

> JETTO
> THIS IS MERMAIN
> OVER
>
> MERMAIN
> THIS IS JETTO
> OVER
>
> THIS IS MERMAIN
> PLEASE RENDEZVOUS AT HAMBLE SPIT BUOY
>   AT ONE NINE ZERO ZERO HOURS
> OVER
>
> THIS IS JETTO
> MESSAGE RECEIVED
> OUT

Special channels

Channel 6 is for intership search and rescue and, with channel 16, is mandatory in multi-channel sets.

Channel 13 is used for bridge-to-bridge communication between merchant vessels.

Channel 67 is used in UK waters for exchange of safety information between HM Coastguard and small craft.

Channel 80 is used by marinas to control berthing.

Channel M2 is used by yacht clubs to control safety boats, or for running regattas, etc.

Channel M (which is also channel 37) is a reserve channel for both channel 80 and channel M2.

Channel 70 is the channel reserved for use by automatic equipment in the Global Maritime Distress and Safety System (GMDSS).

Public correspondence (radio telephone calls) can be made by direct contact with Coast Radio Stations, whose operating frequencies are shown in the Admiralty *List of Radio Signals*, Volume 1, and in some almanacs.

Global Maritime Distress and Safety System

The Global Maritime Distress and Safety System (GMDSS) is a vessel-to-shore alert system; Rescue Co-ordination Centres (RCCs) receive distress alerts from vessels and then co-ordinate an appropriate rescue response. Vessel-to-vessel distress alerting is also a feature of GMDSS as are urgency, safety and routine communications and safety information broadcasts (navigation warnings, weather forecasts, and search and rescue messages, etc).

GMDSS is designed to provide an automatic means of transmitting and receiving distress alerts by using Digital Selective Calling (DSC) via conventional radio or via the Inmarsat satellite communications system. DSC communication is much faster and has a greater probability of reception than the manually operated distress system.

GMDSS also provides facilities with which to send distress alerts and locating signals using Emergency Position Indicating Radio Beacons (EPIRBs) and Search and Rescue Radar Transponders (SARTs).

GMDSS uses four coverage areas: A1, A2, A3 and A4 to cover the sea areas of the world for distress watch keeping.

- *Sea Area A1* is within very high frequency (VHF) range of a coast station fitted with DSC (about 30 to 40 miles).
- *Sea Area A2* is within medium frequency (MF) range of a coast station fitted with DSC (about 150 miles).
- *Sea Area A3* is covered by the Inmarsat Satellite System (excluding A1 and A2 areas).
- *Sea Area A4* is basically the Polar Regions not covered by the above.

Watch keeping at sea

VHF DSC radios automatically keep watch on VHF channel 70 and will sound an alarm if there is:

- An incoming call for your vessel
- An *all ships* call
- Urgency or safety traffic
- A distress call or distress relay

The radio will indicate which channel to use for the subsequent communication, such as channel 16 for distress working or channel 72 for ship-to-ship.

A small craft fitted with VHF DSC should keep an automatic watch on channel 70 and, if practicable, on channels 16 and 13 to ensure that distress, safety and shipping traffic are monitored. When you are within an area which

The Global Maritime Distress and Safety System (GMDSS) is an emergency system which picks up distress alerts from vessels automatically using Digital Selective Calling (DSC) via conventional radio. PHOTO: ICS ELECTRONICS LTD.

has a port operation or vessel traffic service (to oversee the movement of ships), the appropriate channel should be monitored rather than channel 13.

Merchant ships keep an automatic watch on channel 70 for DSC calls; they also keep a watch on channel 13 for bridge-to-bridge communications at sea.

DSC types

Small craft should carry class D controllers for VHF operation; these are capable of sending and receiving distress, safety and routine calls. The class F controller is designed for use in hand-held VHF radios fitted with a DSC option. They only provide a send function for distress purposes and cannot receive DSC calls.

Radio procedures

A VHF DSC radio transmits the initial call to another station with a DSC VHF radio; channel 16 must be used if either or both stations are not fitted for DSC. The DSC call on channel 70 contains the proposed channel for further communication.

A vessel in distress transmits a DSC Distress Alert before the MAYDAY procedure. The Distress Alert will activate all alarms on any DSC radios within range and alert any radio operators to listen on the distress-working channel (channel 16) for the subsequent MAYDAY call. The DSC alert contains the identification number of the vessel (the Maritime Mobile Service Identity – MMSI) and should contain a valid position (preferably as an automatic input from the navigation receiver). Any DSC alert should be immediately followed by the MAYDAY procedure on channel 16.

Emergency Position Indicating Radio Beacons (EPIRBs)

▲ This Emergency Position Indicating Radio Beacon (EPIRB) is designed to float free if the vessel sinks and automatically issue a distress signal via satellite. PHOTO: MCMURDO.

As discussed, GMDSS provides the seafarer with at least two independent means of transmitting a distress alert. An EPIRB is the simplest method of alerting rescue authorities; the most common system is operated on 406 MHz by the COSPAS/SARSAT organisation, which uses polar orbiting satellites.

If a vessel sinks, most 406 MHz EPIRBs are designed to detach themselves, automatically float free, and transmit a distress signal via the satellite system, which calculates the position of the casualty and relays the information to the nearest Rescue Co-ordination Centre. In order to co-ordinate a rescue, the Centres require that you must register your EPIRB(s); each one carries a unique identification number. EPIRBs are sold complete with the necessary forms for registration – in the UK with the Coastguard headquarters in Falmouth.

Most EPIRBs also transmit a signal on 121.5 MHz, which enables search and rescue vessels and helicopters to obtain a radio bearing of the EPIRB when homing in on you.

Search And Rescue Radar Transponders (SARTs)

A SART is a personal locator beacon and should be carried by any crewmember who could possibly fall overboard (whilst changing a headsail in heavy weather, for example). SARTs provide a homing signal by transmitting a coded response to a radar signal. These signals are displayed on the rescue vessel's radar screen.

◄ A 9 GHz Search and Rescue Transponder (SART). On receiving a pulse from any standard 9 GHz x-band radar, the SART locator beacon immediately transmits a signal which clearly identifies the survival craft on the radar screen. PHOTO: MCMURDO.

Navtex

NAVTEX receivers operate on medium frequency 518 KHz and receive search and rescue information, navigation warnings and weather forecasts. This information is displayed either on screen or as a paper printout.

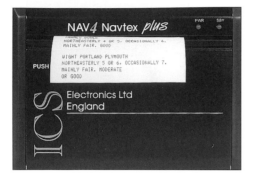

◀ *Navtex enables the boat to receive navigation warnings, weather broadcasts and search and rescue information.*
PHOTO: ICS ELECTRONICS LTD.

Inmarsat

The Inmarsat Organisation operates a constellation of four geo-stationary communications satellites, capable of relaying voice, telex, fax and data transmissions and broadcasting the same type of information as NAVTEX. Any small craft contemplating a passage outside MF range of a coast station should consider satellite communication. Inmarsat C satellite radios are probably the most suitable equipment for small craft but are only capable of sending text messages.

QUESTIONS

13.1 In GMDSS what is the procedure to cancel a false distress alert?

13.2 At sea you see a merchant vessel closing on a steady bearing. Which VHF channel could you use to communicate with her?

13.3 A small fishing vessel flashes SOS at you. Indicate how you would contact the Coastguard.

13.4 You have a crewmember whose head is hit by the boom and is unconscious. How would you call for medical assistance?

13.5 You are approaching the entrance of a harbour from which a regular ferry service operates. How would you determine whether it is safe to enter harbour?

14 ▪ ROPEWORK

Ropes

Ropes are used on a boat for a variety of reasons: halyards to hoist sails, sheets to pull sails in, lines to moor the boat and warps to attach to anchors. At one time they were made from natural fibres such as cotton, hemp, manila and sisal, but now they are mostly made from synthetic materials. Compared with natural fibres of the same diameter, man-made fibres are lighter and stronger but can become slippery and difficult to control.

There are several kinds of synthetic materials used in rope making:

> *Nylon* is strong and stretches. It has good shock absorbing qualities and so is ideal for mooring lines and anchor warps.
> *Polyester* (Terylene) is strong but has low stretching properties and can be obtained pre-stretched. It is used for halyards or sheets.
> *Polypropylene* (Courlene) is a light buoyant rope used wherever a floating line is needed, such as a dinghy painter or lifebuoy line.
> *Kevlar* is a strong, non-stretching rope.

Ropes can be constructed in several ways: laid by twisting strands together, plaited or braided (Fig 14.1)

However they are constructed, all ropes are subject to chafe. To help prevent this, sheets should be led over rollers, and anchor warps and mooring lines passed through a length of hose where they go through a fairlead. You should periodically wash them in fresh water and leave them to dry naturally. They can be damaged by heat and chemicals.

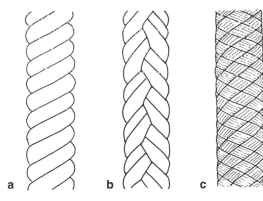

Fig 14.1 Types of rope.
(a) Laid
(b) Plaited
(c) Braided

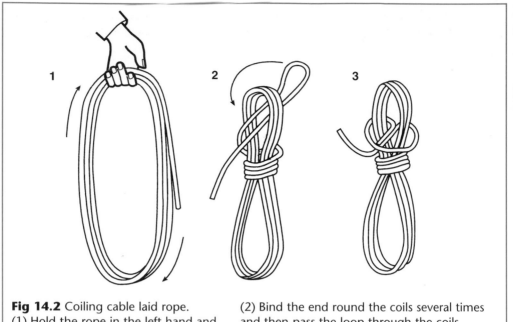

Fig 14.2 Coiling cable laid rope. (1) Hold the rope in the left hand and coil in a clockwise direction. A twist at the top of each coil stops the rope twisting.

(2) Bind the end round the coils several times and then pass the loop through the coils.
(3) Bring the loop back over the top of the coils and push it down to the loops binding the coils. Pull the end tight.

Fig 14.3 Coiling braided or plaited rope. This type of rope twists if coiled as shown for laid rope. It should be coiled in a figure-of-eight so that the twists cancel out.

Coiling rope

Ropes are normally coiled before being stowed, when preparing to come alongside or for a heaving line (Figs 14.2 and 14.3).

Heaving a line

The line is coiled and the coil divided into two, holding half in each hand. Half the coil is swung backwards and forwards, pendulum fashion, and then thrown (heaved). The other half of the coil is allowed to run free until sufficient has run out and the end of the line has reached its target. The heaved end of the line can be made heavier by tying a monkey's fist in the end as shown in Fig 14.12.

Knots

There are many different knots; some of the most useful ones are shown below and overleaf (Figs 14.4 to 14.11).

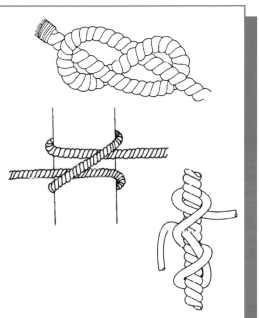

Fig 14.4 Figure-of-eight, sometimes called a stopper knot. It is used on the end of a sheet to stop it accidentally pulling through a block.

Fig 14.5 Clove hitch. It is used to attach the burgee halyard to the burgee pole. Unless under equal tension at both ends this hitch may pull out, and so it is unsuitable to use for mooring or for securing fenders permanently.

Fig 14.6 Rolling hitch. A knot used to fasten a rope to a spar, a chain or a thicker rope to take the strain temporarily. The direction of pull should be lengthwise across the round turn.

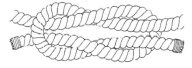

Fig 14.7 Reef knot. Generally used for fastening two ends of the same rope together when reefing a sail.

Fig 14.8a Sheet bend. Useful for joining two ropes of different thicknesses.

Fig 14.8b Double sheet bend. More secure knot than the sheet bend.

Fig 14.9 Bowline. The best all-purpose knot where a temporary loop is required. Some uses are: to fasten the sheets to the headsail; to join two ropes together; to put a temporary eye in a rope. Very secure but difficult to undo under load.

Fig 14.10 Round turn and two half hitches. Used for securing a line to a post or ring or for attaching fenders to a boat. It is secure but easy to undo even under load.

Fig 14.11 Fisherman's bend. For bending a warp onto the ring of an anchor. It is more secure than a round turn and two half hitches, and holds well on a slippery rope.

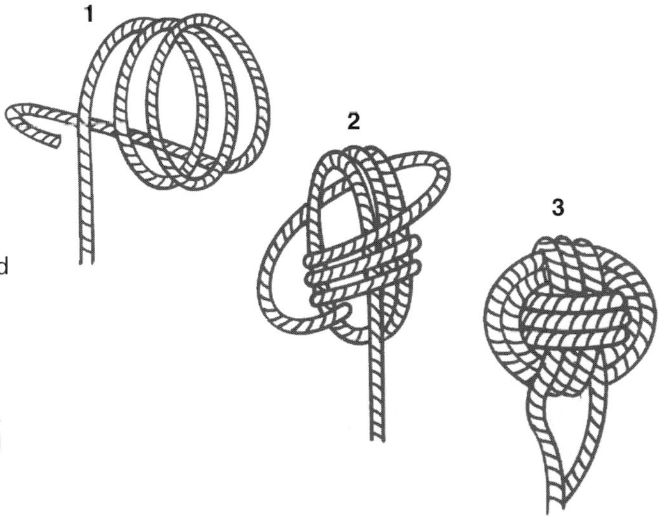

Fig 14.12 Monkey's fist. A monkey's fist is made in the end of a rope to make it heavier for heaving. Sometimes it is made around a piece of lead. (1) Make three loops. (2) Make three more loops outside the first three. (3) Make three final loops over the second three, but inside the first three and splice the end onto the standing part.

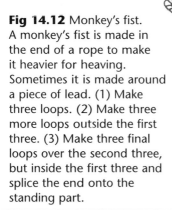

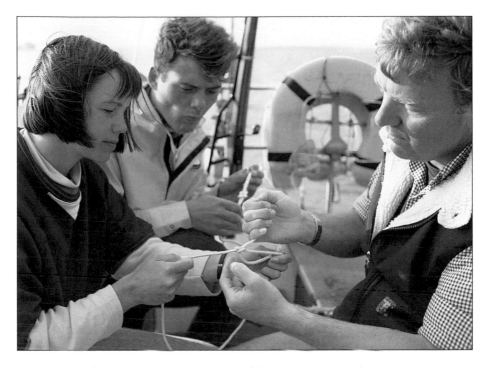

Learning practical knotcraft is an important skill for good seamanship. PHOTO: JOHN GOODE

Winching

A halyard or sheet is turned around a winch drum to take the strain when hoisting or sheeting in a sail. The most important thing to remember when winching is to keep your fingers well away from the winch when there is a strain on the rope. The best way to avoid this is to turn the sheet around the winch drum in the manner shown in Fig 14.13, clenching your fists and keeping them well away from the winch. If the sheet is eased out, use the palm of your hand.

To release a sheet, lift it above the winch and pull the turns off the top (Fig 14.13).

A riding turn

Sometimes one turn of a halyard or sheet on the winch drum slips over another and becomes jammed; this is called a riding turn. It may occur because there are too many turns of rope on the winch drum, or because the lead on to or off the winch is not quite right. It usually frees itself but, if hopelessly jammed, you must attach another line to the halyard or sheet by a rolling hitch and take the tension on this line. With the load off the winch, you can then easily remove the riding turn from the winch drum.

125

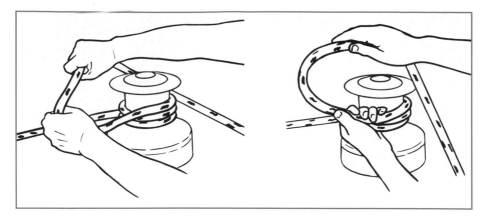

Fig 14.13 Turning a sheet around a winch drum. Left: Correct – the fists are clenched around the sheet and kept well away from the winch drum. Right: Wrong – the fingers will be trapped against the winch drum.

Cleating

Fig 14.14 shows how to secure a halyard to a cleat. For sheets which need to be released quickly, it is usual to have a self-jamming cleat where you only need to turn the rope around the cleat to secure it.

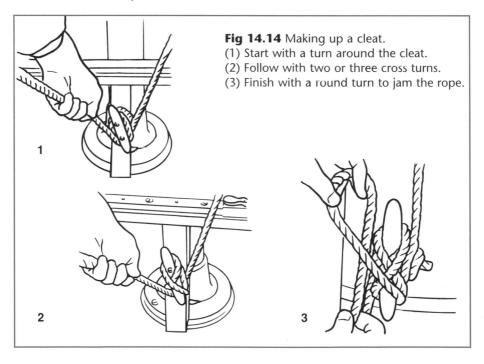

Fig 14.14 Making up a cleat.
(1) Start with a turn around the cleat.
(2) Follow with two or three cross turns.
(3) Finish with a round turn to jam the rope.

On larger boats, winches make lighter work of trimming the jib. PHOTO: DAVID WILLIAMS.

Mooring lines

An alternative to cleating a mooring line is to make an eye on the end of the rope and drop it over a cleat or bollard. Lines used for mooring alongside are shown in the diagram below, and Fig 14.15 shows how you should pass the mooring line through the other boat's lines without fouling them.

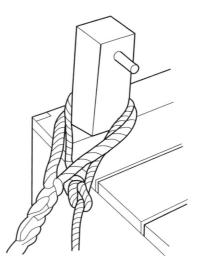

Fig 14.15 Mooring to a bollard. Pass the loop under any existing ones before dropping over bollard.

Fig 14.16 Mooring alongside. Any lines taken ashore must be adjusted as the tide rises or falls. Thus the outside boat must adjust her bow and stern lines, whilst her springs an breast ropes, which are taken to the inside boat, need not be adjusted.
The breast ropes (3) are secured first followed by the bow and stern lines (1 and 2) and then the springs (4 and 5). The breast ropes should then be slackened off.

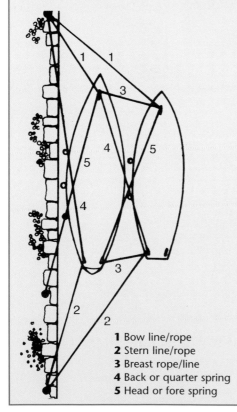

1 Bow line/rope
2 Stern line/rope
3 Breast rope/line
4 Back or quarter spring
5 Head or fore spring

This yacht is well secured with bow, stern and spring lines and two fat fenders to prevent damage alongside.

The Mediterranean moor is commonly used where there is little tide rise or fall; the boat is secured aft to a mooring buoy.

Mediterranean moor

Where there is little rise or fall of tide such as the Mediterranean, it is common to moor the bow or stern to the quayside and drop an anchor or pick up a buoy to hold the boat off.

QUESTIONS

14.1 Which knot would be the most suitable to use in the following cases:
   a) to stop a sheet pulling through a block?
   b) to secure a line to a mooring ring?
   c) to make a temporary loop in a rope?
14.2 What type of line would you use for:
   a) mooring lines?
   b) halyards?
   c) a lifebuoy line?
14.3 What do you consider to be the best all-purpose knot?
14.4 What lines would be required to berth a boat alongside in a marina?
14.5 What is the most important thing to remember when turning a sheet around a winch drum?

15 ■ ANCHORWORK

Anchoring is a way of preventing the boat from drifting when you just want to stop for a while; perhaps for lunch or an overnight stay in a sheltered bay.

Types of anchor

An anchor is made out of heavy metal. A length of chain or warp, or a combination of both, is attached to the anchor and to the boat. There are many different types of anchor. The principal ones are shown in Fig 15.1.

Fisherman
A traditional anchor sometimes called an Admiralty pattern anchor. The drawing shows the names of the parts of the Fisherman: a) shank, b) fluke, c) stock, d) crown, e) ring, f) arm, g) bill.

Advantages
- Can be stowed flat.
- Good holding power in sand and mud.
- Few moving parts to get fouled up or nip fingers.

Disadvantages
- A heavier anchor needed than some other types to give equal holding power.
- When stowed on deck, the flukes can do damage in heavy seas unless well secured.
- Because there is a vertical fluke when it is on the seabed, there is a possibility of the anchor chain or warp fouling this, or the boat settling on it.

Fig 15.1

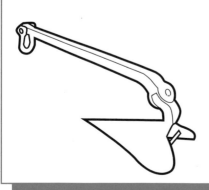

CQR
The CQR is a proprietary type of anchor sometimes also called a plough. Imitations are often not as good.

Advantages
- Holds well in soft sand and mud.
- Lighter anchor required than a Fisherman to give equal holding power.
- Usually digs in well unless the point impales a tin (filling the hollow portion with lead adds extra weight and encourages it to dig into the seabed).

Disadvantages
- There may be stowage difficulties, and special chocks are needed to secure it unless you can fit it over the bow roller.
- Movable parts can become fouled and damage the fingers.
- Can capsize.
- Can be difficult to break out of mud unless a tripping line is used.
- Does not hold too well in kelp or hard sand.

Danforth type
The Danforth type is a flat twin fluke anchor with the stock built into the head.

Advantages
- Good holding power in sand and mud.
- Less weight needed to equal holding power compared with a Fisherman, but about equal to a CQR.
- Can be stowed flat.

Disadvantages
- Movable parts can become fouled and can damage the fingers.
- Not too good on rock.
- Can be difficult to break out of mud unless a tripping line is used.

Bruce type

Advantages
- A much lighter anchor needed to equal the holding power of the other types.
- No movable parts.
- Digs well into the seabed however it lies, and quickly buries itself.
- Good holding power in sand and mud.
- Easy to break out.

Disadvantages
- Difficult to stow without a special chock which, due to lack of space on the foredeck, cannot always be fitted. It can, however, be stowed over the bow roller if well secured.

Grapnel
A good anchor to hold on rock and useful to use as a kedge.

Rond
A one fluke anchor used for permanent mooring, so there is no second fluke left sticking up.

Kedge
A small version of one of the anchors described above used for temporarily anchoring (when racing), for emergencies or for assisting the main anchor.

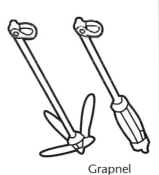

Grapnel

◀ *This CQR anchor is securely held in an offset bracket with pin fastening; the windlass makes life easier when the anchor is being raised.*

Anchoring

Anchors hold best in mud, clay and sand; less well in hard sand, shingle or pebbles; and poorly in rock. Weed can clog movable parts, with consequent loss of holding power. Where there is rock they can become fouled and, if the rock is covered with slippery weed, they can skitter across this without holding. The Fisherman is probably the best for holding in rock. Two main anchors, preferably of different types, should be carried, together with a small kedge.

When selecting an anchorage, the following points should be considered:

- Good holding ground free from obstructions.
- Maximum shelter from all expected winds, and out of strong tidal streams.
- Clear of obstructions and other boats when the boat swings round due to the tidal stream or wind.
- A position where the boat has sufficient chain or warp for the maximum expected depth.
- Sufficient water at low water to avoid grounding.
- Out of areas used frequently by other boats.
- Suitable transits or landmarks for bearings to check periodically that the boat is still in the anchored position.
- Near a suitable landing stage if you intend to go ashore.

Preparing the anchor

Before reaching the anchorage, you must make sure that both ends of the chain or warp have been made fast. The inboard end should be fastened to a fitting in the anchor locker by light line so that it is secure but can be quickly released or cut in an emergency. If chain is used, attach the outboard end to the anchor by means of a shackle. To stop the shackle pin turning a wire is rove through and twisted on to the shackle. This is called mousing. If warp is used, it can either be secured by using a fisherman's bend or an eye can be made around a metal object called a thimble and a shackle used. It is advisable to have at least 6–10m of chain between anchor and warp. The heavy weight of chain gives a horizontal pull on the anchor, which is necessary for the anchor to hold securely. The weight of the chain and elasticity of the warp also provide a damping action (Fig 15.2).

The required amount of chain can be laid out on deck if required, but as this can sometimes cause accidents or damage the boat, then provided it will run out freely it can be marked at 5m intervals and left in the anchor locker until needed.

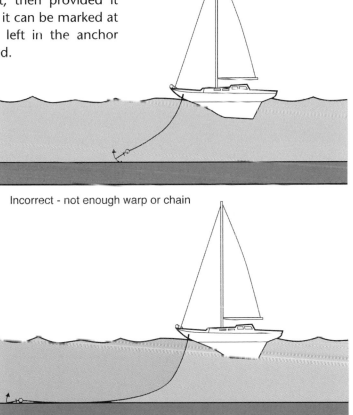

Fig 15.2 Incorrect (top) and correct (bottom) amounts of cable. If warp is used, then it should be paid out at 6 times the depth of water. The pull on the anchor should be horizontal along the seabed to maximise the anchor's holding power. This then acts to your advantage when the anchor is broken out.

Incorrect - not enough warp or chain

Correct - at least 4 times the maximum depth for chain, 6 times for warp

Lowering the anchor

When you reach the anchorage, and the boat has stopped moving forward, lower the anchor to the seabed, and as the boat falls back, let out the required length of chain or warp. If all chain is used, then at least four times the maximum expected depth is needed; for warp allow at least six times; and if bad weather is expected allow at least eight times. The inboard end of the chain or warp is temporarily made fast to a strong cleat or samson post and, when the boat is steady, transits or bearings are observed to make sure that the anchor is holding. If the anchor is dragging, you must let out more chain or warp or the anchor must be raised and the boat re-anchored.

When the boat is secure, the inboard end of the anchor chain or warp is made fast. It is important to check the boat's position at frequent intervals and the circle through which she will swing worked out. A black ball, or by night an all round white light, should be exhibited as high as possible in the fore part of the boat to show she is anchored.

Fouled anchor

If the anchor is likely to become fouled on obstructions, a trip line should be rigged (Fig 15.3). If you have not rigged a trip line and you find that the anchor is fouled, you can sometimes free it by motoring in the direction opposite to that in which it was laid. Alternatively the chain can be hauled in until it is vertical, and a separate clump of chain secured to a line which is dropped down around the original chain until it reaches the anchor, where it should slip down the shank (Fig 15.4). The inboard end of the anchor chain is buoyed and dropped into the water. The line attached to the clump of chain is then made fast to a strong cleat or post on the stern of the boat and the boat

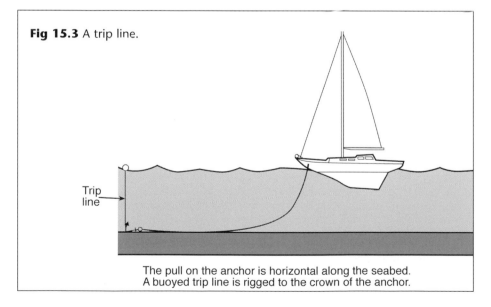

Fig 15.3 A trip line.

Trip line

The pull on the anchor is horizontal along the seabed.
A buoyed trip line is rigged to the crown of the anchor.

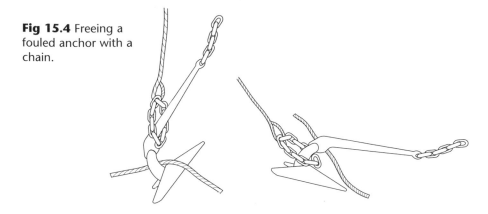

Fig 15.4 Freeing a fouled anchor with a chain.

motored in the opposite direction to that in which you laid the anchor. The slightly lower point of purchase on the anchor will often drag it free.

Laying a second anchor

Sometimes it is necessary to lay a second anchor to reduce the swing or yaw of the boat due to tidal stream or strong wind, especially if you are in a confined anchorage (the boat is then technically said to be moored). Unfortunately not all boats, because of their different hull configurations, lie at the same angle in identical conditions. Some will lie more to wind and some more to tidal stream.

One method of laying two anchors is to lead both from the bows, the heaviest one in the direction of the strongest tidal stream and the other in the opposite direction (Fig 15.5). This method is only suitable for a strong tidal stream with little or no wind. If there is a cross wind, both anchors will drag.

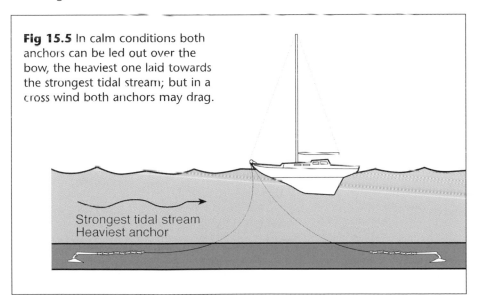

Fig 15.5 In calm conditions both anchors can be led out over the bow, the heaviest one laid towards the strongest tidal stream; but in a cross wind both anchors may drag.

Strongest tidal stream
Heaviest anchor

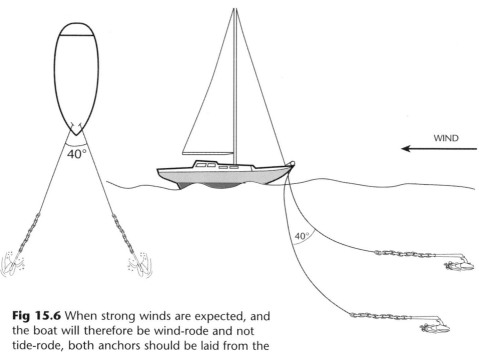

Fig 15.6 When strong winds are expected, and the boat will therefore be wind-rode and not tide-rode, both anchors should be laid from the bow, with about 40° of spread.

Another way is to position the two anchors well forward from the bows, with not too wide an angle between them. This method is used when strong winds are expected so that the boat will lie to the wind rather than to the tidal stream (Fig 15.6).

Anchoring fore-and-aft is not normally suitable for a small boat as it induces too much strain in a cross tide or a strong cross wind.

QUESTIONS

15.1 Give two situations when a second anchor could be laid.

15.2 How does a Fisherman's anchor differ from a CQR anchor?

15.3 When is it necessary to attach a trip line to an anchor?

15.4 You intend to anchor in a sheltered bay overnight. List the considerations you would take into account.

15.5 How can you indicate to other boats that you are anchored:
    a) by day?
    b) by night?

16 ▪ SAFETY

It is the responsibility of the skipper to ensure the safety of the boat and the crew, not only by making the right decisions at the right time, but by seeing that all personal and boat safety requirements are complied with. The following personal requirements are a necessary minimum:

- Plenty of warm clothes and a change of clothing, including hat, gloves and towelling scarf.
- Windproof and waterproof clothing.
- Waterproof non-slip footwear.
- Sharp knife.
- Lifejacket, BS 3595, in good order.
- Safety harness, BS 4474, in good order, preferably with two safety clips.

Personal safety

In most cases it is better to reduce the possibility of falling overboard by fastening your safety harness line to a strong point on the boat, but in fog, when there is a likelihood of a collision in which the boat might sink rapidly, it may be preferable to wear a lifejacket in place of the safety harness. Additionally, non-swimmers should always wear lifejackets. A lifejacket should also be worn in the dinghy to travel between the boat and the shore, as this is where a number of drownings occur. The dinghy should *never* be overloaded.

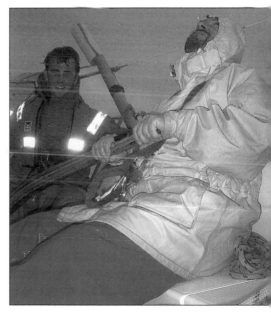

Safety harnesses should be used in rough weather (especially for foredeck

▶ *Make sure that you are kitted out with adequate personal safety equipment and good quality wet-weather gear – there is nothing worse than a flood of cold seawater down your neck or wet feet – it tends to dampen your enthusiasm.*
PHOTO: JOHN GOODE.

work), at night or when alone at the helm. A sharp knife should always be carried (on a lanyard) to cut the safety line if necessary.

The lines on the safety harness should be too short to allow the wearer to fall in the water and be dragged along, as drowning or serious injury can occur.

Many designs of lifejacket are actually made with an integral harness, so it is possible to wear both at the same time, and thus avoiding the choice as to which is better.

General safety

The amount and type of safety equipment you carry depends upon the size and type of your boat and where you will be cruising. There are recommended lists in RYA booklet C8 for craft under 13.7m. Racing boats may be subject to special rules.

Any boat of 13.7m and over must conform to the standards laid down in the Merchant Shipping Rules; below this size the safety equipment is not compulsory but strongly recommended. A general guide is given below:

- Liferaft of a size suitable to carry all persons on board, approved and tested to date, carried on deck where one person can quickly launch it (most liferafts are launched in cases of collision and fire, not, as one would suppose, through heavy weather).
- A half-inflated dinghy can be carried, but is a poor alternative to a liferaft and, in anything but sheltered inshore waters, is totally inadequate.
- Lifebuoys, preferably two, one with a self-igniting smoke float and a drogue, one with 30m of floating line attached ('U' shape is best, because this will fit under the arms of most people, whereas the ring type may not).
- Dan buoy with light.
- Rescue quoit with buoyant line.
- Boarding ladder.
- Two strong buckets with strong handles and lanyards.
- At least 2 multi-purpose fire extinguishers of suitable type and capacity, BS 5423.
- Fire blanket, BS 6575.
- Adequate efficient navigation lights of approved installation.
- Two anchors of sufficient size, and enough chain and/or warp for all expected depths and conditions. There should be a strong point on the deck for attachment.
- One fixed and 1 portable bilge pump.
- An approved, up-to-date pack of pyrotechnics (flares).
- Radar reflector.

There should be at least two of these ▶
horse-shoe shaped lifebuoys on board –
preferably with a self-igniting smoke float.

- First aid box.
- Waterproof torch.
- Safety harness anchor points, one located near the main hatch for use as the crew step into the cockpit.
- Strong and adequate guardrails and lifelines.
- A method of securing and releasing the hatch boards and cover from on deck or down below.
- The name of the boat displayed on the dodgers and on a piece of canvas to display on the coach roof if necessary.
- A method of securing all equipment such as batteries and other heavy gear liable to do damage in heavy weather.
- Radio receiver.
- Marine band VHF radio.
- Radio navigational system.
- An efficient steering and hand-bearing compass.
- Reliable clock or watch.
- Distance log.
- Echo sounder.
- Lead line.
- Up-to-date charts, sailing directions, tide tables and other relevant nautical publications.
- Plotting instruments.
- Tool kit.
- Bolt croppers.
- Engine spares.
- A separate battery, used only for engine starting.
- Tow rope.
- Emergency water supply.
- Rigid tender or inflatable dinghy.
- A mainsail capable of being deeply reefed or a trysail, and a storm jib.

Man overboard

Sometimes, in spite of all precautions, a person will fall overboard. You need to perfect an efficient method of recovery both under sail and motor, which can be done by each member of the crew in all weather conditions. Your pre-ferred method will depend upon the conditions, what type of boat you are sailing, the ability of the helmsman and the availability of other crewmembers.

Immediately a person falls overboard the following actions must be carried out:

- The lifebuoy (and dan buoy), must be thrown in as near to the person as possible.
- As this is being done, *Man Overboard* is shouted loudly to alert all crewmembers.
- If there are sufficient crew, a lookout is appointed immediately who points to the person in the water and continuously calls out his position. (In a rough sea or at night anyone in the water is quickly lost to sight.)

The lifebuoy (and dan buoy) should have a powerful light for night use. It is well worthwhile making sure you have retro-reflective materials on all safety equipment and clothing.

To help guide the helmsman to the pick up point, any buoyant object can be thrown in periodically to form a trail. If available immediately, a buoyant orange smoke canister makes a good marker for day use, or a white para-chute rocket flare to illuminate the area by night.

One method of returning to the man overboard under sail is given as follows:

> Whatever point of sailing the boat is on, she immediately goes on to a reach (wind across the boat at a right angle) and sails on for a sufficient distance to enable the crew to tack and return at a slow speed under full control. After tacking the boat reaches back, dropping slightly to leeward for the final approach, which is made on a close reach with the sails flying so that the boat will stop with the person in the water to leeward.

Using this method, the boat is always under full control, though it is neces-sary to travel some distance before tacking to give the boat room to manoeuvre and stop. It is, therefore, not a good method to use at night or in a rough sea when the person in the water will be lost to sight. In this case it is better to stop the boat quickly by heaving-to to windward of the person and then drifting towards him, or motoring back to him. It may not be pos-sible to bring the boat safely alongside the person in the water in heavy seas

The helmsperson here has sailed back to the casualty, freed off the sheets to slow the boat and skilfully thrown a lifebuoy.

and so a rescue quoit attached to a buoyant line should be prepared ready to throw if required.

The pick up

It is extremely difficult to lift a waterlogged person back on board, especially if he is unconscious. As soon as the person is alongside, secure him to the boat so that he does not drift away. A ladder should be used for recovery, or a line in which a bowline has been tied can either be placed around his waist or hung over the side for him to step into to make recovery easier. If the person is unconscious, another crewmember, who *must* be secured to the boat, may have to go into the water to help. In this case, if the dinghy is available the person in the water can be pulled into it before being winched onto the boat, though this can be quite a tricky manoeuvre. Alternatively a small sail can be attached by its luff to the guardrail, lowered into the water and passed under him. A halyard is attached to the clew of this sail so that he can be hauled in over the guardrail.

Helicopter rescue

Preparations – before the helicopter arrives
- Lower and stow all sails. Lower boom to starboard quarter. Remove runners and any other obstruction possible, topping lift etc.
- Your crew should be wearing lifejackets and harnesses.
- Get the crew to prepare to abandon ship, while waiting, in case things become worse. Wear lifejackets, warm clothes and only take small valuables.
- Clear the area of the deck of dan buoys, aerials, etc, from where the helicopter will pick up.
- Prepare any casualty. If any medical treatment has been given to an unconscious casualty, tie a label on, explaining what has been done. Put them on deck ready to go.
- If the weather conditions permit, place casualty in dinghy or liferaft and tow behind the boat.

Communications
- If you have VHF, contact the helicopter pilot as soon as possible. He will want to know the number of people to lift and the wind speed and direction at the scene.
- Agree a procedure for the lift-strop or stretcher.
- He may ask for a long call on the radio. Helicopters can 'home in' on your VHF radio transmissions or EPIRB signal – so keep transmitting.
- When you see the helicopter, tell him what direction he is from you.
- By day have orange smokeflare ready, by night red pinpoint flare – do not use rocket flares.

When the helicopter arrives
Don't touch the winchman, stretcher, hook until earthed.
Don't secure anything from the helicopter to the boat.
Don't fire anything into the air when the helicopter is near.
Don't use your radio when winching is in progress unless it is urgent. The words **BREAK OFF!** will warn the helicopter off if things are going wrong.
Don't shine strong lights at the helicopter.

Do as you are told
- Steer with the wind 40° on the port bow if the wind is less than force 4, or 30° on the starboard quarter in strong winds. Keep on a steady course.
- At night indicate heading with light shining forward.
- Detail a crewmember to take care of the *high line*. If winching aft in light winds flake the line down in the bottom of the cockpit. If winching forward flake down in a large bucket (lashed to the pulpit). **Do not attach the line to the boat**. Make sure it is clear to run.

Before the rescue helicopter arrives, make sure that the crew are wearing lifejackets and clear the deck of any loose items. Follow the instructions given to you by the helicopter pilot. PHOTO: COURTESY OF HM COASTGUARD.

- A boathook to hand may be useful to grab it.
- When the high line arrives, just grab it and pull (*hard*).
- If the weather is very bad, the pilot may ask you to leave the boat. If it is an abandon ship situation, do so one at a time so that there is only one person in the water at a time.

Aftercare

Anyone who has fallen from a boat will be in a distressed condition. He may be unconscious, not breathing, suffering from shock or cardiac arrest. It is essential that there are crewmembers on board qualified to render first aid for these conditions; all Day Skipper students are strongly advised to attend a recognised course.

Resuscitation

When breathing has stopped it is necessary to start resuscitation. Unless this is done within four minutes, brain damage may occur.

Fig 16.1 shows the correct position of the head for mouth-to-mouth resuscitation.

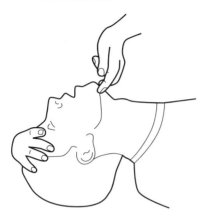

Fig 16.1 The correct position of the head for mouth-to-mouth resuscitation.

Expired Air Resuscitation (EAR)

- Lie the patient on his back.
- Clear his mouth of obstructions and check whether he has swallowed his tongue (but do not waste time).
- Tilt his head back and lift his jaw as shown in Fig 16.1. This lifts the tongue away from the back of the throat and creates an open airway.
- Pinch his nose and blow firmly into his mouth or close his mouth with your thumb and blow gently but firmly into his nose. Whichever method is used, see that a good seal is made. His chest should rise; if it does not, check for obstructions.
- Turn your head away, wait for his chest to fall, take a breath and repeat. Initially give 4 to 6 quick breaths and then one every 5 seconds.
- Continue until he is breathing normally or until there is no hope of recovery.
- If normal breathing is resumed, put him in the recovery position (Fig 16.2) and watch him carefully to see that his breathing does not fail again.

Fig 16.2 Recovery position.

For small children and babies more rapid breathing is needed. Be careful not to blow too hard as you may damage the lungs. If a person's heart has stopped beating, closed chest cardiac massage should be applied. This needs to have been properly learned, however, if it is to be successful.

An alternative method of resuscitation should have been learned in case your casualty has a facial injury and EAR cannot be done.

Any person who has suffered a blow to the head and become unconscious, had severe hypothermia, or recovered from an apparent drowning should be referred to a doctor as soon as possible.

Contents of a first aid kit

The first aid kit should be kept in a watertight box and a list of the contents should be on the outside of the box. The following is a basic kit:

Roll of plaster	Scissors	Aspirin
Individual plasters	Tweezers	Seasickness tablets
Large triangular bandages	Eye lotion and eye bath	Indigestion tablets
	Calamine lotion	Exposure bag
Small bandages	Safety pins	First aid book
Lint and cotton wool	Disinfectant	

First aid has been dealt with here only briefly. During the winter months it is a good idea to attend a first aid course and learn how to administer it thoroughly.

Fire

A fire on a boat at sea can be very alarming. If the fire looks as though it might get out of hand, prepare to abandon ship. Get the dinghy inflated and tow it astern. See that the liferaft is ready to launch immediately. Don lifejackets and then stand by to initiate distress procedures.

The best way to deal with a fire is to smother it (thus starving it of oxygen) and prevent it spreading by cooling the surrounding areas.

The number and type of extinguishers you should carry on board depends upon the type and size of the boat. For extinguishers made to BS 5423, capacity is expressed as a number, whilst a letter shows the type. The letter A denotes an extinguisher suitable for fires caused by paper, wood etc; B is for burning liquids such as oil and fuel; whilst C is for flammable gases. Most extinguishers deal with at least two types of fire. A minimum requirement for a boat fitted with a galley and engine is 2 multi-purpose extinguishers with a fire rating of 5A/34B. Fire authorities recommend that one 13A/113B should also be carried. Fire extinguishers should be stowed in a readily accessible place and maintained regularly.

Water may be used on non-oil, non-electric fires such as bedding. A bedding fire may appear to be extinguished but can often smoulder and restart, so use plenty of water. Smoking below deck often causes this type of fire.

A fire blanket is useful for cooker fires. Do not throw a burning frying pan overboard as there is a possibility of spillage, thus spreading the fire. You should smother it with a fire blanket, which should be applied over the fire away from the person holding it so that the flames are not fanned towards them. A heavy piece of damp material can also be used.

Prevention

To help prevent fire occurring, you should keep the bilges clean and well ventilated so that gas fumes do not accumulate. Gas bottles should be outside the cockpit where any leaks will drain overboard and not into the bilges. They should be turned off at the bottle when not in use. Turning the gas off at the bottle before turning it off at the cooker is recommended to burn out the gas in the pipes.

The engine compartment should be closed when refuelling and if any fuel spillage occurs the boat should be hosed down and ventilated.

The liferaft

Everyone on board should know how to inflate and board the liferaft.

Launching

Do not launch the liferaft until the last minute as it may capsize in rough weather. Do not leave the boat if it is still afloat: abandoned boats have been found still floating with no survivors.

- Make sure that the liferaft's painter is secured to a strong point on the boat before it is launched.

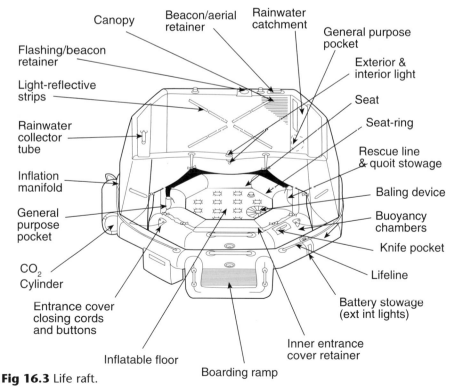

Fig 16.3 Life raft.

- Release the fastening which secures the raft to the boat, and launch it.
- When it is in the water take up the slack on the painter and then tug sharply: this should inflate the raft.

Boarding
- Do not *jump* into the raft.
- Get the heaviest person in first to stabilise it.
- When everyone is aboard, cut the painter and paddle away from the boat.
- Stream the drogue.
- Elect a leader.
- Take seasickness tablets.
- Check for leaks.
- Locate the first aid kit, flares, repair kit, survival kit.
- Do not issue drinking water for 24 hours unless someone is injured and bleeding.
- Do not drink seawater or urine.
- Keep warm.
- Keep a lookout and try to estimate your position.

Pyrotechnics

Red flares
A red hand flare (pinpoint flare) is for use when within sight of land or another boat, or to pinpoint your position when the rescuers are within visible range. It burns for 1 minute. Do not point it into the wind or you will be covered with sparks and smoke. Do not look directly at it.

Fig 16.4 Operating a red rocket flare

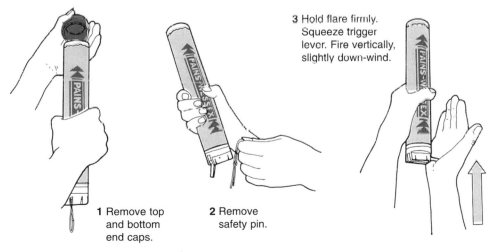

3 Hold flare firmly. Squeeze trigger lever. Fire vertically, slightly down-wind.

1 Remove top and bottom end caps.

2 Remove safety pin.

A parachute rocket flare is for use when out of sight of land to raise the alarm. It projects a bright red parachute-suspended flare to a height of 300m for 40 seconds. A rocket turns towards the wind and so should be fired vertically, or in strong winds 15° downwind. If there is low cloud it should be fired 45° downwind so that it ignites below the cloud base.

Orange smoke flare

This is a daytime distress signal, which produces a dense cloud of orange smoke easily seen from the air. In strong winds, however, the smoke blows along the sea surface and may not be visible from the shore or other boats. Hand smokes burn for 50 seconds and are used when rescuers are within visible range. Buoyant smokes, which consist of a container with a ring pull, can be thrown into the water and burn for 3 minutes. A smoke marker is available which can be attached to a lifebuoy and mounted on deck for man overboard situations; it burns for 15 minutes.

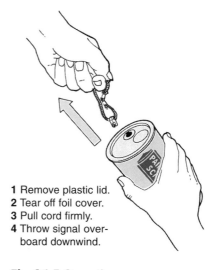

1 Remove plastic lid.
2 Tear off foil cover.
3 Pull cord firmly.
4 Throw signal over-
  board downwind.

Fig 16.5 Operating an orange smoke signal.

White handflare

This is not used for distress but to warn other boats of your position. It burns for 50 seconds. Do not look directly at it, as it is very bright. White parachute flares are also available. These are generally used for demonstration purposes. They are very useful to illuminate the area in a man overboard situation.

White parachute flare

White parachute flares are available, used mainly for demonstration, but prove very useful to illuminate the area by night.

Minimum recommended flare packs

Inshore waters less than 3 miles from land:
2 red hand flares
2 orange hand smokes

Coastal waters up to 7 miles from land:
2 red parachute rockets
2 red hand flares
2 handheld orange smokes

Offshore over 7 miles from land:
4 red parachute rockets
4 red hand flares
2 buoyant orange smokes

For collision warning:
4 white hand flares

Flare safety
- Learn the purpose of the flares carried and how to use them.
- Read and memorise the operating instructions on the flares and always follow these instructions EXACTLY.
- Stow flares in a secure, cool dry place, which is easily accessible, and make sure that all crewmembers know where this is.
- Always have at least the minimum required number and type of flares on board, and make sure they are within their use-by date.
- If a signal fails, hold it in the firing position for at least 30 seconds. Remove the caps and drop it into the sea.
- Never point flares at another person.

VHF radio telephony

See Chapter 13.

QUESTIONS

16.1 When should a safety harness be worn?

16.2 What should you do immediately a person falls overboard?

16.3 What precautions should be taken to minimise the risk of fire?

16.4 What is the recommended flare pack for a boat in coastal waters within 7 miles of the coast?

16.5 You are in motorboat *Jetto*, which is about to sink. There are 3 other crewmembers as well as yourself on board. The boat is 3 miles southwest of the Needles lighthouse. Write down the appropriate VHF call you would send and state the channel on which you would send it.

17 ■ INTERNATIONAL REGULATIONS FOR PREVENTING COLLISIONS AT SEA

It is absolutely necessary to have a sound knowledge of all collision rules, and this chapter should be read in conjunction with a copy of International Regulations for Preventing Collisions At Sea. Some of the rules particularly relevant to yachtsmen are given here and explained in the tinted boxes.

Extracts of the Convention on the International Regulations for Preventing Collisions at Sea, 1972 are reprinted by permission of IMO.

Steering and sailing rules 5, 7, 8, 9, 10, 12 to 19, 34 and 37

RULE 5 Look-out

Every vessel shall at all times maintain a proper look-out by sight and hearing as well as by all available means appropriate in the prevailing circumstances and conditions so as to make a full appraisal of the situation and of the risk of collision.

> *It is very easy in bad weather when there is a lot of spray, especially at night, to be blind to things forward of the boat. There is also a temptation, when self-steering is used, to abandon the helm. It is vital in both of these situations that a good and adequate look-out is kept. In fog, when visibility is lost, a good hearing watch should be kept. At night the helmsman may be temporarily blinded by thoughtless use of the cabin lights or matches struck close to him.*

RULE 7 Risk of collision

(d) In determining if risk of collision exists the following considerations shall be among those taken into account:

   (i) such risk shall be deemed to exist if the compass bearing of an approaching vessel does not appreciably change;

   (ii) such risk may sometimes exist even when an appreciable bearing change is evident, particularly when approaching a very large vessel or a tow or when approaching a vessel at close range.

RULE 8 Action to avoid collision

(a) Any action taken to avoid collision shall, if the circumstances of the case admit, be positive, made in ample time and with due regard to the observance of good seamanship.

(b) Any alteration of course and/or speed to avoid collision shall, if the circumstances of the case admit, be large enough to be readily apparent to another vessel observing visually or by radar; a succession of small alterations of course and/or speed should be avoided.

A small alteration of course by the give-way vessel may not be seen by the other vessel, a series of small alterations will be confusing, possibly causing a collision. Any alterations to be made should be bold and made in plenty of time.

RULE 9 Narrow channels

(a) A vessel proceeding along the course of a narrow channel or fairway shall keep as near to the outer limit of the channel or fairway which lies on her starboard side as is safe and practicable.

(b) A vessel of less than 20 metres in length or a sailing vessel shall not impede the passage of a vessel, which can safely navigate only within a narrow channel or fairway.

(c) A vessel engaged in fishing shall not impede the passage of any other vessel navigating within a narrow channel or fairway.

This ferry is proceeding along a narrow channel and has limited ability to manoeuvre so it is up to you, in your sailing boat with less draft, to keep clear

(d) A vessel shall not cross a narrow channel or fairway if such crossing impedes the passage of a vessel which can safely navigate only within such channel or fairway. The latter vessel may use the sound signal prescribed in Rule 34 (d) if in doubt as to the intention of the crossing vessel.

(e) (i) In a narrow channel or fairway when overtaking can take place only if the vessel overtaken has to take action to permit safe passage, the vessel intending to overtake shall indicate her intention by sounding the appropriate signal prescribed in Rule 34 (c) (i). The vessel to be overtaken shall, if in agreement, sound the appropriate signal prescribed in Rule 34 (c) (ii) and take steps to permit safe passing. If in doubt she may sound the signals prescribed in Rule 34 (d).

(ii) This Rule does not relieve the overtaking vessel of her obligation under Rule 13.

(f) A vessel nearing a bend or an area of a narrow channel or fairway where other vessels may be obscured by an intervening obstruction shall navigate with particular alertness and caution and shall sound the appropriate signal prescribed in Rule 34 (e).

(g) Any vessel shall, if the circumstances of the case admit, avoid anchoring in a narrow channel.

As no definition of a 'narrow channel' is given, the appropriate action depends upon the type and size of vessels using the channel. Generally speaking, there is usually enough depth of water for a sailing vessel to navigate outside a buoyed channel used by deep draught vessels.

RULE 10 Traffic separation schemes
(a) This Rule applies to traffic separation schemes adopted by the Organisation and does not relieve any vessel of her obligation under any other rule.

(b) A vessel using a traffic separation scheme shall:
(i)   proceed in the appropriate traffic lane in the general direction of traffic flow for that lane;
(ii) so far as practicable keep clear of a traffic separation lane or separation zone;
(iii) normally join or leave a traffic lane at the termination of the lane, but when joining or leaving from either side shall do so at as small an angle to the general direction of traffic flow as practicable.

(c) A vessel shall, so far as practicable, avoid crossing traffic lanes, but if obliged to do so shall cross on a heading as nearly as practicable at right angles to the general direction of traffic flow.

(d) (i)   A vessel shall not use an inshore traffic zone when she can safely use the appropriate traffic lane within the traffic separation scheme. However, vessels of less than 20 metres in length, sailing vessels and vessels engaged in fishing may use the inshore traffic zone.

(ii) Notwithstanding sub-paragraph (d) (i), a vessel may use as inshore traffic zone when *en route* to or from a port, offshore installation or structure, pilot station, or any other place situated within the inshore traffic zone or to avoid immediate danger.

(e) A vessel other than a crossing vessel or a vessel joining or leaving a lane shall not normally enter a separation zone or cross a separation line except:

(i) in case of emergency to avoid immediate danger;

(ii) to engage in fishing within a separation zone.

(f) A vessel navigating in areas near the terminations of traffic separation schemes shall do so with particular caution.

(g) A vessel shall so far as practicable avoid anchoring in a traffic separation scheme or in areas near its terminations.

(h) A vessel not using a traffic separation scheme shall avoid it by as wide a margin as is practicable.

(i) A vessel engaged in fishing shall not impede the passage of any vessel following a traffic lane.

(j) A vessel of less than 20 metres in length or a sailing vessel shall not impede the safe passage of a power-driven vessel following a traffic lane.

(k) A vessel restricted in her ability to manoeuvre when engaged in an operation for the maintenance of safety of navigation in a traffic separation scheme is exempted from complying with this Rule to the extent necessary to carry out the operation.

(l) A vessel restricted in her ability to manoeuvre when engaged in an operation for the laying, servicing or picking up a submarine cable, within a traffic separation scheme, is exempted from complying with this Rule to the extent necessary to carry out the operation.

RULE 12 Sailing vessels

(a) When two sailing vessels are approaching one another, so as to involve risk of collision, one of them shall keep out of the way of the other as follows:

(i) When each has the wind on a different side, the vessel which has the wind on the port side shall keep out of the way of the other;

(ii) When both have the wind on the same side, the vessel which is to windward shall keep out of the way of the vessel which is to leeward;

(iii) If a vessel with the wind on the port side sees a vessel to windward and cannot determine with certainty whether the other vessel has the wind on the port or on the starboard side, she shall keep out of the way of the other.

The boat to windward may have a large sail such as a spinnaker blanketing a view of the other sails. In this rule the give way boat is on port tack, and, as she cannot determine which tack the other boat is on, it must be assumed that it is

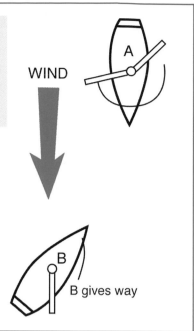

Fig 17.1 Rule 12 (iii) Sailing vessels. Because vessel B cannot clearly see which tack vessel A is on (the spinnaker blocks her view of A's mainsail) she must assume that A is on starboard and B therefore has to give way since she is on port tack. Had B been on starboard tack, she would hold her course under Rule 12(ii).

WIND

A

B

B gives way

on starboard and has right of way. Had the leeward boat been on starboard tack she would have held her course and speed as the windward rule (ii) would have applied (Fig 17.1).

RULE 13 Overtaking

(a) Notwithstanding anything contained in the Rules of this section, any vessel overtaking any other shall keep out of the way of the vessel being overtaken.

The Rule states any *vessel overtaking, which is one of several instances when sail gives way to power. The give-way vessel must continue on her course until she is past and clear. As she is overtaking, the situation could go on for a long time (though it may seem to change; if a sailing boat overtakes a small motor boat and the wind suddenly dies so that the two are abreast, and then the motor boat again goes ahead, the sailing boat is still the give-way vessel).*

RULE 14 Head-on situation

(a) When two power-driven vessels are meeting on reciprocal or nearly reciprocal courses so as to involve risk of collision each shall alter her course to starboard so that each shall pass on the port side of the other (Fig 17.2).

RULE 15 Crossing situation

When two power-driven vessels are crossing so as to involve risk of collision, the vessel which has the other on her own starboard side shall keep out of the way and shall, if the circumstances of the case admit, avoid crossing ahead of the other vessel (Fig 17.3).

The give-way vessel should alter course to starboard and pass astern of the other vessel unless she is prevented from doing so, in which case an alteration to port will have to be made which will need to be considerable if she is to avoid crossing ahead.

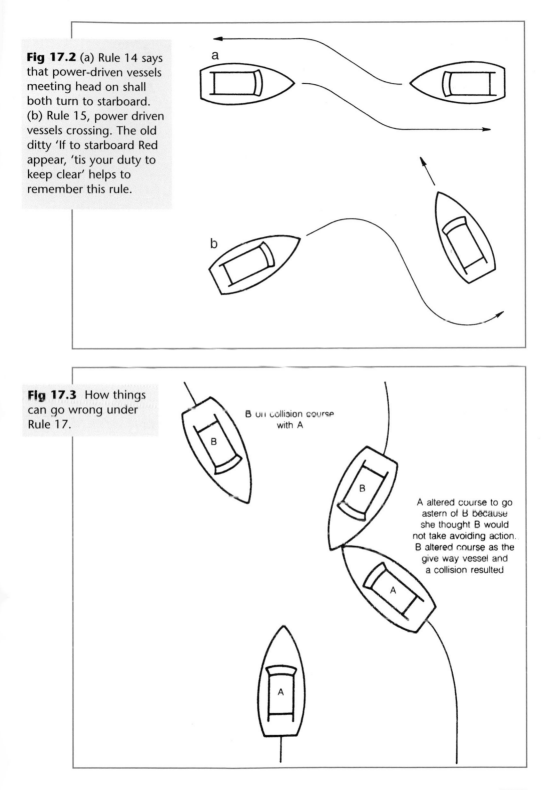

Fig 17.2 (a) Rule 14 says that power-driven vessels meeting head on shall both turn to starboard. (b) Rule 15, power driven vessels crossing. The old ditty 'If to starboard Red appear, 'tis your duty to keep clear' helps to remember this rule.

a

b

Fig 17.3 How things can go wrong under Rule 17.

B on collision course with A

B

B

A altered course to go astern of B because she thought B would not take avoiding action. B altered course as the give way vessel and a collision resulted

A

A

In this crossing situation the helmsperson has changed course to pass to the stern of the ship. Any alteration in course should be taken early and be obvious.

RULE 16 Action by give-way vessel

Every vessel which is directed to keep out of the way of another vessel shall, so far as possible, take early and substantial action to keep well clear.

An early alteration of course and a bold one so that the intentions of the give-way vessel are clear in good time.

RULE 17 Action by stand-on vessel

(a) (i) Where one of two vessels is to keep out of the way the other shall keep her course and speed.

(ii) The latter vessel may however take action to avoid collision by her manoeuvre alone, as soon as it becomes apparent to her that the vessel required to keep out of the way is not taking appropriate action in compliance with these Rules.

(b) When from any cause, the vessel required to keep her course and speed finds herself so close that collision cannot be avoided by the action of the give-way vessel alone, she shall take such action as will best aid to avoid collision.

(c) A power-driven vessel which takes action in a crossing situation in accordance with sub-paragraph (a) (ii) of this Rule to avoid collision with another power-driven vessel shall, if the circumstances of the case admit, not alter course to port for a vessel on her own port side.

(d) This Rule does not relieve the give-way vessel of her obligation to keep out of the way.

In Fig 17.3, vessel A has right of way but is not sure whether vessel B will take avoiding action. If vessel A decides that she must alter course to avoid collision and does so to port, B may suddenly decide that as give-way vessel she will take avoiding action, and if she also alters course to port to pass behind A, a collision will result. A better course of action for A if she must take avoiding action would be to stop or go astern, or turn to starboard.

RULE 18 Responsibilities between vessels

Except where Rules 9, 10 and 13 otherwise require:

(a) A power-driven vessel underway shall keep out of the way of:
- (i) a vessel not under command;
- (ii) a vessel restricted in her ability to manoeuvre;
- (iii) a vessel engaged in fishing;
- (iv) a sailing vessel.

(b) A sailing vessel underway shall keep out of the way of:
- (i) a vessel not under command;
- (ii) a vessel restricted in her ability to manoeuvre;
- (iii) a vessel engaged in fishing.

(c) A vessel engaged in fishing when underway shall, so far as possible, keep out of the way of:
- (i) a vessel not under command;
- (ii) a vessel restricted in her ability to manoeuvre.

(d) (i) Any vessel other than a vessel not under command or a vessel restricted in her ability to manoeuvre shall, if the circumstances of the case admit, avoid impeding the safe passage of a vessel constrained by her draught, exhibiting the signals in Rule 28;

(ii) A vessel constrained by her draught shall navigate with particular caution having full regard to her special condition.

(e) A seaplane on the water shall, in general, keep well clear of all vessels and avoid impeding their navigation. In circumstances, however, where risk of collision exists, she shall comply with the Rules of this Part.

Sailing vessels must also keep clear when they are the overtaking vessel whether they are overtaking power or sail, and must not impede any vessel, which has a deep draught and cannot navigate outside her channel.

The signals (in Rule 28) exhibited by a vessel constrained by her draught are: three all round red lights in a vertical line, or a cylinder.

RULE 19 Conduct of vessels in restricted visibility

(a) This Rule applies to vessels not in sight of one another when navigating in or near an area of restricted visibility.

(b) Every vessel shall proceed at a safe speed adapted to the prevailing circumstances and conditions of restricted visibility. A power-driven vessel shall have her engines ready for immediate manoeuvre.

(c) Every vessel shall have due regard to the prevailing circumstances and conditions of restricted visibility when complying with the Rules of Section 1 of this Part.

(d) A vessel which detects by radar alone the presence of another vessel shall determine if a close-quarter situation is developing and/or risk of collision exists. If so, she shall take avoiding action in ample time, provided that when such action consists of an alteration of course, so far as possible the following shall be avoided: (i) an alteration of course to port for a vessel forward of the beam, other than for a vessel being overtaken (ii) an alteration of course towards a vessel abeam or abaft the beam.

(e) Except where it has been determined that a risk of collision does not exist, every vessel which hears apparently forward of her beam the fog signal of another vessel, or which cannot avoid a close-quarters situation with another vessel forward of her beam, shall reduce her speed to the minimum at which she can be kept on her course. She shall if necessary take all her way off and in any event navigate with extreme caution until the danger of collision is over.

Great care is necessary by small boats caught in fog (see Chapter 12).

RULE 34 Manoeuvring and warning signals

(a) When vessels are in sight of one another, a power-driven vessel underway, when manoeuvring as authorized or required by these Rules, shall indicate that manoeuvre by the following signals on her whistle:
- one short blast to mean 'I am altering my course to starboard';
- two short blasts to mean 'I am altering my course to port';
- three short blasts to mean 'I am operating astern propulsion'.

(b) Any vessel may supplement the whistle signals prescribed in paragraph (a) of this Rule by light signals, repeated as appropriate, whilst the manoeuvre is being carried out:

(i)   these light signals shall have the following significance:
- one flash to mean 'I am altering my course to starboard';
- two flashes to mean 'I am altering my course to port';
- three flashes to mean 'I am operating astern propulsion';

(ii)   the duration of each flash shall be about one second, the interval between flashes shall be about one second, and the interval between successive signals shall be not less than ten seconds;

(iii) the light used for this signal shall, if fitted, be an all-round white light, visible at a minimum range of 5 miles, and shall comply with the provisions of Annex I to these Regulations.

(c) When in sight of one another in a narrow channel or fairway:

(i) a vessel intending to overtake another shall in compliance with Rule 9 (e)(i) indicate her intention by the following signals on her whistle:

- two prolonged blasts followed by one short blast to mean 'I intend to overtake you on your starboard side';
- two prolonged blasts followed by two short blasts to mean 'I intend to overtake you on your port side',

(ii) the vessel about to be overtaken when acting in accordance with Rule 9 (e)(i) shall indicate her agreement by the following signal on her whistle:

- one prolonged, one short, one prolonged and one short blast, in that order.

(d) When vessels in sight of one another are approaching each other and from any cause either vessel fails to understand the intentions or actions of the other, or is in doubt whether sufficient action is being taken by the other to avoid collision, the vessel in doubt shall immediately indicate such doubt by giving at least five short and rapid blasts on the whistle. Such a signal may be supplemented by a light signal of at least five short and rapid flashes.

(e) A vessel nearing a bend or an area of a channel or fairway where other vessels may be obscured by an intervening obstruction shall sound one prolonged blast. Such signal shall be answered with a prolonged blast by any approaching vessel that may be within hearing around the bend or behind the intervening obstruction.

(f) If whistles are fitted on a vessel at a distance apart of more than 100 metres, one whistle only shall be used for giving manoeuvring and warning signals.

RULE 37 Distress signals

When a vessel is in distress and requires assistance she shall use or exhibit the signals described in Annex IV to these Regulations.

Annex IV

1 The following signals, used or exhibited either together or separately, indicate distress and need of assistance:

(a) a gun or other explosive signal fired at intervals of about a minute;

(b) a continuous sounding with any fog signalling apparatus;

(c) rockets or shells, throwing red stars fired one at a time at short intervals;

(d) a signal made by radiotelegraphy or by any other signalling method consisting of the group ··· --- ··· (SOS) in the Morse Code;

(e) a signal sent by radiotelephony consisting of the spoken word 'Mayday';

Fig 17.4 Distress signals

(f) The International Code Signal of distress indicated by NC;

(g) a signal consisting of a square flag having above or below it a ball or anything resembling a ball;

(h) flames on the vessel (as from a burning tar barrel, oil barrel, etc);

(i) a rocket parachute flare or a hand flare showing a red light;

(j) a smoke signal giving off orange-coloured smoke;

(k) slowly and repeatedly raising and lowering arms outstretched to each side;

(l) the radio telegraph alarm signal;

(m) the radiotelephone alarm signal;

(n) signals transmitted by emergency position-indicating radio beacons.

2 The use or exhibition of any of the foregoing signals except for the purpose of indicating distress and need of assistance and the use of other signals which may be confused with any of the above signals is prohibited.

3 Attention is drawn to the relevant sections of the International Code of Signals, the Merchant Ship Search and Rescue Manual and the following signals; (a) a piece of orange coloured canvas and either a black square and circle or other appropriate symbol (for identification from the air); (b) a dye marker.

QUESTIONS

17.1 What are you required to do at all times?

17.2 If you are required to alter course to avoid another boat, what three things should you do?

17.3 Study these sketches and state which boat has right of way:

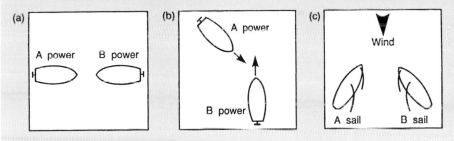

17.4 Give three instances when a sailing boat must keep clear of a motorboat.

17.5 How can you determine whether there is a risk of collision with another boat?

18 ■ GLOSSARY OF NAUTICAL TERMS AND DEFINITIONS

Aback: A sail is aback when the wind strikes it on what would normally be its lee side.

Abaft the beam: The sector on both sides of a boat from abeam to astern.

Abeam: The direction at right angles to the fore-and-aft line.

Abate: The true wind abates or moderates when it blows less strongly than before.

Adrift: Not attached to the seabed.

Afloat: Floating; at sea.

Aft: Near or towards the stern.

Ahead: The direction of an object beyond the stem of a boat.

Ahoy!: Shout to attract attention of another vessel.

Alee: To leeward.

Almanac: An annual publication containing information on, for example, buoyage, tides, signals, glossaries, and positions of heavenly bodies.

Aloft: Above deck.

Amidships: The centre part of the boat.

Anchor buoy: Buoy or float secured by a tripping line to the crown of the anchor.

Anchor cable: Chain or rope connection between a boat and her anchor.

Anchor light: An all-round white light usually shackled to the forestay of a boat and hoisted to a suitable height by the jib halyard.

Anchor locker: A locker where the anchor and anchor chain are kept.

Anchor roller: A roller over which the cable is passed when at anchor.

Anchor watch: Watch kept when a boat is at anchor to check whether the anchor is dragging.

Anchor well: *See* anchor locker.

Answer the helm: A boat answers the helm when she alters course in response to the helmsman's deflection of the rudder.

Apparent wind: The wind felt by the crew in a boat that is moving over the ground.

Ashore: On the land; or aground.

Astern: Direction beyond the stern; or a movement through the water in that direction.

Athwartships: At right angles to the centreline of the boat inside the boat.

Autopilot: Equipment that allows the boat to follow automatically a compass course or a course relative to wind direction.

Auxiliary: A term for a sailing boat that has auxiliary power, ie an engine.

Avast!: Order to stop an activity.

Awash: Level with the surface of the water which just washes over an object.

Babystay: An inner forestay.

Back: To back a sail: it is sheeted or held to windward so that the wind strikes it on the side which is normally to leeward. Of wind: it backs when it shifts to blow from a direction that is further anticlockwise.

Back splice: The end of a rope that has been finished by unlaying the strands, making a crown knot and tucking the strands back down the rope.

Backstay: A stay that supports the mast from aft.

Backwind: Airflow that is deflected on to the lee side of a sail, such as a jib backwinding the mainsail.

Bail: To remove water from the bilges or cockpit.

Bailer: A utensil used to bail water out of a boat.

Deck areas and fittings.

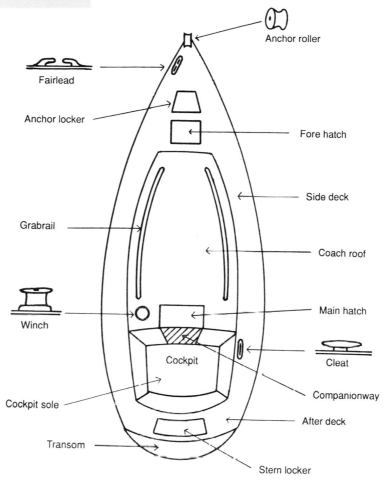

Anchor roller

Fairlead

Anchor locker

Fore hatch

Side deck

Grabrail

Coach roof

Main hatch

Winch

Cleat

Cockpit

Cockpit sole

Companionway

After deck

Transom

Stern locker

Ball: A black signal shape normally displayed by day when a boat is at anchor.

Ballast: Additional weight placed low in the hull to improve stability.

Bar: A shoal close by a river mouth or harbour entrance; a measure of barometric pressure usually noted as 1000 millibars.

Bare poles: No sails are set and the boat is driven by the force of the wind on the spars and rigging.

Barnacle: A marine crustacean that attaches itself to the bottom of a boat.

Batten: A flexible strip of wood or plastic used to stiffen the leech of a mainsail.

Batten pocket: A pocket on the leech of a mainsail to contain a batten.

Beach: To run a boat ashore deliberately.

Beacon: A mark erected on land or on the bottom in shallow waters to guide or warn shipping.

Beam: The breadth of a boat.

Beam reach: A point of sailing with the wind roughly at right angles to the fore-and-aft line.

Bear: The direction of an object from an observer.

Bear away: To put the helm to windward so that the boat alters course to leeward away from the wind.

Bearing: The direction of an object from an observer given as an angle from a line of reference (true north or magnetic north).

Bearings (3 figure notation): Bearings and courses are given in a 3 figure notation, that is: 180°C or 180°T depending on whether it is a Compass or True bearing.

Beating: Sailing towards an objective to windward following a zigzag course on alternate tacks.

Beaufort scale: A scale for measurement of the force of the wind.

Belay: To make fast a line round a cleat or bollard.

Bell: In restricted visibility a bell is rung to indicate that a boat is at anchor or aground.

Below deck: Beneath the deck.

Bend: To connect two ropes with a knot; to prepare a sail for hoisting, a type of knot.

Berth: A place where a boat can lie for a period; a sleeping place on a boat; to given an obstruction a wide berth by keeping well clear.

Bight: A loop or curve in a rope or line.

Bilge: The rounded part of a boat where the bottom curves upwards towards the sides.

Bilges: The lowest part inside the hull below the cabin sole where bilge water collects.

Bilge keel: One of two keels fitted on either side of a boat's hull to resist rolling and provide lateral resistance.

Binnacle: Strong housing to protect the steering compass.

Blanket: To take the wind from another boat's sails.

Blast (foghorn): A sound signal – a short blast lasts 1 second, a prolonged blast 4 to 6 seconds.

Block: A pulley made of wood, metal or plastic.

Boat-hook: A pole, generally of wood or light alloy, with a hook at one end, used for picking up moorings and buoys.

Bollard: Strong fitting, firmly bolted to the deck, to which mooring lines are made fast. Large bollards are on quays, piers and pontoons.

Bolt rope: Rope sewn to one or more edges of a sail either to reinforce the sides or so that the sail can be fed into a grooved spar.

Boom: Spar that supports the foot of a sail.

Boom out: On a run to thrust the genoa out to windward so that it fills with wind.

Boot top: A narrow strip just above the waterline between the bottom and side of the hull. Usually of contrasting colour.

Bottlescrew: A rigging screw to tension the standing rigging or guardrails.

Bow: The forward part of a boat. A direction 45° either side of right ahead.

Bowline: A knot tied in the end of a line to make a loop that will neither slip nor jam.

Breakwater: A structure to protect a harbour or beach from the force of the sea.

Breast rope: A mooring line that runs at right angles to the centreline; one runs from the bow and another from the stern to the shore or a boat alongside.

Breather: A pipe fitted to a water or fuel tank which allows air to escape.

Broach: With heavy following seas the boat can slew round uncontrollably, heeling dangerously.

Broad reach: The point of sailing between a beam reach and a run.

Broken out: The anchor, when pulled out of the seabed by heaving on the cable, is broken out.

Bulkhead: A vertical partition below decks.

Bunk: A built-in sleeping place.

Buoy: A floating object used to indicate the position of a channel, wreck, danger, etc., or the position of an object on the seabed.

Buoyancy aid: A life-preserver to help

a person float if he falls in; less effective than a lifejacket.

Burgee: A triangular flag worn at the masthead.

Cabin: The sheltered area in which the crew live and sleep.

Cable: Chain or rope that is made fast to the anchor. A measure of distance equivalent to one tenth of a nautical mile.

Capsize: The boat overturns.

Cast off: To let go a rope or line.

Cavita line: A decorative line of contrasting colour on the hull of the boat, near the rubbing strake.

Centreboard: A board lowered through a slot in the keel to reduce leeway by providing lateral resistance.

Chafe: Damage or wear resulting from friction.

Chain locker: *See* anchor locker.

Chainplate: A fitting which is bolted to the hull, to which the shrouds are attached.

Chandler: A shop which sells nautical gear.

Channel: A waterway through shoals, rivers or harbours.

Chart: Printed map giving many details about the area covered by water and details about the adjacent land.

Chart datum: Reference level on charts and for use in tidal predictions.

Clear: To disentangle a line; to avoid a danger or obstruction; improved weather.

Cleat: A fitting with two horns round which a rope is secured.

Clevis pin: A locking pin with an eye at one end through which a slip ring is fitted to prevent accidental withdrawal.

Clew: The after lower corner of a sail to which the sheets are fitted.

Clew outhaul: The line which tensions the foot of the mainsail.

Close hauled: The point of sailing when the boat is as close to the wind as she can lie with advantage in working to windward.

Coachroof: The part of the cabin that is raised above the deck to provide height in the cabin.

Coaming: Vertical structure surrounding a hatch or cockpit to prevent water entering.

Coast radio station: A radio station for communication between ships at sea and the public telephone network.

Coastguard: The organisation responsible for search and rescue operations in UK waters.

Cocked hat: In navigation the triangle formed when three position lines fail to meet at a single point.

Cockpit: A space lower than deck level in which the crew can sit or stand.

Collision course: The course of a boat which, if maintained relative to that of another, would result in a collision.

Compass rose: A circle printed on a chart representing the true compass and graduated clockwise from 0° to 360°.

Cone: A signal shape displayed either point upwards or point downwards.

Counter: Above the waterline where the stern extends beyond the rudder post forming a broad afterdeck abaft the cockpit.

Course: The direction in which the boat is being, or is to be, steered.

Courtesy ensign: The national flag of the country being visited by a foreign boat; it should be flown from the starboard spreader.

CQR anchor: A patented anchor with good holding power.

Cringle: A rope loop, usually with a metal thimble, worked in the edge of a sail.

Crutch: A U-shaped fitting with a pin, which fits into a hole in the gunwale and provides a fulcrum for the oar.

Dan buoy: A temporary mark to indicate a position, say, or a man overboard. A flag flies from a spar passing through a float weighted at the bottom.

Deck log: A book in which all matters concerning navigation are entered.

Depth sounder: *See* echo sounder.

Deviation: The deflection of the needle of a magnetic compass caused by the proximity of ferrous metals, electrical circuits or electronic equipment.

Diaphone: A powerful two-tone fog signal with a grunt at the end.

Dip the ensign: To lower the ensign briefly as a salute. It is not rehoisted until the vessel saluted has dipped and rehoisted hers in acknowledgement.

Direction finder: A radio receiver with a directional antenna with which the bearing of a radio beacon can be found.

Displacement: The weight of a boat defined as the weight of water displaced by that boat.

Distance made good: The distance covered over the ground having made allowance for tidal stream and leeway.

Dividers: Navigational instrument for measuring distances on charts.

Dodger: Screen fitted to give the crew protection from wind and spray.

Dolphin: A mooring post or group of piles.

Double up: To put out extra mooring lines when a storm is expected.

Douse: To lower a sail or extinguish a light quickly.

Downhaul: A rope or line with which an object such as a spar or sail is pulled down.

Downstream: The direction towards which the stream flows.

Downwind: Direction to leeward.

Drag: The anchor drags when it fails to hold and slides over the seabed.

Draught: The vertical distance from the lowest part of the keel to the waterline.

Dredger: A vessel for dredging a channel.

Dress ship: On special occasions ships in harbour or at anchor dress overall with International Code flags from the stem to the top of the mast and down to the stern.

Drift: To be carried by the tidal stream. The distance that a boat is carried by the tidal stream in a given time.

Drifter: A fishing vessel that lies to her nets.

Drop astern: To fall astern of another boat.

Drop keel: A keel that can be drawn up into the hull.

Ease out: To let a rope out gradually.

Ebb: The period when the tidal level is falling.

Echo sounder: An electronic depth-finding instrument.

Ensign: The national flag worn at or near the stern of a boat to indicate her nationality.

EPIRB: An Emergency Position Indicating Radio Beacon that transmits a distinctive signal on a distress frequency.

Even keel: A boat floating so that her mast is more or less vertically upright.

Eye: A loop or eye splice. The eyes of a boat: right forward.

Eyelet: A small hole in a sail with metal grommet through which lacing is passed.

Eye splice: A permanent eye spliced in the end of a rope or wire rope.

Fair: Advantageous or favourable, as of wind or tidal stream.

Fairlead: The lead through which a working line is passed in order to alter the direction of pull.

Fairway: The main channel in a body of water such as an estuary or river.

Fender: Any device hung outboard to absorb the shock when coming alongside and to protect the hull when moored alongside.

Fetch: The distance travelled by the wind when crossing open water: the height of the waves is proportional to the fetch and strength of the wind.

Fin keel: A steel keel bolted to the hull.

Fix: The position of a boat as plotted on the chart from position lines obtained by compass bearings, direction finder, echo sounder, etc.

Flake down: Rope laid down on deck in a figure of eight pattern so that it will run out easily.

Flashing: A light used as an aid to navigation that flashes repeatedly at regular intervals.

Flood: The period when the tidal level is rising.

Fluke: The shovel-shaped part of an anchor that digs into the ground.

Flying out: A sail is flying out in a breeze when it has no tension in the sheets.

Focsle (Forecastle): The part of the accommodation below the foredeck and forward of the mast.

Fog: Visibility reduced to less than 1000 metres (approximately 0.5 nautical miles).

Foghorn: A horn with which fog signals are made.

Following sea: Seas that are moving in the same direction as the boat is heading.

Foot: The lower edge of a sail.

Fore-and-aft: Parallel line between the stem and the stern.

Foredeck: The part of the deck that is forward of the mast and coachroof.

Forefoot: The area below the water where the stem joins the keel.

Forehatch: A hatch forward, usually in the foredeck.

Forepeak: The most forward compartment in the bows of the boat.

Foresail: The headsail set on the forestay.

Forestay: The stay from high on the mast to the stemhead providing fore-and-aft support for the mast.

Foul: The opposite of clear; adverse (wind or tide); unsuitable.

Foul anchor: An anchor whose flukes are caught on an obstruction on the seabed or tangled with the cable.

Frap: Tie halyards to keep them off the mast to stop them rattling noisily in the wind when in harbour.

Freeboard: The vertical distance between the waterline and the top of the deck.

Free wind: The wind when it blows from a direction abaft the beam.

Front (air mass): Boundary between air masses at different temperatures.

Full and by: Close-hauled with all sails full and drawing; not pinching.

Full rudder: The maximum angle to which the rudder can be turned.

Furling: Rolling up or gathering and lashing a lowered sail using sail ties or shock-cord to prevent it from blowing about.

Gale: In the Beaufort scale, wind force 8, 34 to 40 knots. Severe gale, force 9, is 41 to 47 knots.

Galley: An area where food is prepared and cooked.

Gelcoat: The outer unreinforced layer of resin in a GRP hull.

Genoa: A large overlapping headsail set in light breezes.

Ghoster: A light full headsail set in light breezes.

Give-way vessel: The vessel whose duty it is to keep clear of another; she should take early and substantial action to avoid a collision.

Go about: To change from one tack to another by luffing and turning the bows through the wind.

Gong: A fog signal sounded in conjunction with a bell in a vessel over 100m in length when at anchor or aground.

Gooseneck: Fitting which attaches the boom to the mast.

Goosewing: To fly the headsail on the opposite side to the mainsail (using a spinnaker pole or whisker pole perhaps) when running.

Grab rail: Rails fitted above and below decks to grab at when the boat heels.

Ground: To run aground or touch the bottom either accidentally or deliberately.

Ground tackle: A general term for the anchors, cables and all the gear required when anchoring.

Groyne: *See* breakwater.

GRP: Glass Reinforced Plastic.

Guardrail: Safety line fitted round the boat to prevent the crew from falling overboard.

Gunwale: The upper edge of the side of a boat.

Guy: A line attached to the end of a spar to keep it in position.

Gybe: To change from one tack to another by turning the stern through the wind.

Gybe-oh!: The call to indicate that the helm is being put across to gybe.

Hail: To shout loudly to crew in another boat.

Half hitch: A simple knot.

Halyard: A line or rope with which a sail, spar or flag is hoisted up a mast.

Hand-bearing compass: Portable magnetic compass with which visual bearings are taken.

Handrail: A wooden or metal rail on the coachroof or below deck which can be grabbed to steady a person.

Hanks: Fittings made of metal or nylon by which the luff of a staysail is held to a stay.

Hard: Hard ground where boats can be launched.

Hard and fast: Said of a boat that has run aground and is unable to get off immediately.

Harden in: To haul in the sheets to bring the sail closer to the centreline; the opposite of ease out.

Hatch: An opening in the deck that allows access to the accommodation.

Haul in: To pull in.

Hawse pipe: A hole in the bow of a vessel through which the anchor cable passes.

Haze: Visibility reduced to between 0.5 and 2 nautical miles by dry particles in suspension in the air.

Head: The bow or forward part of the boat. The upper corner of a triangular sail.

Head line: The mooring line or rope leading forward from the bows.

Head to wind: To point the stem of the boat into the wind.

Heading: The direction in which the boat's head is pointing, her course.

Headland: A fairly high and steep part of the land that projects into the sea.

Heads: The lavatory on a boat.

Headsail: Any sail set forward of the mast or of the foremast if there is more than one mast.

Headway: Movement through the water stem first.

Heat seal: To fuse the ends of the strands of a man-made fibre rope by heating.

Heaving line: A light line coiled ready for throwing; sometimes the end is weighted.

Heaving-to: A boat heaves-to when she goes about leaving the headsail sheeted on the original side so it is backed. Ideal manoeuvre for reefing in heavy weather.

Heel: To lean over to one side.

Height of tide: The vertical distance at any instant between sea level and chart datum.

Helmsman: The member of the crew who steers the boat.

Hitch: A type of knot.

Hoist: To raid an object vertically with a halyard.

Holding ground: The composition of the seabed that determines whether the anchor will hold well or not.

Hull: The body of a boat excluding masts, rigging and rudder.

Hull down: Said of a distant vessel when only the mast, sail and/or superstructure is visible above the horizon.

Hurricane: In the Beaufort scale, wind of force 12, 64 knots or above.

Hydrofoil: A boat with hydrofoils to lift the wetted surface of her hull clear of the water at speed.

Hydrography: The science of surveying the waters of the earth and adjacent land area, and publishing the results in charts, pilots, etc, for example Admiralty charts.

IALA: The International Association of Lighthouse Authorities which is responsible for the international buoyage system.

Impeller: Screw-like device which is rotated by water flowing past: used for measuring boat speed and distance travelled through the water.

In irons: Said of a boat that stops head to wind when going about.

Inflatable dinghy: A dinghy of synthetic rubber filled with air; can be deflated for stowage on board.

Inshore: Near to or towards or in the direction of the shore.

Isobar: On a synoptic chart, a line joining points of equal pressure.

Isophase: A light where the duration of light and darkness are equal.

Jackstay: A wire secured between two points.

Jam cleat (self jamming): A cleat with one horn shorter than the other designed so that a rope can be secured with a single turn.

Jib: Triangular headsail set on a stay forward of the mast.

Jury rig: A temporary but effective device that replaces lost or damaged gear.

Kedge anchor: A lightweight anchor used to move a boat or anchor temporarily in fine weather.

Keel: The main longitudinal beam on a boat between the stem and the stern.

Ketch: A two-masted boat where the after (mizzen) mast is smaller and is stepped forward of the rudder stock.

kHz (kilohertz): A measurement of frequency of radio waves equivalent to 1000 cycles per second.

Kicking strap: Line or tackle to pull the boom down to keep it horizontal.

Kink: A sharp twist in a rope or wire rope; can be avoided by coiling the rope properly.

Knot: The unit of speed at sea; one nautical mile per hour; a series of loops in a rope or line.

Landfall: Land first sighted after a long voyage at sea.

Lanyard: A short length of line used to secure an object such as a knife.

Lash down: To secure firmly with a rope or line.

Lay: Strands twisted together to form a rope. To lay a mark is to sail direct to it without tacking.

Lead line: A line marked with knots at regular intervals and attached to a heavy weight; used to determine the depth of water.

Lee: The direction towards which the wind blows.

Leeboard: A board or strip of canvas along the open side of a berth to prevent the occupant from falling out.

Lee helm: The tendency of a boat to turn her bow to leeward.

Leech: The trailing edge of a triangular sail.

Lee-oh!: The action of putting the helm across to go about.

Lee shore: A coastline towards which the onshore wind blows; the shore to leeward of a boat.

Leeward: Downwind, away from the wind, the direction towards which the wind blows.

Leeward boat: When two boats are on the same tack, the leeward boat is that which is to leeward of the other.

Leeway: The angular difference between the water track and the boat's heading. The effect of wind moving the boat bodily to leeward.

Lifeline: A wire or line attached at either end to a strong point and rigged along the deck to provide a handhold or to clip on a safety harness.

Line: Alternative name for small rope or for a rope used for mooring a boat.

Line of soundings: Numerous soundings taken at regular intervals.

List: A permanent lean to one side or the other.

List of lights: Official publication giving details of lights exhibited as aids to navigation.

Lively: Said of a boat that responds rapidly to the seas.

LOA: Length overall.

Loafer: A lightweight sail used when reaching or running in light winds.

Lock: A chamber with gates at each end in which the water level can be raised or lowered.

Locker: An enclosed stowage anywhere on board.

Locking turns: A reversed turn on a cleat to make a rope more secure; not advisable for halyards which may need to be cast off quickly.

Log: A device to measure a boat's speed or distance travelled through the water. *See* deck log.

Log reading: The reading of distance travelled through the water usually taken every hour from the log and recorded in the deck log.

Look-out: Visual watch; or the member of the crew responsible for keeping it.

Loom: The glow from a light below the horizon usually seen as a reflection on the clouds.

Lop: Short choppy seas.

Lose way: A boat loses way when she slows down and stops in the water.

Lubber line: The marker in the compass which is aligned with the fore-and-aft line of the boat against which the course can be read off on the compass card.

Luff: The leading edge of a fore-and-aft sail.

Lull: A temporary drop in wind speed.

Mainsail: The principal sail.

Mainsheet traveller: The athwartships slider to which the mainsheet tackle is made.

Make fast: To secure a line or rope to a cleat, mooring ring, bollard, etc.

Make heavy weather: Said of a yacht which rolls and pitches heavily, making slow and uncomfortable progress.

Make sail: To hoist the sails and get under way.

Make water: To leak but not by shipping water over the side.

Marina: Artificial boat harbour usually consisting of pontoons.

Mark: An object that marks a position.

Maroon: An explosive signal used to summon the crew when a lifeboat is called out.

Mast: The most important vertical spar without which no sail can be set.

Mast step: Fitting into which the mast heel fits.

Masthead light: A white light exhibited near the masthead by a power-driven vessel under way.

Masthead rig: A boat with the forestay attached to the masthead.

Mayday: The internationally recognised radio telephone distress signal.

Medico: When included in an urgency call (Pan Pan) on the radio telephone, medico indicates that medical advice is required.

MHWS (Mean High Water Springs): The average level of all high water at spring tides throughout the year: used as the datum level for heights of features on the chart.

Mist: Visibility reduced to between 0.5 and 2 nautical miles due to suspension of water particles in the air.

Mizzen mast: The smaller aftermast of a ketch or yawl.

Mole: A breakwater made of stone or concrete.

Monohull: A boat with a single hull.

Mooring: The ground tackle attached to a mooring buoy.

Mooring buoy: A non-navigational buoy to which a boat can moor.

Mooring ring: A ring on a mooring buoy.

Multihull: A boat with more than one hull such as a catamaran or trimaran.

Nautical almanac: Official publication giving positions of heavenly bodies and other information to enable a boat's position to be established.

Nautical mile: Unit of distance at sea based on the length of one minute of latitude.

Navel pipe: A pipe which passes through the deck to the anchor chain locker.

Navigation lights: Lights exhibited by all vessels between sunset and sunrise.

Neap tide: Tides where the range is least and the tidal streams run least strongly.

Near gale: Wind of Beaufort force 7, 28 to 33 knots.

Parts of the sail.

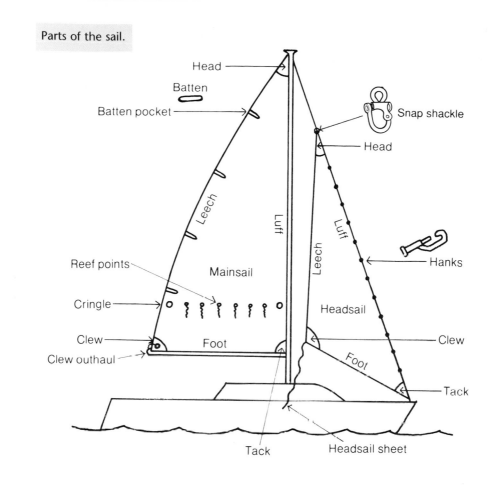

Head — Batten — Batten pocket — Snap shackle — Head — Leech — Luff — Luff — Leech — Reef points — Mainsail — Hanks — Cringle — Headsail — Clew — Clew — Foot — Clew outhaul — Foot — Tack — Tack — Headsail sheet

Nominal range of a light: Nominal range of a light is dependent on its intensity: it is the luminous range when the meteorological visibility is 10 nautical miles.

No sail sector: An area either side of the wind, towards which a boat cannot sail.

Not under command: A vessel unable to manoeuvre such as one whose rudder has been damaged.

Notice to mariners: Official notices issued weekly or at other times detailing corrections to charts and hydrographic publications.

Occulting light: A rhythmic light eclipsing at regular intervals so that the duration of light in each period is greater than the duration of darkness.

Offing: The part of the sea that is visible from the shore. To keep an offing is to keep a safe distance from the shore.

Oilskins: Waterproof clothing worn in foul weather.

On the bow: A direction about 45° from right ahead on either side of the boat.

On the quarter: A direction about 45° from right astern on either side of the boat.

Open: When two leading marks are not in line they are said to be open.

Osmosis: Water absorption through tiny pinholes in a GRP hull causing deterioration of the moulding.

Outhaul: A line with which the mainsail is hauled out along the boom.

Overcanvas: A boat carrying too much sail for the weather conditions.

Overfalls: Turbulent waters where there is a sudden change in depth or where two tidal streams meet.

Overtaking light: The white stern light; seen by an overtaking vessel when approaching from astern.

Painter: The line at the bow of a dinghy.

Pan pan: The internationally recognised radio telephone urgency signal which has priority over all the other calls except Mayday.

Parallel rules: Navigational instrument used in conjunction with the compass rose on a chart to transfer bearings and courses to plot a boat's position.

Pay off: The boat's head pays off when it turns to leeward away from the wind.

Pay out: To let out a line or rope gradually.

Period: Of a light, the time that it takes a rhythmic light to complete one sequence.

Pile: A stout timber or metal post driven vertically into a river or seabed.

Pilot: An expert in local waters who assists vessels entering or leaving harbour. An official publication listing details of, for example, local coasts, dangers and harbours.

Pilot berth: A berth or bunk for use at sea.

Pinch: To sail too close to the wind so that the sails lose driving power.

Pipe cot: A spare berth on a pipe frame that hinges up when not in use.

Piston hanks: A hank on the luff of a staysail.

Pitch: The up and down motion of the bow and stern of a boat.

Pitchpole: A capsize in a following sea where the stern is lifted over the bow.

Play: To adjust a sheet continuously rather than cleating it. Movement of equipment such as the rudder in its mounting or housing.

Plot: To find a boat's position by laying off bearings on a chart.

Plough anchor: An anchor shaped like a ploughshare similar to a CQR anchor.

Point: The ability of a boat to sail close-hauled: the closer she sails the better she points. A division of 11° 15′ on the compass.

Poling out: Using a spar to push a foresail out when running.

Pontoon: A watertight tank, usually between piles, that rises and falls with the tide.

Pooped: A condition of a boat in which a following sea has broken over the stern into the cockpit.

Port hand: A direction on the port or left hand side of the boat.

Port side: The left hand side of a boat when looking towards the bow.

Position line: A line drawn on a chart by the navigator.

Pound: A boat pounds in heavy seas when the bows drop heavily after being lifted by a wave.

Prevailing wind: The wind direction that occurs most frequently at a place over a certain period.

Preventer: A line rigged from the end of the boom to the bow in heavy weather to prevent an accidental gybe.

Privileged vessel: The stand-on vessel in a collision situation: she should maintain her course and speed.

Pull: To row.

Pulpit: Stainless steel frame at the bow encircling the forestay to which the guardrails are attached.

Pushpit: Colloquial term for the stern pulpit.

Pyrotechnic: Any type of rocket or flare used for signalling.

Quarter: The side of the hull between amidships and astern.

Quarter berth: A berth that extends under the deck between the cockpit and the hull.

Race: A strong tidal stream.

Radar reflector: A device hoisted or fitted up the mast to enhance the reflection of radar energy.

Radio direction finder: A radio receiver with a directional aerial that enables the navigator to find the direction from which a radio signal arrives.

Raft of boats: Two or more boats tied up alongside each other.

Range of tide: The difference between sea level at high water and sea level at the preceding or following low water.

Rate: The speed of a tidal stream or current given in knots and tenths of a knot.

RDF: Radio Direction Finder.

Reach: A boat is on a reach when she is either close-hauled or running. It is her fastest point of sail.

Ready about: The helmsman's shout that he intends to go about shortly.

Reciprocal course: The course (or bearing) that differs by 180°.

Reed: A weak high-pitched fog signal.

Reef: To reduce the area of sail, particularly the mainsail.

Reef points: Short light lines sewn into the sail parallel with the boom that are tied under the foot (or under the boom itself) when the sail is reefed in high winds.

Reefing pendants: A strong line with which the luff and leech are pulled down to the boom when a sail is reefed.

Relative bearing: The direction of an object relative to the fore-and-aft line of a boat measured in degrees from right ahead.

Relative wind: *See* apparent wind.

Restricted visibility: Visibility restricted by rain, drizzle, fog, etc, during which vessels are required to proceed at a safe speed and to navigate with extreme caution.

Rhumb line: A line on the surface of the earth that cuts all meridians at the same angle. On a standard (Mercator) chart the rhumb line appears as a straight line.

Ride: To lie at anchor free to swing to the wind and tidal stream.

Ridge: On a synoptic chart, a narrow area of relatively high pressure between two low pressure areas.

Riding light: Alternative term for anchor light.

Riding turn: On a winch the situation where an earlier turn rides over a later turn and jams.

Rigging: All ropes, lines, wires and gear used to support the masts and to control the spars and sails.

Right of way: Term used for the vessel which does not give way.

Risk of collision: A possibility that a collision may occur; usually established by taking a compass bearing of an approaching vessel.

Roads: An anchorage where the holding ground is known to be good and there is some protection from the wind and sea.

Roll: The periodic rotating movement of a boat that leans alternatively to port and starboard.

Roller reef: A method of reefing where the sail area is reduced by rolling part of the sail around the boom.

Rolling hitch: A knot used to attach a small line to a larger line or spar.

Rotator: A metal spinner with vanes which rotates when a boat moves through the water actuating the log on board to which it is attached by a log line.

Round: To sail around a mark.

Round turn: A complete turn of a rope or line around an object. The rope completely encircles the object.

Round up: To head up into the wind.

Roving fender: A spare fender held ready by a crewmember in case of emergencies.

Rowlock: A space in the gunwhale in which the oar is placed.

Rubbing strake: A projecting strake round the top of a hull to protect the hull when lying alongside.

Rudder: A control surface in the water at or near the stern, used for altering course.

Run: The point of sailing where a boat sails in the same direction as the wind is blowing with her sheets eased right out.

Run down: To collide with another boat.

Runner: A backstay that supports the mast from aft and can be slacked off.

Running fix: A navigational fix when only a single landmark is available. Two bearings are taken and plotted at different times, making allowance for distance travelled.

Running rigging: All rigging that moves and is not part of the standing rigging.

Sacrificial anode: A zinc plate fastened to the hull to prevent corrosion of metal fittings on the hull.

Sail locker: Place where sails are stowed.

Sail ties: Light lines used to lash a lowered sail to the boom or guardrails to prevent it blowing about.

Sailing directions: Also called Pilots. Official publications covering specific areas containing navigational information concerning, for example, coasts, harbours and tides.

Sailing free: Not close-hauled; sailing with sheets eased out.

Saloon: The main cabin.

Salvage: The act of saving a vessel from danger at sea.

Samson post: Strong fitting bolted firmly to the deck around which anchor cables, mooring lines or tow ropes are made fast.

SAR: Search and Rescue.

Scend: Vertical movement of waves or swell against, for example, a harbour wall.

Scope: The ratio of the length of anchor cable let out to the depth of water.

Scupper: Drain hole in the toe-rail.

Sea anchor: A device, such as a conical canvas bag open at both ends, streamed from bow or stern to hold a boat bow or stern on to the wind or sea.

Sea breeze: A daytime wind blowing across a coastline from the sea caused by the rising air from land heated by the sun.

Sealegs: The ability to keep one's feet in spite of the motion of the boat.

Seacock: A stop-cock next to the hull to prevent accidental entry of water.

Searoom: An area in which a vessel can navigate without difficulty or danger of hitting an obstruction.

Seaway: A stretch of water where there are waves.

Securité: An internationally recognised safety signal used on the radio telephone preceding an important navigational or meteorological warning.

Seize: To bind two ropes together.

Serve: To cover and protect a splice on a rope by binding with small line or twine.

Set (sails): To hoist a sail.

Set (tidal stream): The direction to which a tidal stream or current flows.

Set sail: To start out on a voyage.

Shackle: A metal link for connecting ropes, wires or chains to sails, anchors, etc. To shackle on is to connect using a shackle.

Shape: A ball, cone or diamond shaped object, normally black, hoisted by day in a vessel to indicate a special state or occupation.

Sheave: A wheel over which a rope or wire runs.

Sheer off: To turn away from another vessel or object in the water.

Sheet: Rope or line fastened to the clew of a sail or the end of the boom supporting it. Named after the sail to which it is attached.

Sheet bend: A knot used to join two ropes of different size together.

Sheet in: To pull in on a sheet till it is taut and the sail drawing.

Shelving: A gradual slope in the seabed.

Shipping forecast: Weather forecast broadcast four times each day by the British Broadcasting Corporation for the benefit of those at sea.

Shipping lane: A busy track across the sea or ocean.

Shipshape: Neat and efficient.

Shoal: An area offshore where the water is so shallow that a ship might run aground. To shoal is to become shallow.

Shock cord: Elastic rubber bands enclosed in a sheath of fibres, very useful for lashing.

Shorten in: Decrease the amount of anchor cable let out.

Shorten sail: To reduce the amount of sail set either by reefing or changing to make a smaller sail.

Shrouds: Parts of the standing rigging that support the mast laterally.

Sidedeck: The deck alongside the coachroof.

Sidelight: The red and green lights exhibited either side of the bows by vessels under way and making way through the water.

Sill: A wall which acts as a dam, to keep water in a marina.

Siren: The fog signal made by vessels over 12 metres in length when under way.

Skeg: A false keel fitted near the stern which supports the leading edge of the rudder.

Skylight: A framework fitted on the deck of a boat with glazed windows to illuminate the cabin and provide ventilation.

Slab reef: A method of reefing a boomed sail where the sail is flaked down on top of the boom.

Slack off: To ease or pay out a line.

Slack water: In tidal waters, the period of time when the tidal stream is non-existent or negligible.

Slam: The underpart of the forward part of the hull hitting the water when pitching in heavy seas.

Slide: A metal or plastic fitting on the luff or foot of a sail running in a track on the mast or boom.

Sliding hatch: A sliding hatch fitted over the entrance to the cabin.

Slip: To let go quickly.

Sliplines: Mooring ropes or lines doubled back so that they can be let go easily from on board.

Slipway: An inclined ramp leading into the sea.

Snap hook: A hook that springs shut when released.

Snap shackle: A shackle that is held closed by a spring-loaded plunger.

Snarl up: Lines or ropes that are twisted or entangled.

Snatch: Jerk caused by too short an anchor cable in a seaway. To take a turn quickly around a cleat, bollard or Samson post.

Snug down: To prepare for heavy weather by securing all loose gear.

Soldier's wind: A wind that enables a sailing boat to sail to her destination and return without beating.

Sole: The floor of a cabin or cockpit.

SOS: International distress signal made by light, sound or radio.

Sound: To measure the depth of water.

Sounding: The depth of water below chart datum.

Sou'wester: A waterproof oilskin hat with a broad brim.

Spar: General term for all poles used on board such as mast, boom and yard.

Speed made good: The speed made good over the ground; that is, the boat speed corrected for tidal stream and leeway.

Spill wind: To ease the sheets so that the sail is only partly filled by the wind, the rest being spilt.

Spindrift: Fine spray off wave crests caused by strong winds.

Spinnaker: A large symmetrical balloon shaped sail used when running or reaching.

Spinnaker pole: A spar which is used to hold the spinnaker out.

Spit: A projecting shoal or strip of land connected to the shore.

Splice: A permanent joint made between two ropes.

Split ring: A ring like a key ring that can be fed into an eye to prevent accidental withdrawal.

Spray hood: A folding canvas cover over the entrance to the cabin.

Spreaders: Metal struts fitted either side of the mast to spread the shrouds out sideways.

Spring tide: The tides at which the range is greatest: the height of high water is greater and that for low water is less than those for neap tides.

Springs: Moorings lines fastened to prevent a boat moving forwards or backwards relative to the quay or other boats alongside.

Squall: A sudden increase of wind speed often associated with a line of low dark clouds representing an advancing cold front.

Stanchions: Metal posts supporting the guardrails.

Standby to gybe: A warning, given by the helmsman, that he is about to gybe.

Stand in: To head towards land.

Stand off: To head away from shore.

Standing rigging: Wire rope or solid rods that support masts and fixed spars but do not control the sails.

Starboard side: The right side when looking forward towards the bow.

Stay: Part of the standing rigging which provides support fore-and-aft.

Staysail: A sail set on a stay.

Steady: Order to the helmsman to keep the boat on her present course.

Steaming light: Alternative term for masthead light.

Steep-to: A sharply sloping seabed.

Steerage way: A boat has steerage way when she is moving fast enough to answer to the helm; that is, to respond to deflections of the rudder.

Steering compass: The compass permanently mounted adjacent to the helmsman which he uses as a reference to keep the boat on a given course.

Stem: The forwardmost part of the hull.

Stemhead: The top of the stem.

Stemhead fitting: A fitting on the stemhead, often an anchor roller.

Stern: The afterpart of the boat.

Stern gland: Packing around the propeller shaft where it passes through the hull.

Stern light: A white light exhibited from the stern.

Stern line: The mooring line going aft from the stern.

Sternsheets: The aftermost part of an open boat.

Stiff: A boat that does not heel easily; opposite to tender.

Stopper knot: A knot made in the end of a rope to prevent it running out through a block or fairlead.

Storm: Wind or Beaufort force 10, 48 to 55 knots; or a violent storm force 11, 56 to 63 knots.

Storm jib: Small heavy jib set in strong winds.

Stormbound: Confined to a port or anchorage by heavy weather.

Stove in: A hull that has been broken inwards.

Stow: Put away in a proper place. Stowed for sea implies that all gear and loose equipment has, in addition, been lashed down.

Strand: To run a vessel aground intentionally or accidentally.

Strop: A loop of wire rope fitted round a spar. A wire rope used to add length to the luff of a headsail.

Strum box: A strainer fitted around the suction end of a bilge pump hose to prevent the pump being choked by debris.

Strut: A small projecting rod.

Suit: A complete set of sails.

Surge: To ease a rope out round a winch or bollard.

Swashway: A narrow channel between shoals.

Sweat up: To tauten a rope as much as possible.

Sweep: A long oar.

Swig: To haul a line tight when it is under load, by pulling it out at right angles and quickly taking in the slack.

Swing: To rotate sideways on a mooring in response to a change in direction of the tidal stream or wind.

Hull and rigging terms.

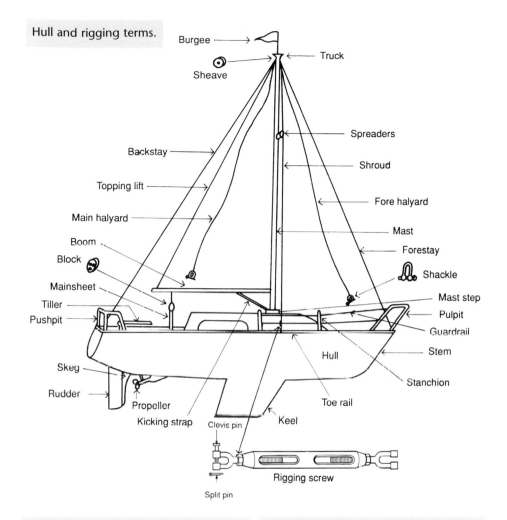

Burgee
Truck
Sheave
Spreaders
Backstay
Shroud
Topping lift
Fore halyard
Main halyard
Mast
Boom
Forestay
Block
Shackle
Mainsheet
Mast step
Tiller
Pulpit
Pushpit
Guardrail
Hull
Stem
Skeg
Stanchion
Rudder
Propeller
Toe rail
Kicking strap
Clevis pin
Keel
Split pin
Rigging screw

Swinging room: The area encompassed by a swing that excludes any risk of collision or of grounding.

Synopsis: A brief statement outlining the weather situation at a particular time.

Synoptic chart: A weather chart covering a large area on which is plotted information giving an overall view of the weather at a particular moment.

Tack: To go about from one course to another with the bow passing through the eye of the wind. A sailing boat is on a tack if she is neither gybing nor tacking; the lower forward corner of a sail.

Tackle: A combination of rope and blocks designed to increase the pulling or hoisting power of a line.

Take in: Lower a sail.

Take the helm: Steer the boat.

Take way off: To reduce the speed of the boat.

Telltales: Lengths of wool or ribbon attached to the sails or shrouds to indicate the airflow or apparent direction of the wind.

Tender: A boat that heels easily is said to be tender; the opposite of stiff.

Thwart: The athwartships seat in a small boat or dinghy.

Tidal stream: The horizontal movement of water caused by the tides.

Tidal stream atlas: An official publication showing the direction and rate of the tidal streams for a particular area.

Tide: The vertical rise and fall of the waters in the oceans in response to the gravitational forces of the sun and moon.

Tide tables: Official annual publication which gives the times and heights of high and low water for standard ports and the differences for secondary ports.

Tideway: The part of a channel where the tidal stream runs most strongly.

Tiller: A lever attached to the rudder head by which the helmsman deflects the rudder.

Time (4 figure notation): Time is given in a four figure notation based on the 24-hour clock.

Toe-rail: A low strip of wood or light alloy that runs round the edge of a deck.

Toggle: A small piece of wood inserted in an eye to make a quick connection.

Topping lift: A line from the base of the mast passing around a sheave at the top thence to the end of the boom to take the weight of the boom when lowering the sail.

Topsides: The part of the boat which lies above the waterline when she is not heeled.

Track: The path between two positions: ground track is that over the ground; water track is that through the water.

Traffic separation scheme: In areas of heavy traffic, a system of one-way lanes. Special regulations apply to shipping in these zones.

Transceiver: A radio transmitter and receiver.

Transducer: A component that converts electric signals into sound waves and vice versa.

Transferred position line: A position line for one time, transferred, with due allowance for the vessel's ground track, to cross with another position line at a later time.

Transit: Two fixed objects are in transit when they are in line.

Transom: The flat transverse structure across the stern of a hull.

Traveller: The sliding car on a track, for example on the main sheet track or adjustable headsail sheet block.

Trawler: A fishing vessel that fishes using nets trawled along the seabed.

Trick: Spell on duty, especially at the helm.

Tri-colour light: A single light at the top of the mast of sailing boats under 20 metres long that can be used in place of the navigation lights.

Trim: To adjust the sails by easing or hardening in the sheets to obtain maximum driving force.

Trip-line: A line attached to the crown of an anchor to enable it to be pulled out backwards if it gets caught fast by an object on the seabed.

Trot: Mooring buoys laid in a line.

Truck: The very top of the mast.

Trysail: A small heavy sail set on the mast in stormy weather in place of the mainsail.

Tune: To improve the performance of a sailing boat or engine.

Twilight: Period before sunrise and after sunset when it is not yet dark.

Twine: Small line used for sewing and whipping.

Unbend: To unshackle sheets and halyards and remove a sail ready to stow.

Underway: A vessel is underway if it is not at anchor, made fast to the shore or aground.

Unshackle: To unfasten.

Unship: To remove an object from its working position.

Up and down: Said of an anchor cable when it is vertical.

Uphaul: A line which is used to raise a spar vertically.

Upstream: The direction from which the wind is blowing.

Vang: A tackle or strap fitted between the boom and the toe-rail to keep the boom horizontal.

Variation: The angle between the true

and the magnetic meridian for any geographical position.

Veer: Of a cable or line, to pay out gradually. Of the wind, to change direction clockwise.

Ventilator (vent): A fitting which allows fresh air to enter the boat.

VHF: Very High Frequency; usually taken as meaning the VHF radio telephone.

Visibility: The greatest distance at which an object can be seen against its background.

Wake: Disturbed water left by a moving boat. The direction of the wake compared with the fore-and-aft line of the boat is often used as a rough measure of leeway.

Warp: Heavy lines used for mooring, kedging or towing, and to move a boat by hauling on warps secured to a bollard or buoy.

Wash: The turbulent water left astern by a moving boat.

Washboards: Removable planks fitted in the cabin entrance to prevent water getting in.

Watch: One of the periods into which 24 hours is divided on board.

Waterline: The line along the hull at the surface of the water in which she floats.

Wear: To change tacks by gybing.

Weather a mark: To succeed in passing to windward of a mark.

Weather helm: The tendency of a boat to turn her bow to windward making it necessary to hold the tiller to the weather side.

Weep: To leak slowly.

Weigh anchor: To raise the anchor.

Well: A sump in the bilges. A small locker for the anchor.

Wheel: The steering wheel that moves the rudder.

Whipping: Twine bound round the ends of a rope to keep it from fraying.

Whisker pole: Light spar to hold out the clew of a headsail when running, particularly when goosewinged.

Whistle: An appliance to make sound signals in restricted visibility and when manoeuvring.

White horses: Breaking waves with foamy crest. Not surf breaking on the shore.

Winch: A fitting designed to assist the crew hauling on a rope or line.

Winch handle: A removable handle used for operating a winch.

Windage: All parts of a boat that contribute to total air drag.

Windlass: The winch used for weighing the anchor.

Windward: The direction from which the wind blows.

Withies: Branches used in small rivers to mark the edges of the channel.

Yankee jib: A large jib set forward of the staysail in light winds.

Yard: A long spar on which a square sail is set.

Yawing: Swinging from side to side of the course set, or at anchor.

Yawl: A two-masted boat where the mizzen mast is aft of the rudder stock.

TEST PAPERS

TEST PAPER A: GENERAL

A1 What are the meanings of the following day shapes?

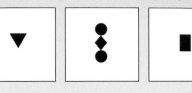

A2 Which vessel has right of way?

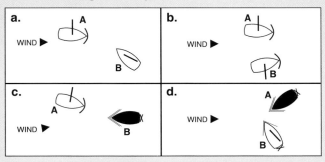

A3 What type of vessel do these lights indicate? Is she under way; what is her aspect and length?

A4 Upon which VHF radio channel will a strong wind warning be announced?

A5 You are listening on the VHF and hear the word *securité*. What type of message would you expect to follow?

A6 The weather forecast reports a large anticyclone stationary centred over England. There is a low pressure to the south over France. Briefly what weather might you expect in the English Channel?

A7 What do the following meteorological terms mean?
- poor visibility
- moving rapidly
- falling slowly
- imminent

A8 You have just recovered a crewmember from the sea. What are your immediate actions?

A9 What basic items would you expect to find in a first aid kit?

A10 You will be mooring to bollards alongside a quay. What type of knot would you use for the head and astern lines? Why?

A11 A crewmember falls over the side of the boat. You have on board a GMDSS transceiver. What is your immediate action?

A12 You are approaching two beacons in transit and would like to check the accuracy of the steering compass, which you suspect might be in error. How can you do this?

A13 Your boat is sinking rapidly and you are about to abandon ship to the dinghy/liferaft. What would you do before entering the dinghy/liferaft?

A14 Use chart 15. You are leaving Poole Harbour. Which side of the Swash Channel should you use?

A15 You are about to enter a Traffic Separation Scheme (TSS). How should you cross the TSS?

A16 For vessels within sight of each other what do the following sound signals signify?
- a) five short blasts.
- b) three short blasts.
- c) two prolonged blasts followed by two short blasts.
- d) one short blast.

A17 What precautions would you take before anchoring if you suspect obstructions on the seabed?

A18 You are about to cross a sandbar drying 1.2m. Your draught is 1.0m and you would like a clearance of 0.5m. What height of tide will you require?

A19 Use chart 15. What are the light characteristics of Anvil Point Light? What do they signify?

A20 Where would you find information on:
- a) tidal streams;
- b) tidal times and heights?

TEST PAPER B: CHARTWORK

On chart 15, chartlet 3, Poole Bay, insert tidal diamond Z at position 50° 41'.9N 1° 44'.6W. Add table as follows:

Tidal streams referred to HW at PORTSMOUTH			
		Z 50°41'9N 1°44'.6W	
Hours	*Dir*	*Rate* *Sp*	*(kn)* *Np*
HW–6	240	0.8	0.4
HW–5	030	0.4	0.2
HW–4	065	1.2	0.5
HW–3	075	1.9	0.9
HW–2	085	2.1	1.0
HW–1	090	1.5	0.7
HW	090	0.4	0.2
HW+1	195	0.6	0.3
HW+2	200	1.2	0.6
HW+3	204	1.8	0.9
HW+4	206	2.4	1.6
HW+5	226	2.0	1.2
HW+6	240	0.8	0.4

All times are BST and variation is 3°W.

B1 On 21 May at 1030, log 7.0, a boat fixes her position by GPS at 50° 43'.6N 1° 41'.4W. From this position what is the bearing and range of Highcliffe Castle? She steers a course of 250°M at a boat speed estimated as 4.2k. What is her estimated position at 1100? Use tidal diamond Z. Leeway nil.

B2 At 1100 the boat takes bearings as follows:

Water Tower	314°M
CG LOOKOUT	005°M
Beacon at end of groyne	047°M

Plot the 1100 position. What are the possible reasons for the difference between the fix and the EP for 1100?

B3 From the 1100 position what is the course to steer for Bar Buoy No 1 at the entrance to Poole Harbour? Boat speed is maintained at 4.2k and the leeway is 5° due to a northwest wind. What is the ETA (estimated time of arrival) at the buoy?

B4 Having reached the Bar Buoy No 1 at 1215, the boat decides to anchor in Studland Bay. What is the course and distance to the anchorage? What will be the approximate height of tide? Assume negligible tidal stream and leeway.

B5 The wind steadily veers round to northeast making the anchorage untenable. At 1600 the boat decides to weigh anchor and enter Poole Harbour. At 1740 she picks up one of the Small Craft Moorings north of Bell Buoy No 20 in Brownsea Road. The depth of water is 3.1m. Over the next 14 hours what will be the maximum and minimum depths on the mooring? Can she remain on the mooring overnight? Use tidal curves for Poole Harbour (Extract 16).

◀ *Southbourne Water Tower.*

Coastguard ▶ lookout on Hengistbury Head.

ANSWERS TO QUESTIONS AND TEST PAPERS

Chapter 1

1.1 Chart 15 is a **much larger scale** than chart 12 so will include more detail.

1.2 **Dorset Harbours and approaches.**

1.3 a) **The latitude scale**
b) **The longitude scale**

1.4 By **using the latitude and longitude scales** as a reference.

1.5 **One nautical mile per hour**.

1.6 During projection distortion occurs on the chart. On a Mercator projection chart the distance scale increases as latitude increases, therefore **one minute of latitude is equivalent to one nautical mile only in the area of the boat's position.**

1.7 **Meridians of longitude** appear as **straight lines** in a north–south direction. **Parallels of latitude** appear as **straight parallel lines** in an east–west direction (at right angles to meridians of longitude). Any **rhumb line course crosses all meridians and parallels of latitude at the same angle.**

1.8 There is **too much distortion**.

1.9 The **Greenwich meridian** which passes through London.

1.10 50° 38'.5.

Chapter 2

2.1 Bar Buoy No 1.

2.2 289°T 3.7M. 0.3M.

2.3 50° 41'.9N 1° 50'.6W. 310°T 1.5M (310°T is the reciprocal of 130°T).

2.4 063°T 7.3M. 2h 17min.

2.5 334°T 1.4M. A caution on the chart states: **BOAT CHANNEL. There is a Boat Channel for use by recreational craft and fishing vessels with a draught of up to 3.0m on the western side of the Swash Channel. Recreational craft and fishing vessels are to use this channel whenever possible.**

Chapter 3

3.1 3°W. For 2001 the variation is 3° 35'W decreasing about 9' annually. In 2005 it will have decreased by about 36', giving a variation of 2° 59'W.

3.2 a) **224°M; 143°M; 009°M.**

b) **352°T; 185°T; 012°T.**

3.3 a) **001°C; 004°C; 158°C.**

b) **231°M; 066°M; 289°M.**

3.4 For a course of 120°C, deviation is 4°E.

a) **089°T; 165°T; 328°T.**

b) **2°W.**

3.5 Well away from anything likely to cause deviation (electrical equipment, magnets, ferrous metal); accurately aligned with the fore-and-aft line of the boat; where it can easily be seen by the helmsman; and where it will not suffer damage.

Chapter 4

4.1 Admiralty Tide Tables; nautical almanacs for yachtsmen; local tide tables from marinas or harbourmasters.

4.2 3.0m.

4.3

	LW		HW		Range
	Time	*Height*	*Time*	*Height*	
Dover	1406 GMT	2.3	1927 GMT	5.4	3.1
Add 1 hour	+ 0100		+ 0100		(neaps)
Dover	1506 BST		2027 BST		

Interval   – 4h 00min

Time **1627**

4.4

	HW		LW		Range
	Time	*Height*	*Time*	*Height*	
Dover	0401 GMT	6.0	1113 GMT	1.5	4.5
add 1 hour	+0100		+ 0100		(mid-range)
Dover	0501 BST		1213 BST		

Interval   + 4h 30min

Height **2.3m**

4.5

	HW		LW		Range
	Time	*Height*	*Time*	*Height*	
Dover	0454 GMT	5.5	1149 GMT	2.0	3.5
Differences	+ 0010	−1.3		− 0.7	(neaps)
Ramsgate	0504 GMT	4.2		1.3	
Add 1 hour	+ 0100				
Ramsgate	0604 BST				

Interval + 3h 50min
Time **0954**

4.6 Boat draught 0.5m
Berth dries 0.5m
Clearance <u>0.5m</u>
Height of tide required 1.5m

	LW		HW		LW		Range
	Time	*Height*	*Time*	*Height*	*Time*	*Height*	
Portsmouth	0606 GMT	0.6	1320 GMT	4.5	1829 GMT	0.9	3.9
Differences	− 0003	0.0		− 0.5	− 0005	0.0	(Springs)
Cowes	0603 GMT	0.6		4.0	1824 GMT	0.9	
Add 1 hour	+ 0100				+ 0100		
Cowes	0703 BST				1924 BST		

Berth cannot be entered from 0603 to 0842.

4.7

	LW		HW		Range
	Time	*Height*	*Time*	*Height*	
Portsmouth	1114 GMT	1.9	1825 GMT	3.8	1.9
Differences	− 0030	−0.		−1.2	(neaps)
Yarmouth	1044 GMT	1.6		2.6	
Add 1 hour	+ 0100				
Yarmouth	1144 BST				

Interval LW +4h 00min
Time **1544**

4.8 Chart 15, chartlet 2, St Alban's Ledge, tidal diamond G. Tidal stream west-going from HW Plymouth +6 to HW Plymouth −1.
Tidal stream west-going from 0250 to 0821 and from 1521 to 2034.

4.9 In Studland Bay there is a back eddy and the tidal stream is very much weaker than that in the main channel. In the absence of wind the boats will be tide rode. If coming in to anchor, always observe carefully the direction towards which the other boats are pointing.

4.10 Look at the base of the buoy.

Chapter 5

5.1 Tide tables, tidal stream atlas, list of lights, sailing directions. Yachtsman's nautical almanacs contain all relevant information.

5.2 Two fixed red in a vertical line.

5.3 No. It is obscured north of 057°T.

5.4 The ferry shows a black ball above the leading control cabin when it is about to get under way or is under way. All non-piloted craft must keep clear of the ferry.

5.5 There are two fixed red lights in a vertical line on Swanage Pier and a Quick Flashing Red light on Peveril Ledge buoy. Due to background lights in the town they may both be difficult to see. However, if Anvil Point light (White Flashing every 10 seconds) is kept in sight until the lights in the town are clearly visible, and then course altered to 275°T, there will be no danger as the north-going tidal stream will keep the boat well clear of Peveril Ledge.

Chapter 6

6.1 50° 42'2N 1° 44'.4W. Water track 305°T, distance run 2.1M, speed made good 6.3k, elapsed time 20 minutes. She could continue on the same course for a further 7 minutes.

6.2 50° 42'.7N 1° 49'.9W. Water track 284°T, distance run 2.7M, distance made good 3.2M, **speed made good 6.4k.**

6.3 50° 41'.3N 1° 48'.6W. Water tracks 272°T and 284°T, distances run 3.2M/0.9M, boat speed 4.0k, distance made good 4.9M, speed made good 4.9k.

6.4 50° 38'.8N 1° 54'.9W. Log 19.8. Water tracks 041°T and 286°T, distances run 1.8M/1.4M, tidal stream 179°T 0.4k.

6.5 50°41'1N 1°51'.5W. Water track 065°T, distance run 2.7M, tidal stream 347°T 1.2k, ground track 053°T, distance made good 2.9M, speed made good 5.8k. Distance to go to buoy abeam 1.9M. **Yellow buoy abeam at 0700.** Note that the ground track was plotted to determine when the yellow buoy was abeam.

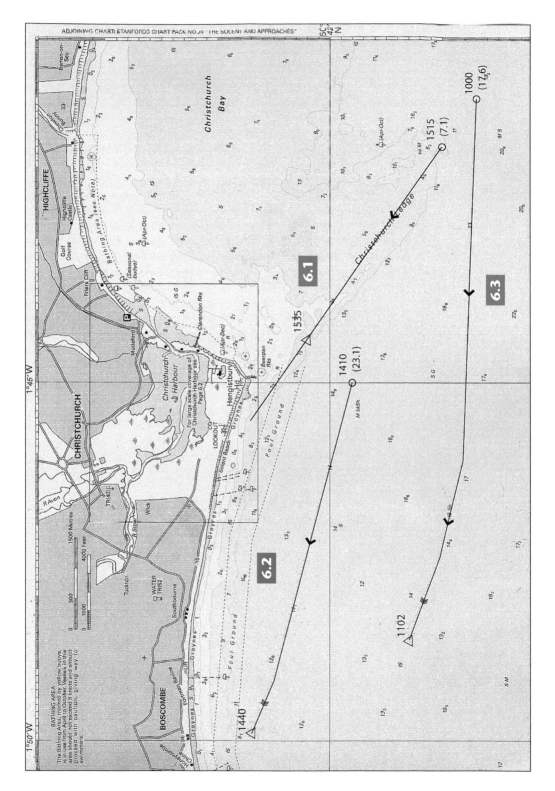

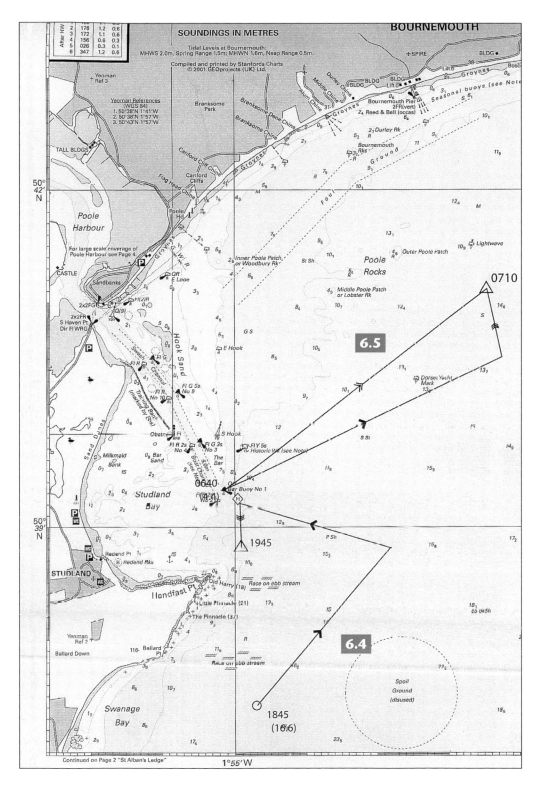

Chapter 7

7.1   50° 42'.5N 1° 45'.3W. As only two bearings are used any errors will not be obvious. However there is a good angle of cut between the position lines.

7.2   087°T 1.1M.

7.3   50° 34'.6N 2° 00'.2W. Over the high land the church spire at Worth Matravers might be difficult to identify. The bearings of St Alban's Head and Anvil Point intersect at a narrow angle so a third crossing bearing is necessary. Provided there are no errors in the bearings the position should be fairly accurate as there are three position lines with a reasonable angle of cut. Also, there is no cocked hat.

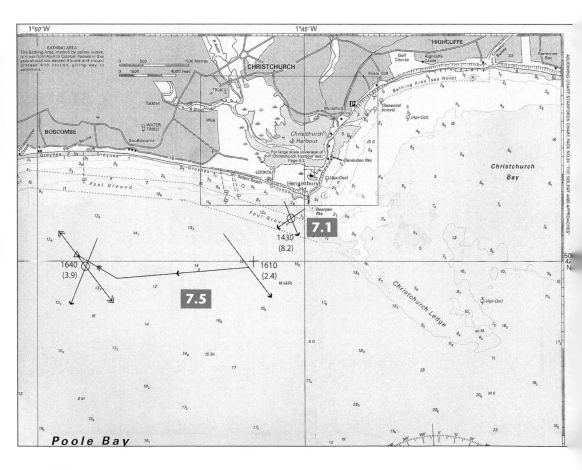

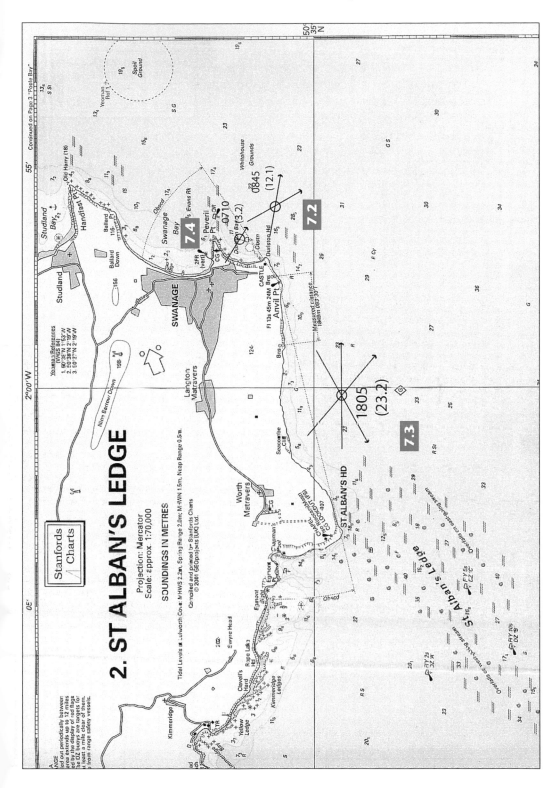

2. ST ALBAN'S LEDGE

Stanfords Charts

Projection: Mercator
Scale: approx 1:70,000

SOUNDINGS IN METRES

Tidal Levels at Lulworth Cove: M HWS 2.2m, Spring Range 2.0m; M HWN 1.5m, Neap Range 0.5m.

Compiled and printed by Stanfords Charts
© 2001 GEOprojects (UK) Ltd.

7.4 50° 36'.1N 1° 56'.7W. A transit is always very accurate. The bearing confirms that the two marks in transit have been correctly identified. The true bearing of the transit should be the same as that of the hand-bearing compass after allowing for variation, so the accuracy of the compass is confirmed. The bottom of Durlston Bay is fairly flat with no clearly defined depth contours so the echo sounder reading is not helpful and the boat's position cannot be regarded as accurate. The indicated depth also has to be adjusted for height of tide, which could make quite a difference. (Note: In practice, because of the cliffs, the transit of the two churches would not be visible from seaward.)

7.5 50° 41'.9N 1° 49'.1W. A transferred position line should only be used if it is not possible to get a good two- or three-bearing fix. Any inaccuracies of the course steered, distance run and the estimate of tidal stream will affect the final position. (Answer plot page 190.)

Chapter 8

8.1 **Course to steer 035°T or 038°M. ETA 1149.** Distance to go 4.8M. Elapsed time 64 minutes. (Answer plot page 195.)

8.2 **Course to steer 279°T or 282°M. ETA 1539.** Distance to go 6.0M. Tidal stream 355° 0.7k. Approximate passage time 1 hour. Water track 279°T. Speed made good 5.2k. Elapsed time 69 minutes.

8.3 **Course to steer 284°T or 287°M. ETA 1152.** Distance to go 8.4M. Approximate passage time 1½ hours. Tidal streams 251° 1.0k (for 30 minutes plot 251°T 0.5M), 257° 1.6k. Water track 289°T. Leeway 5°. Distance made good 7.8M. Speed made good 5.2k. Elapsed time 1 hour 37 minutes. (Answer plot page 194.)

8.4 a) **Course to steer 127°T or 130°M. ETA 1311.** Distance to go 2.8M, tidal stream 280°T 1.1k. Water track 127°T, speed made good 4.1k, elapsed time 41 minutes.

   b) **Course to steer 001°T or 004°M. ETA 1336.** Distance to go 2.1M, tidal stream 280°T 1.1k. Water track 011°T, speed made good 5.0k, elapsed time 25 minutes. (Answer plot page 195.)

8.5 **Course to steer 096°T or 099°M. ETA 0908.** Distance to go 7.2M. Approximate passage time 2 hours. Tidal streams 102° 0.4k, 069°T 1.7k. Water track 096°T. Distance made good 7.0M. Speed made good 3.5k. Elapsed time 2 hours 3 minutes. (Answer plot page 194.)

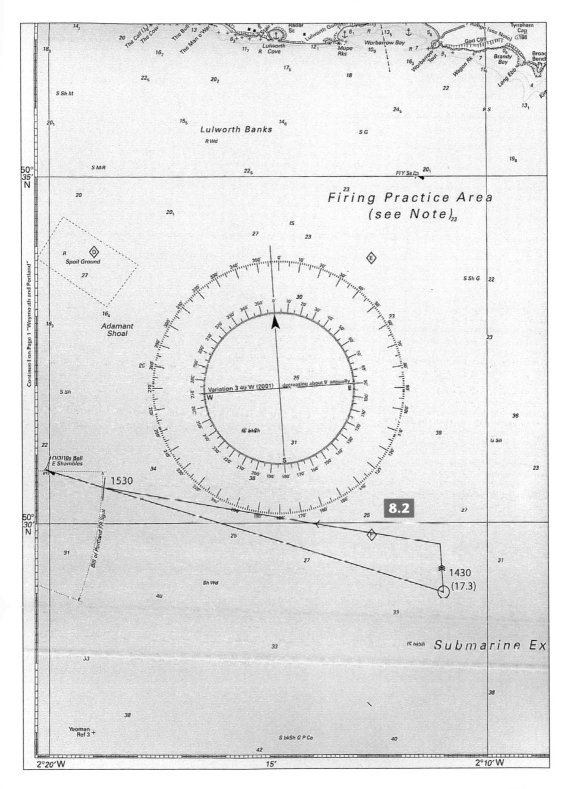

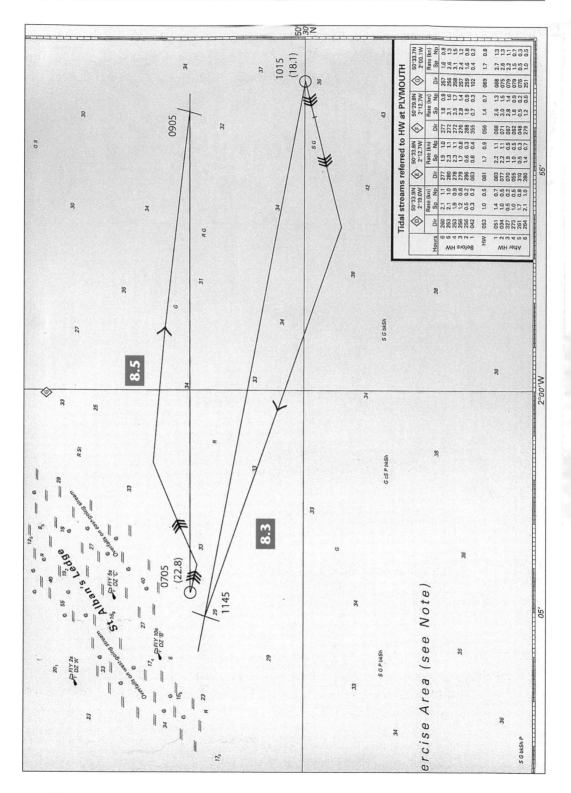

Tidal streams referred to HW at PLYMOUTH

		50°33.9N 2°19.0W			50°33.8N 2°12.7W			50°29.8N 2°12.7W			50°33.7N 2°00.1W		
			Rate (kn)			Rate (kn)			Rate (kn)			Rate (kn)	
Hours		Dir	Sp	Np	Dir	Sp	Np	Dir	Sp	Np	Dir	Sp	Np
Before HW	6	260	2.1	1.1	277	1.9	1.0	277	1.8	0.9	257	1.6	0.8
	5	253	2.1	1.0	280	2.3	1.1	272	3.1	1.6	256	2.6	1.3
	4	253	1.9	0.8	278	2.3	1.1	272	3.5	1.7	258	3.1	1.5
	3	256	1.2	0.6	279	1.7	0.9	276	2.8	1.4	257	2.4	1.2
	2	256	0.5	0.2	296	0.6	0.3	288	1.8	0.9	259	1.6	0.8
	1	042	0.3	0.2	063	0.8	0.4	355	0.7	0.3	102	0.4	0.2
HW		053	1.0	0.5	081	1.7	0.9	056	1.4	0.7	069	1.7	0.8
After HW	1	051	1.4	0.7	083	2.2	1.1	068	2.6	1.3	068	2.7	1.3
	2	034	1.0	0.5	077	2.1	1.0	077	3.0	1.5	075	2.6	1.3
	3	327	0.5	0.2	070	1.9	0.9	067	2.8	1.4	079	2.2	1.1
	4	273	1.0	0.5	055	1.0	0.3	062	1.8	0.9	079	1.5	0.7
	5	261	1.7	0.8	310	0.3	0.1	048	0.5	0.2	076	0.8	0.3
	6	264	2.1	1.0	280	1.4	0.7	279	1.2	0.6	251	1.0	0.5

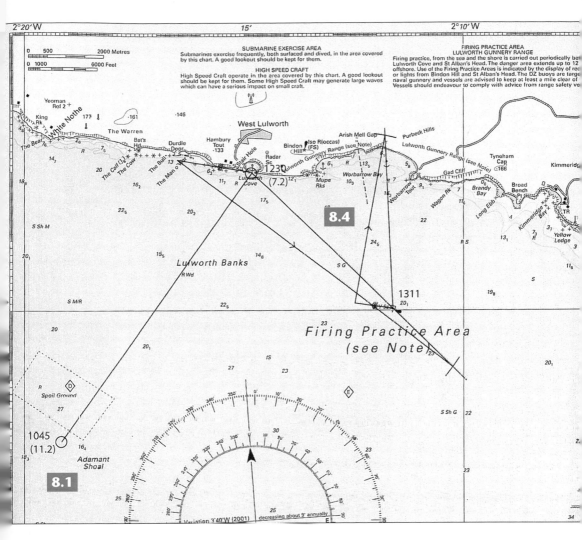

Chapter 9

9.1 Winds in Portland and Plymouth are SW 5–6 at time of forecast. Channel Light Vessel Auto reported WSW 5 whereas Scilly Auto is reporting WSW 6 with heavy showers with greatly improved visibility with rapidly rising barometer, so it would appear that the cold front is about to pass over Plymouth and is approaching Portland. Although there are no gale warnings for the area concerned for the passage, winds of SW 5–6 becoming NW 7 would make for a very uncomfortable if not dangerous passage. There will be choppy seas with wind over tide conditions, and as the cold front passes over Plymouth and Portland there could be confused seas as the wave pattern caused by the NW wind is superimposed across the SW wave pattern. **The boat should stay in Poole Harbour and wait for conditions to improve**, which will be after the cold front passes. She should listen to further shipping forecasts and, if possible, visit the harbour office or yacht club to view a surface analysis chart.

9.2 This is **radiation fog** which has drifted off the land as the land warms. It can extend to about 2 miles offshore. It usually disperses by midday. **Stay in the anchorage until the fog lifts**.

9.3 These are ideal conditions for an **onshore sea breeze**. Around midday a steady onshore breeze will develop, reaching a peak of about force 3 between 1500 and 1600, then gradually dying away to calm around sunset. The ideal timing for a passage would be from around 1030 to 1830.

9.4 By observing the isobars on a surface analysis chart, **high pressure areas and depressions can be readily identified. Also evident are the warm and cold fronts which imply rain, cloud cover and reduced visibility**. From the isobars the approximate direction and strength of the wind can be determined. By studying a sequence of surface analysis charts, the rate of movement of the depressions and fronts can be estimated, from which a general forecast can be made for any particular area over the next few days.

9.5 Close to a mountainous coast onshore anabatic winds (which are similar to sea breezes) develop during the day and can reach force 7 in mid-afternoon. At sunset they die away. During the night the land at high altitude cools rapidly, forming a blanket of cold air. If this blanket is displaced, a katabatic wind develops which rushes down the mountainside towards the sea. This can happen late at night or during the following morning. Within a mile of the land these offshore winds can reach gale force for about 20 minutes or so. Though very local they can be devastating to a boat at anchor or one making a close inshore passage.

Chapter 10

10.1 Check with www.admiraltyleisure.com, www.imray.com, or www.allweathercharts.com for any corrections for charts held on board.

10.2 Charts – small scale for planning; large scale for navigation and pilotage.

Publications – *Yachtsman's Nautical Almanac* **or**
Admiralty List of Lights
Admiralty Tide Tables
Tidal Stream Atlas

Admiralty List of Radio Signals
Sailing Directions or Pilots

10.3 Get five-day forecasts, shipping forecasts and local forecasts and observe weather trends, looking out for any deepening depressions approaching. Obtain surface analysis charts from MetFAX Marine.

10.4 • Fill up with water, fuel and gas.
• Stow and secure all loose gear above and below decks.
• Issue safety harnesses and lifejackets to all crewmembers.
• Pump bilges.
• Complete Coastguard Form CG66 and ensure someone ashore has details of your proposed passage.
• Check victuals.
• Check first aid kit.
• Check, and service where necessary, sails, engine, and electronic equipment.

10.5 Enter waypoints into navigation computer, Yeoman plotter and mark on chart. Work out times of high water and low water for all ports to be visited plus any alternative destinations. Check tidal streams and work out ideal departure and arrival times.

Chapter 11

11.1 **Blood Alley Lake**: shallow but protected from a north wind.
Redhorn Quay
Goathorn Point: can be uncomfortable in certain combinations of wind and current.
West of Goathorn Point: more sheltered than off Goathorn Point.
Shipstal Point: sheltered from the west.
Pottery Pier

11.2 **Salterns Marina, Town Quay (Dolphin) Boat Haven, Cobbs Quay Marina, Lake Yard Marina**.

11.3 After passing the chain ferry with the Haven Hotel to port, turn to port leaving the green starboard-hand beacons to port and the Swash west cardinal buoy and North Hook port-hand buoy to starboard. Locate and steer for East Looe port-hand buoy leaving it to starboard. Beyond East Looe buoy a course to the east can be set.

11.4 All round the coastline from Poole Harbour entrance to St Alban's Head there are tide races on all the headlands. The sea is turbulent when a strong tidal stream is running, in particular downstream of the ebb or flood tide. In calm conditions these tide races do not present a danger, but if a wind of force 4 or above is blowing in the opposite direction to the tidal stream, conditions can be rough and dangerous and the area should be avoided.

11.5 **Lulworth Cove**: a pleasant anchorage in fair conditions. If the wind is from the south and above force 4, there will be a swell and swirling gusts.

Mupe Bay: deep-water anchorage protected from the west.

Worbarrow Bay: a pleasant anchorage sheltered from the east.

Chapman's Pool: an attractive anchorage when the wind is offshore and the swell low. There is a mooring for the range safety vessel in the bay.

Chapter 12

12.1 In the event of electrical failure it is always a requirement to carry paper charts.

12.2 The log that under reads. A landfall would be made sooner than expected which would put the boat in danger on a rocky or shoaling shore.

12.3 Waypoints are selected positions, usually at keypoints on a passage. Electronic position indicating systems can be programmed with waypoints particularly at positions where a course change may be necessary, such as close to buoys or off headlands. A digital display will show the bearing and range of the waypoint from the present position of the boat. An electronic chart will show the waypoints together with the tracks.

12.4 a) Most electronic position indicating systems identify the direct track from one waypoint to the next. They can tell whether the boat is to the right or the left of the track and the distance off this track. This is cross track error. They will also show which way to steer to bring the boat back on track.

b) Electronic position indicating systems calculate speed over the ground. Speed through the water is only valid where the tidal stream is negligible.

12.5 The man overboard facility gives the latitude and longitude of the position at which the man overboard button was pressed. This position is stored as a waypoint. In strong tidal streams the man overboard might drift a considerable distance from the man overboard position.

Chapter 13

13.1 Make an **all stations** call on channel 16. Give the boat name, callsign, MMSI number and state that you are cancelling the false alert sent at the date and time.

13.2 Communication with a merchant vessel for purposes of safety and collision avoidance is conducted on channel 13.

13.3 Make a MAYDAY RELAY call on channel 16. Small craft fitted with GMDSS do not have a facility to use DSC for a Mayday Relay. It is of utmost importance to contact the Coastguard Rescue Coordination Centre, who will alert the appropriate rescue services.

13.4 A VHF radio with DSC has an Urgency message category. The announcement of the Urgency message is carried out by DSC on channel 70 followed by transmission of the Urgency message on channel 16. Once the announcement of the call has been made by DSC, the channel indicated within the DSC message (usually channel 16) should be automatically selected. The broadcast urgency message will be in the format:

> **PAN PAN PAN PAN PAN PAN MEDICO**
> **All Stations All Stations All Stations**
> **This is** (the nine digit MMSI and the callsign or other identity)
> **My position is** (either latitude and longitude or relative to a significant navigational mark)
> **I require urgent medical advice** (plus brief details of casualty)
> **Over**

13.5 On the approach to the harbour select and monitor the Port Operations Channel (usually either channel 12 or 14). When about half a mile from the harbour entrance make a call in this format:

> **Jersey Port Radio Jersey Port Radio**
> **This is Yacht Starlight**
> **I am ½ mile west of harbour entrance**
> **I should be at the entrance in 10 minutes**
> **Am I clear to enter?**
> **Over**

Chapter 14

14.1 a) A stopper knot, such as a figure-of-eight.
b) A round turn and two half hitches.
c) A bowline.

14.2 a) Nylon, because of its strength and shock absorbing qualities.
b) Polyester, because it is strong with low stretching properties.

c) Polypropylene, because it is buoyant.

14.3 A bowline, which is used to make a temporary loop in a rope.

14.4 Bow and stern lines; bow and stern spring lines; and bow and stern breast lines.

14.5 To keep your fingers clear of the winch drum to avoid getting them trapped and causing an injury.

Chapter 15

15.1 a) To stop the boat yawing in a strong wind, when the boat is wind-rode. Both anchors will be laid from the bows with an angle between them of 40°.

b) To reduce the swinging circle of the boat in a strong tidal stream when there is not much wind. Both anchors will be laid from the bows, the heavier in the direction from which the strongest tidal stream is expected. The second is in the opposite direction.

15.2 *Fisherman anchor*

1 Can be stowed flat.

2 Few moving parts to trap the fingers.

3 Heavier anchor required to give the same holding power as a CQR anchor.

4 Anchor chain may be fouled on the vertical fluke when the anchor is on the seabed.

CQR anchor

1 Cannot be stowed flat.

2 Movable parts which can trap fingers.

3 Lighter anchor required to give the same holding power as a Fisherman anchor.

4 Digs in well unless the point becomes impaled.

15.3 A trip line is used if the anchor is likely to become fouled on an obstruction. The trip line is used to haul up the anchor by the crown.

15.4 a) Good holding ground free from obstructions.

b) Maximum shelter from all expected wind directions.

c) Out of strong tidal streams.

d) Clear of other boats at all states of the tide.

e) A position where the boat does not ground and where there is sufficient anchor chain for the maximum expected depth.

f) Out of busy areas.

g) Where there are suitable transits or landmarks for bearings to check the boat's position.

h) If going ashore, near a suitable landing place.

15.5 a) By exhibiting a black ball as high as possible in the fore part of the boat.

b) By exhibiting an all-round white light as high as possible in the fore part of the boat.

Chapter 16

16.1 In rough weather, especially when on deck, at night, and when alone in the cockpit. The safety line should be clipped to a strong point.

16.2 Shout 'man overboard' to alert crew, and throw in the dan buoy to mark the position.

16.3 a) No smoking below deck.

b) Engine compartment and bilges cleaned and ventilated regularly.

c) Gas bottles installed outside in the cockpit where any leaks drain overboard and not in the bilges.

d Gas should be burned out of pipes after cooker is used and gas turned off at bottle.

e) Engine checked regularly for oil and fuel leaks.

f) Hatches should be closed when fuelling and the boat well ventilated afterwards. If there is any spillage, this should be hosed down.

g) The correct up-to-date fire appliances should be carried in readily accessible positions.

16.4 2 red parachute flares, 2 red hand flares, 2 handheld orange smoke flares.

16.5   **MAYDAY MAYDAY MAYDAY**
This is MOTORBOAT JETTO JETTO JETTO
MAYDAY MOTORBOAT JETTO
My position is 3 miles southwest of Needles lighthouse
I am sinking and require immediate assistance
I have 4 persons on board
OVER
The call should be sent on channel 16.

Chapter 17

17.1 Keep a good look-out.

17.2 a) Make a large enough alteration of course to be immediately apparent to the other boat.

b) Make the alteration in good time.

c) Make the alteration with due regard to the observance of good seamanship.

17.3 a) Neither. Both must alter course to starboard.
   b) B has right of way. A should go astern of B.
   c) B has right of way as she is on starboard tack. A should bear away or go astern of B or tack.

17.4 a) When she is overtaking the motorboat.
   b) When the motorboat is hampered in any way and cannot manoeuvre freely.
   c) When the motorboat, because of its draught, cannot navigate outside a deep-draught channel.

17.5 By taking repeated compass bearings of the approaching boat. If the bearing does not appreciably alter, then a risk of collision is deemed to exist.

Test Paper A: General

A1 a) A vessel under power and sail.
   b) A vessel restricted in her ability to manoeuvre.
   c) A vessel constrained by her draught.

A2 a) A has right of way. If a vessel with the wind on the port side sees a vessel to windward and cannot determine with certainty whether the other vessel has the wind on the port or starboard side she will keep out of the way of the other.
   b) Boat A is on starboard tack and has right of way.
   c) Boat A under sail has right of way over power boat B.
   d) The two boats are both under power, so A has right of way as she is on the starboard bow of B.

A3 a) A power vessel under way; bow aspect; less than 50m in length.
   b) A vessel at anchor; starboard side; more than 50m in length.
   c) A vessel not under command making no way through the water; all round; no indication of length.

A4 Coastguard announces warning on VHF channel 16 and broadcasts full details on channel 67.

A5 On VHF channel 16 *securité* is the code word announcing that a navigation warning will be broadcast on a separate channel.

A6 Winds circulate in a clockwise direction around an anticyclone in the northern hemisphere and anti-clockwise around a low pressure system. With no other weather factors, over the English Channel there would be light winds from an easterly direction. However if the low pressure system is moving towards the anticyclone, then the pressure gradient will increase (the isobars will be squeezed closer together) causing strong winds from the east. Possibility of poor visibility.

A7 a) between 1000m and 2 nautical miles

b) between 35 and 45 knots

c) 0.1mb to 1.5mb in preceding 3 hours

d) within 6 hours

A8   Check that the casualty is breathing and that his heart is beating. If not, apply artificial resuscitation.

A9   Contents of a first aid kit (these should be kept in a watertight box with a list on the lid):

roll of plasters	tweezers	aspirin
individual plasters	eye lotion and eye	seasickness tablets
large triangular	bath	indigestion tablets
bandages	calamine lotion	exposure bag
small bandages	safety pins	first aid manual
lint and cotton wool	disinfectant	

A10   A bowline to make a loop in the rope. It can be passed quickly over a bollard if necessary under existing lines. It is secure and can be easily slipped off a bollard on departure.

A11   Shout **'Man Overboard'** and press man overboard button on the GMDSS.

A12   Steer the boat along the transit and note the heading on the steering compass. Compare with true bearing of transit from the chart. When variation has been applied any remaining difference is deviation.

A13   If you have a VHF radio, initiate a MAYDAY call. Don lifejackets. Launch the dinghy/liferaft. Take flare pack and spare water and board dinghy/liferaft.

A14   Neither: if your draught allows you must use the small craft channel to the west of the red buoys. See caution on chart.

A15   You should cross on a heading as nearly as practicable at right angles to the general direction of traffic flow.

A16   a) I am unsure of your intentions.

b) I am engaging astern propulsion.

c) I intend to overtake you on your port side.

d) I am altering course to starboard.

A17   From the crown of the anchor rig a trip line either attached to an anchor buoy or led back to bows of boat.

A18   A height of tide of 2.7m is required.

A19   **Fl 10s 45m 24M**. Single flash white every 10 seconds. Height of light 45 metres above Mean High Water Springs. Nominal range of light (brightness) 24 miles.

A20   a) Tidal stream atlas, tidal diagrams or diamonds on chart.

b) Tide tables.

These are all based on UK Hydrographic Office publications, but are included in yachtsman's almanacs. Local tide tables can often be obtained from harbour or marina offices.

Test Paper B: Chartwork

B1 306°T 1.1M. HW Portsmouth 0559 GMT or 0659 BST (neap tides).
Water track 247°T distance 2.1M. Tidal stream 206°T 0.8M.
50° 42'.2N 1° 45'.1W.

B2 Tidal streams around headlands can be very variable.

B3 Distance to go 6.6M. Favourable tidal stream estimated at just
over 1 knot. Boat speed 4.2k. Estimated time just over one hour.

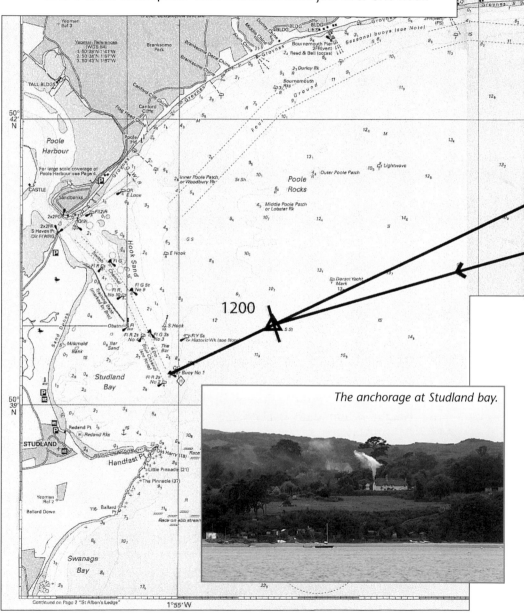

The anchorage at Studland bay.

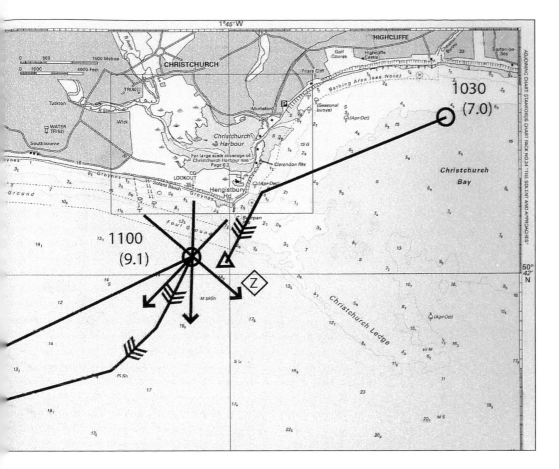

Tidal streams 206°T 0.8M (206°T 1.6k) and 226°T 0.6M (226° 1.2k). Water track 254°T or 257°M. Leeway 5°. Course to steer **262°M**. Distance made good 5.5M. Speed made good 5.5k. Elapsed time = 6.6/5.5 x 60 = 72 minutes. FTA **1212 BST**.

B4 216°T or **219°M 0.8M**. ETA at Studland Bay will be shortly after LW. Height of tide at LW is 1.0m.

B5 21/22 May.

	LW		HW	LW		HW	Range
	Time	Height	Height	Time	Height	Height	
Poole	1141 GMT	1.0	1.9	0021 GMT	1.0	1.9	0.9
	1241 BST			0121 BST			(mid-range)

1740 is LW + 4h 59min. From Poole Harbour tidal curve the height of tide is 1.9m. Charted depth: 3.1 – 1.9 = 1.2m. At the next LW (0121 BST 22 May) depth will be 1.2 + 1.0 = **2.2m**. At the next HW the depth will be 1.2 + 1.9 = **3.1m**. Unless her draught is greater than 2.2m, the boat can safely remain overnight.

EXTRACTS

TIME ZONE (UTC)	ENGLAND – DOVER	Extract 1
For Summer Time add ONE hour in non-shaded areas	LAT 51°07′N LONG 1°19′W TIMES AND HEIGHTS OF HIGH AND LOW WATERS	

MAY

Time	m		Time	m
1 0132 / 0901 / W 1355 / 2114	6.7 / 0.9 / 6.5 / 1.1	**16** 0048 / 0820 / TH 1310 / 2038	6.4 / 1.2 / 6.4 / 1.3
2 0217 / 0937 / TH 1443 / 2153	6.3 / 1.3 / 6.1 / 1.5	**17** 0127 / 0856 / F 1354 / 2119	6.3 / 1.4 / 6.2 / 1.4
3 0309 / 1017 / F 1537 / 2241	5.9 / 1.8 / 5.8 / 1.9	**18** 0215 / 0939 / SA 1449 / 2208	6.0 / 1.6 / 5.9 / 1.7
4 0408 / 1110 / SA 1638 / 2350	5.5 / 2.2 / 5.4 / 2.2	**19** 0320 / 1033 / SU 1603 / 2313	5.7 / 1.9 / 5.7 / 1.8
5 0516 / 1227 / SU 1748	5.1 / 2.4 / 5.2	**20** 0454 / 1149 / M 1728	5.5 / 2.0 / 5.6
6 0111 / 0642 / M 1344 / 1909	2.3 / 5.1 / 2.4 / 5.3	**21** 0037 / 0621 / TU 1317 / 1846	1.8 / 5.6 / 1.9 / 5.7
7 0224 / 0810 / TU 1450 / 2018	2.1 / 5.3 / 2.1 / 5.6	**22** 0153 / 0732 / W 1427 / 1953	1.6 / 5.8 / 1.7 / 6.0
8 0325 / 0859 / W 1546 / 2106	1.8 / 5.6 / 1.8 / 5.8	**23** 0257 / 0830 / TH 1529 / 2049	1.3 / 6.1 / 1.4 / 6.3
9 0414 / 0934 / TH 1633 / 2143	1.5 / 5.8 / 1.6 / 6.1	**24** 0400 / 0921 / F 1630 / 2138	1.0 / 6.3 / 1.1 / 6.6
10 0455 / 1005 / F 1712 / 2216	1.3 / 6.0 / 1.4 / 6.2	**25** 0501 / 1007 / SA 1726 / 2225	0.8 / 6.5 / 0.9 / 6.7
11 0531 / 1035 / SA 1747 / 2246	1.2 / 6.2 / 1.2 / 6.3	**26** 0557 / 1050 / SU 1816 / ○ 2309	0.7 / 6.6 / 0.8 / 6.8
12 0605 / 1105 / SU 1820 / ● 2315	1.1 / 6.3 / 1.1 / 6.4	**27** 0644 / 1132 / M 1901 / 2352	0.6 / 6.7 / 0.8 / 6.8
13 0640 / 1134 / M 1854 / 2344	1.1 / 6.3 / 1.1 / 6.4	**28** 0726 / 1213 / TU 1941	0.7 / 6.7 / 0.8
14 0714 / 1203 / TU 1928	1.1 / 6.4 / 1.1	**29** 0034 / 0805 / W 1256 / 2020	6.7 / 0.9 / 6.6 / 1.0
15 0014 / 0746 / W 1234 / 2002	6.4 / 1.1 / 6.4 / 1.1	**30** 0117 / 0841 / TH 1339 / 2058	6.5 / 1.2 / 6.4 / 1.2
		31 0201 / 0917 / F 1424 / 2137	6.2 / 1.5 / 6.2 / 1.5

JUNE

Time	m		Time	m
1 0249 / 0954 / SA 1513 / 2220	5.9 / 1.8 / 5.9 / 1.8	**16** 0218 / 0940 / SU 1450 / 2211	6.1 / 1.5 / 6.2 / 1.4
2 0343 / 1037 / SU 1606 / 2314	5.5 / 2.0 / 5.6 / 2.0	**17** 0320 / 1033 / M 1551 / 2310	5.9 / 1.6 / 6.0 / 1.5
3 0442 / 1138 / M 1705	5.3 / 2.3 / 5.4	**18** 0431 / 1136 / TU 1657	5.8 / 1.7 / 5.9
4 0021 / 0547 / TU 1249 / 1811	2.1 / 5.2 / 2.3 / 5.4	**19** 0015 / 0546 / W 1245 / 1807	1.5 / 5.7 / 1.7 / 5.9
5 0126 / 0657 / W 1353 / 1917	2.1 / 5.2 / 2.2 / 5.4	**20** 0121 / 0658 / TH 1351 / 1917	1.5 / 5.8 / 1.7 / 6.0
6 0224 / 0756 / TH 1450 / 2011	1.9 / 5.4 / 2.0 / 5.6	**21** 0225 / 0801 / F 1455 / 2021	1.4 / 5.9 / 1.5 / 6.1
7 0315 / 0842 / F 1541 / 2055	1.7 / 5.6 / 1.8 / 5.8	**22** 0329 / 0856 / SA 1600 / 2117	1.3 / 6.1 / 1.4 / 6.3
8 0404 / 0920 / SA 1628 / 2132	1.5 / 5.8 / 1.5 / 6.0	**23** 0435 / 0947 / SU 1702 / 2209	1.1 / 6.2 / 1.2 / 6.4
9 0449 / 0957 / SU 1711 / 2208	1.3 / 6.0 / 1.4 / 6.2	**24** 0535 / 1035 / M 1756 / ○ 2257	1.0 / 6.4 / 1.1 / 6.5
10 0533 / 1033 / M 1753 / ● 2245	1.2 / 6.2 / 1.2 / 6.3	**25** 0625 / 1119 / TU 1843 / 2341	1.0 / 6.5 / 1.0 / 6.5
11 0614 / 1109 / TU 1833 / 2322	1.1 / 6.3 / 1.1 / 6.4	**26** 0709 / 1200 / W 1920	1.0 / 6.5 / 1.0
12 0654 / 1145 / W 1912	1.1 / 6.4 / 1.1	**27** 0023 / 0748 / TH 1242 / 2006	6.4 / 1.1 / 6.5 / 1.1
13 0000 / 0733 / TH 1225 / 1952	6.4 / 1.1 / 6.4 / 1.1	**28** 0104 / 0825 / F 1323 / 2044	6.3 / 1.3 / 6.4 / 1.3
14 0041 / 0812 / F 1308 / 2034	6.4 / 1.2 / 6.4 / 1.1	**29** 0144 / 0859 / SA 1404 / 2120	6.1 / 1.5 / 6.3 / 1.4
15 0126 / 0853 / SA 1355 / 2119	6.3 / 1.3 / 6.3 / 1.2	**30** 0226 / 0930 / SU 1445 / 2155	5.9 / 1.6 / 6.1 / 1.6

JULY

Time	m		Time	m
1 0310 / 1003 / M 1528 / 2233	5.7 / 1.8 / 5.9 / 1.8	**16** 0303 / 1023 / TU 1529 / 2255	6.2 / 1.3 / 6.4 / 1.1
2 0359 / 1043 / TU 1614 / 2319	5.5 / 2.0 / 5.6 / 1.9	**17** 0401 / 1113 / W 1626 / 2348	6.0 / 1.5 / 6.2 / 1.3
3 0454 / 1133 / W 1708	5.3 / 2.1 / 5.5	**18** 0506 / 1210 / TH 1730	5.8 / 1.7 / 6.0
4 0016 / 0554 / TH 1239 / 1809	2.0 / 5.2 / 2.2 / 5.4	**19** 0047 / 0618 / F 1315 / 1841	1.5 / 5.7 / 1.8 / 5.8
5 0120 / 0656 / F 1349 / 1911	2.0 / 5.3 / 2.2 / 5.4	**20** 0152 / 0731 / SA 1424 / 1957	1.6 / 5.6 / 1.8 / 5.8
6 0223 / 0752 / SA 1452 / 2005	1.9 / 5.4 / 2.0 / 5.6	**21** 0301 / 0837 / SU 1536 / 2105	1.6 / 5.7 / 1.7 / 5.9
7 0321 / 0841 / SU 1549 / 2054	1.7 / 5.6 / 1.8 / 5.8	**22** 0415 / 0935 / M 1646 / 2204	1.5 / 6.0 / 1.5 / 6.1
8 0415 / 0926 / M 1641 / 2139	1.5 / 5.9 / 1.5 / 6.1	**23** 0520 / 1025 / TU 1744 / 2253	1.4 / 6.2 / 1.3 / 6.3
9 0506 / 1008 / TU 1729 / 2223	1.3 / 6.1 / 1.3 / 6.3	**24** 0612 / 1108 / W 1833 / ○ 2335	1.3 / 6.4 / 1.2 / 6.3
10 0554 / 1051 / W 1815 / ● 2307	1.2 / 6.3 / 1.1 / 6.4	**25** 0656 / 1148 / TH 1915	1.2 / 6.5 / 1.1
11 0640 / 1133 / TH 1901 / 2351	1.1 / 6.5 / 1.0 / 6.5	**26** 0013 / 0733 / F 1227 / 1953	6.3 / 1.2 / 6.5 / 1.1
12 0725 / 1216 / F 1947	1.1 / 6.6 / 0.9	**27** 0049 / 0807 / SA 1304 / 2026	6.3 / 1.3 / 6.5 / 1.2
13 0035 / 0809 / SA 1301 / 2033	6.5 / 1.1 / 6.6 / 0.9	**28** 0124 / 0836 / SU 1340 / 2056	6.2 / 1.4 / 6.4 / 1.3
14 0121 / 0854 / SU 1347 / 2119	6.5 / 1.1 / 6.6 / 0.9	**29** 0158 / 0901 / M 1412 / 2123	6.0 / 1.4 / 6.3 / 1.4
15 0210 / 0938 / M 1436 / 2206	6.4 / 1.1 / 6.5 / 1.0	**30** 0230 / 0929 / TU 1442 / 2153	5.9 / 1.5 / 6.1 / 1.5
		31 0303 / 1002 / W 1515 / 2229	5.7 / 1.7 / 5.9 / 1.7

AUGUST

Time	m		Time	m
1 0341 / 1041 / TH 1558 / 2312	5.5 / 1.9 / 5.6 / 1.9	**16** 0430 / 1136 / F 1658	5.8 / 1.7 / 5.9
2 0435 / 1130 / F 1657	5.3 / 2.1 / 5.4	**17** 0014 / 0542 / SA 1242 / 1812	1.7 / 5.5 / 2.0 / 5.6
3 0011 / 0554 / SA 1240 / 1814	2.1 / 5.2 / 2.3 / 5.3	**18** 0123 / 0703 / SU 1359 / 1941	2.0 / 5.4 / 2.1 / 5.5
4 0131 / 0709 / SU 1406 / 1927	2.2 / 5.2 / 2.3 / 5.4	**19** 0241 / 0823 / M 1524 / 2105	2.0 / 5.5 / 2.0 / 5.7
5 0245 / 0810 / M 1517 / 2028	2.0 / 5.5 / 2.0 / 5.7	**20** 0407 / 0927 / TU 1642 / 2205	1.8 / 5.8 / 1.7 / 6.0
6 0348 / 0903 / TU 1616 / 2121	1.7 / 5.8 / 1.6 / 6.0	**21** 0514 / 1016 / W 1738 / 2249	1.6 / 6.1 / 1.4 / 6.2
7 0444 / 0951 / W 1709 / 2210	1.4 / 6.1 / 1.3 / 6.3	**22** 0602 / 1055 / TH 1824 / ○ 2325	1.4 / 6.4 / 1.2 / 6.3
8 0537 / 1036 / TH 1759 / ● 2256	1.2 / 6.4 / 1.0 / 6.5	**23** 0642 / 1132 / F 1902 / 2357	1.3 / 6.6 / 1.1 / 6.4
9 0627 / 1119 / F 1850 / 2340	1.0 / 6.7 / 0.8 / 6.6	**24** 0716 / 1207 / SA 1934	1.2 / 6.6 / 1.1
10 0716 / 1202 / SA 1939	0.9 / 6.8 / 0.7	**25** 0027 / 0743 / SU 1241 / 2000	6.4 / 1.3 / 6.6 / 1.1
11 0023 / 0801 / SU 1246 / 2025	6.7 / 0.8 / 6.9 / 0.6	**26** 0057 / 0806 / M 1311 / 2024	6.3 / 1.3 / 6.5 / 1.2
12 0106 / 0843 / M 1329 / 2108	6.7 / 0.8 / 6.9 / 0.6	**27** 0124 / 0828 / TU 1335 / 2048	6.2 / 1.3 / 6.4 / 1.3
13 0150 / 0923 / TU 1415 / 2149	6.6 / 0.9 / 6.8 / 0.7	**28** 0146 / 0855 / W 1357 / 2116	6.1 / 1.4 / 6.3 / 1.4
14 0237 / 1002 / W 1503 / 2231	6.3 / 1.1 / 6.6 / 1.0	**29** 0208 / 0926 / TH 1424 / 2148	6.0 / 1.5 / 6.1 / 1.6
15 0330 / 1045 / TH 1556 / 2317	6.2 / 1.3 / 6.3 / 1.3	**30** 0239 / 1001 / F 1501 / 2225	5.8 / 1.8 / 5.9 / 1.9
		31 0320 / 1042 / SA 1551 / 2312	5.5 / 2.1 / 5.5 / 2.2

Extract 2

FOLKESTONE *9.3.13*

Kent **51°04'·59N 01°11'·67E** ✿✿⚓⚓✿✿

CHARTS AC *5605, 1991, 1892*; Imray C8, C12; Stanfords 9, 20; OS 179

TIDES –0010 Dover; ML 3·9; Duration 0500; Zone 0 (UT)

Standard Port DOVER (⟶)

Times				Height (metres)			
High Water		Low Water		MHWS	MHWN	MLWN	MLWS
0000	0600	0100	0700	6·8	5·3	2·1	0·8
1200	1800	1300	1900				
Differences FOLKESTONE							
–0020	–0005	–0010	–0010	+0·4	+0·4	0·0	–0·1
DUNGENESS							
–0010	–0015	–0020	–0010	+1·0	+0·6	+0·4	+0·1

Extract 3

RAMSGATE *9.3.16*

Kent **51°19'·51N 01°25'·50E** ✿✿✿⚓⚓⚓✿✿✿

CHARTS AC *5605*, 1827, *1828, 323*; Imray C1, C8, C30, 2100 series; Stan 5, 9, 20; OS 179

TIDES +0030 Dover; ML 2·7; Duration 0530; Zone 0 (UT)

Standard Port DOVER (⟵)

Times				Height (metres)			
High Water		Low Water		MHWS	MHWN	MLWN	MLWS
0000	0600	0100	0700	6·8	5·3	2·1	0·8
1200	1800	1300	1900				
Differences RAMSGATE							
+0030	+0030	+0017	+0007	–1·6	–1·3	–0·7	–0·2
RICHBOROUGH							
+0015	+0015	+0030	+0030	–3·4	–2·6	–1·7	–0·7

HW Broadstairs = HW Dover +0037 approx.

Extract 4

TIME ZONE (UTC)
For Summer Time add ONE hour in **non-shaded areas**

ENGLAND – PORTSMOUTH

LAT 50°48'N   LONG 1°07'W

TIMES AND HEIGHTS OF HIGH AND LOW WATERS

MAY

Day	Time m	Time m	Time m	Time m		Day	Time m	Time m	Time m	Time m
1 W	0150 4.7	0722 0.8	1420 4.5	1941 1.1		16 TH	0116 4.4	0643 1.0	1346 4.4	1903 1.2
2 TH	0230 4.4	0803 1.1	1506 4.3	2026 1.4		17 F	0153 4.3	0724 1.1	1429 4.3	1949 1.4
3 F	0313 4.1	0851 1.4	1557 4.0	2122 1.8		18 SA	0238 4.2	0814 1.3	1521 4.2	2046 1.6
4 SA	0403 3.8	0953 1.7	1701 3.8	2235 2.0		19 SU	0333 4.0	0917 1.5	1625 4.1	2158 1.7
5 SU	0510 3.6	1114 1.9	1825 3.8	2359 2.1		20 M	0441 3.9	1035 1.5	1740 4.0	2319 1.7
6 M	0645 3.6	1235 1.9	1942 3.9			21 TU	0559 3.9	1156 1.5	1856 4.2	
7 TU	0112 1.9	0802 3.7	1336 1.7	2036 4.1		22 W	0036 1.5	0715 4.1	1307 1.3	2000 4.4
8 W	0205 1.6	0853 3.9	1421 1.5	2118 4.2		23 TH	0140 1.3	0819 4.3	1405 1.0	2056 4.6
9 TH	0246 1.4	0933 4.0	1501 1.2	2154 4.3		24 F	0235 1.0	0916 4.5	1457 0.8	2147 4.7
10 F	0323 1.2	1009 4.1	1538 1.1	2228 4.4		25 SA	0325 0.8	1009 4.6	1545 0.7	2235 4.8
11 SA	0359 1.0	1044 4.2	1613 1.0	2301 4.4		26 SU	0413 0.6	1059 4.7	1631 0.6	○ 2322 4.9
12 SU	0433 0.9	1119 4.3	1647 0.9	● 2334 4.5		27 M	0458 0.6	1147 4.7	1716 0.7	
13 M	0505 0.9	1154 4.4	1719 0.9			28 TU	0006 4.8	0542 0.6	1234 4.7	1758 0.8
14 TU	0007 4.5	0536 0.9	1231 4.4	1750 1.0		29 W	0048 4.7	0623 0.7	1318 4.6	1840 1.0
15 W	0041 4.5	0607 0.9	1307 4.4	1824 1.1		30 TH	0128 4.6	0704 0.9	1402 4.5	1921 1.2
						31 F	0207 4.4	0744 1.1	1446 4.3	2005 1.4

JUNE

Day	Time m	Time m	Time m	Time m		Day	Time m	Time m	Time m	Time m
1 SA	0249 4.1	0828 1.4	1533 4.1	2054 1.7		16 SU	0233 4.3	0814 1.1	1516 4.4	2042 1.3
2 SU	0335 3.9	0919 1.6	1625 4.0	2152 1.9		17 M	0326 4.2	0911 1.2	1614 4.3	2143 1.4
3 M	0429 3.7	1021 1.8	1726 3.9	2301 2.0		18 TU	0427 4.1	1013 1.3	1717 4.3	2249 1.5
4 TU	0534 3.6	1131 1.9	1832 3.9			19 W	0534 4.1	1120 1.3	1824 4.3	2359 1.5
5 W	0012 2.0	0645 3.6	1237 1.8	1932 4.0		20 TH	0644 4.1	1228 1.3	1929 4.4	
6 TH	0112 1.8	0749 3.7	1330 1.6	2022 4.1		21 F	0107 1.3	0751 4.2	1333 1.2	2029 4.5
7 F	0200 1.6	0841 3.9	1416 1.5	2106 4.2		22 SA	0209 1.2	0854 4.3	1432 1.1	2124 4.6
8 SA	0242 1.4	0926 4.0	1457 1.3	2147 4.3		23 SU	0304 1.0	0951 4.4	1524 1.0	2215 4.6
9 SU	0322 1.2	1009 4.2	1537 1.2	2226 4.4		24 M	0354 0.9	1044 4.5	1613 1.0	○ 2303 4.7
10 M	0400 1.1	1050 4.3	1615 1.1	● 2305 4.5		25 TU	0442 0.8	1134 4.6	1659 1.0	2347 4.6
11 TU	0437 1.0	1131 4.4	1653 1.1	2343 4.5		26 W	0526 0.8	1219 4.6	1742 1.0	
12 W	0515 0.9	1211 4.5	1733 1.0			27 TH	0028 4.6	0608 0.9	1302 4.6	1823 1.1
13 TH	0022 4.5	0555 0.9	1253 4.5	1814 1.0		28 F	0107 4.5	0647 1.0	1343 4.5	1902 1.2
14 F	0102 4.5	0637 0.9	1337 4.5	1858 1.1		29 SA	0145 4.3	0725 1.1	1423 4.4	1942 1.4
15 SA	0145 4.4	0723 1.0	1424 4.5	1947 1.2		30 SU	0224 4.2	0802 1.3	1503 4.3	2023 1.5

JULY

Day	Time m	Time m	Time m	Time m		Day	Time m	Time m	Time m	Time m
1 M	0305 4.0	0842 1.4	1546 4.1	2107 1.7		16 TU	0315 4.4	0855 0.9	1554 4.5	2122 1.2
2 TU	0349 3.9	0927 1.6	1632 4.0	2158 1.9		17 W	0408 4.3	0948 1.1	1649 4.4	2220 1.3
3 W	0439 3.8	1019 1.6	1723 3.9	2258 1.9		18 TH	0507 4.1	1048 1.3	1749 4.3	2326 1.5
4 TH	0536 3.7	1121 1.9	1821 3.9			19 F	0614 4.0	1155 1.5	1856 4.2	
5 F	0005 1.9	0641 3.7	1228 1.8	1921 4.0		20 SA	0038 1.5	0727 4.0	1308 1.5	2004 4.2
6 SA	0107 1.8	0747 3.8	1327 1.7	2018 4.1		21 SU	0148 1.4	0839 4.1	1414 1.5	2107 4.3
7 SU	0200 1.6	0846 4.0	1418 1.6	2109 4.2		22 M	0249 1.3	0942 4.2	1512 1.3	2202 4.4
8 M	0247 1.4	0938 4.1	1505 1.4	2156 4.3		23 TU	0342 1.1	1037 4.4	1602 1.2	2250 4.5
9 TU	0332 1.2	1026 4.3	1550 1.2	2240 4.5		24 W	0429 1.0	1124 4.5	1646 1.1	○ 2332 4.5
10 W	0416 1.0	1111 4.5	1635 1.1	● 2323 4.5		25 TH	0512 0.9	1206 4.5	1728 1.1	
11 TH	0500 0.9	1156 4.6	1720 1.0			26 F	0011 4.5	0550 0.9	1245 4.5	1805 1.1
12 F	0006 4.6	0545 0.8	1241 4.6	1805 0.9		27 SA	0047 4.4	0627 0.9	1321 4.5	1841 1.1
13 SA	0051 4.6	0631 0.7	1327 4.7	1852 0.9		28 SU	0121 4.3	0701 1.0	1355 4.4	1916 1.2
14 SU	0136 4.6	0717 0.7	1414 4.7	1940 0.9		29 M	0156 4.3	0733 1.1	1429 4.4	1949 1.3
15 M	0224 4.5	0805 0.8	1503 4.6	2029 1.0		30 TU	0233 4.2	0804 1.3	1505 4.3	2023 1.5
						31 W	0311 4.0	0838 1.4	1543 4.2	2101 1.7

AUGUST

Day	Time m	Time m	Time m	Time m		Day	Time m	Time m	Time m	Time m
1 TH	0351 3.9	0917 1.7	1624 4.0	2148 1.8		16 F	0440 4.1	1018 1.4	1714 4.2	2256 1.6
2 F	0440 3.8	1009 1.9	1716 3.9	2250 2.0		17 SA	0546 3.9	1129 1.7	1825 4.0	
3 SA	0542 3.7	1118 2.0	1821 3.9			18 SU	0016 1.7	0711 3.9	1251 1.8	1947 4.0
4 SU	0010 2.0	0659 3.7	1240 2.0	1934 4.0		19 M	0136 1.7	0835 4.0	1406 1.7	2058 4.1
5 M	0125 1.8	0814 3.9	1349 1.8	2038 4.1		20 TU	0241 1.5	0939 4.2	1504 1.5	2154 4.3
6 TU	0223 1.5	0915 4.1	1445 1.6	2132 4.3		21 W	0332 1.2	1029 4.4	1551 1.3	2239 4.4
7 W	0313 1.2	1007 4.4	1534 1.3	2219 4.5		22 TH	0414 1.0	1111 4.5	1632 1.2	○ 2318 4.5
8 TH	0400 0.9	1054 4.6	1621 1.1	● 2305 4.6		23 F	0453 0.9	1149 4.6	1709 1.0	2352 4.5
9 F	0446 0.7	1140 4.7	1707 0.9	2350 4.7		24 SA	0529 0.8	1222 4.6	1744 1.0	
10 SA	0532 0.6	1225 4.8	1753 0.7			25 SU	0024 4.4	0602 0.8	1254 4.5	1817 1.0
11 SU	0036 4.7	0617 0.5	1311 4.8	1838 0.7		26 M	0056 4.4	0633 0.8	1303 4.5	1847 1.1
12 M	0122 4.7	0702 0.5	1357 4.8	1923 0.7		27 TU	0128 4.4	0701 1.0	1354 4.4	1914 1.2
13 TU	0209 4.7	0747 0.6	1442 4.8	2009 0.8		28 W	0200 4.3	0727 1.2	1425 4.4	1942 1.3
14 W	0256 4.5	0832 0.8	1528 4.6	2057 1.0		29 TH	0233 4.2	0755 1.3	1457 4.2	2015 1.5
15 TH	0345 4.4	0921 1.1	1617 4.4	2151 1.3		30 F	0309 4.0	0830 1.4	1532 4.1	2055 1.7
						31 SA	0351 3.9	0916 1.9	1618 3.9	2151 2.0

Extract 5

YARMOUTH *9.2.19*

Isle of Wight **50°42'·42N 01°30'·05W** ✹✹✹⬦⬦⬦✿✿✿

CHARTS AC *5600, 2021, 2037*; Imray C3, C15; Stanfords 11, 24, 25; OS 196

TIDES Sp −0050, +0150, Np +0020 Dover; ML 2·0; Zone 0 (UT)

Standard Port PORTSMOUTH (⟶)

Times				Height (metres)			
High Water		Low Water		MHWS	MHWN	MLWN	MLWS
0000	0600	0500	1100	4·7	3·8	1·9	0·8
1200	1800	1700	2300				
Differences YARMOUTH							
−0105	+0005	−0025	−0030	−1·7	−1·2	−0·3	0·0

NOTE: Double HWs occur at or near sp; at other times there is a stand lasting about two hrs. Predictions refer to the first HW when there are two; otherwise to the middle of the stand. See 9.2.12.

Extract 6

COWES/RIVER MEDINA *9.2.23*

Isle of Wight 50°45'·89N 01°17'·80W ✹✹✹⬦⬦⬦✿✿✿

CHARTS AC *5600, 2793, 2035, 2036*; Imray C3, C15; Stanfords 11, 24, 25; OS 196

TIDES +0029 Dover; ML 2·7; Zone 0 (UT)

Standard Port PORTSMOUTH (⟶)

Times				Height (metres)			
High Water		Low Water		MHWS	MHWN	MLWN	MLWS
0000	0600	0500	1100	4·7	3·8	1·9	0·8
1200	1800	1700	2300				
Differences COWES							
−0015	+0015	0000	−0020	−0·5	−0·3	−0·1	0·0
FOLLY INN							
−0015	+0015	0000	−0020	−0·6	−0·4	−0·1	+0·2
NEWPORT							
No data		No data		−0·6	−0·4	+0·1	+0·8

NOTE: Double HWs occur at or near sp. On other occasions a stand occurs lasting up to 2hrs; times given represent the middle of the stand. See 9.2.12, especially for Newport.

Extract 7

LYMINGTON *9.2.20*

Hampshire 50°45'·13N 01·31'·40W ✹✹✹⬦⬦⬦✿✿✿

CHARTS AC *5600, 2021, 2035*; Imray C3, C15; Stanfords 11, 25, 25; OS 196

TIDES Sp −0040, +0100, Np +0020 Dover; ML 2·0; Zone 0 (UT)

Standard Port PORTSMOUTH (⟶)

Times				Height (metres)			
High Water		Low Water		MHWS	MHWN	MLWN	MLWS
0000	0600	0500	1100	4·7	3·8	1·9	0·8
1200	1800	1700	2300				
Differences LYMINGTON							
−0110	+0005	−0020	−0020	−1·7	−1·2	−0·5	−0·1

NOTE: Double HWs occur at or near sp and on other occasions there is a stand lasting about 2hrs. Predictions refer to the first HW when there are two. At other times they refer to the middle of the stand. See 9.2.12.

Extract 8

TIME ZONE (UTC)
For Summer Time add ONE hour in **non-shaded areas**

ENGLAND – POOLE HARBOUR

LAT 50°42′N LONG 1°59′W

HIGH WATER HEIGHTS AND TIMES AND HEIGHTS OF LOW WATERS

MAY

Date	Day	Time	m	Time	m	Time	m	Time	m
1	W		2.2	0707	0.6		2.1	1926	0.8
2	TH		2.0	0748	0.8		2.0	2011	0.9
3	F		1.9	0836	0.9		1.8	2107	1.2
4	SA		1.7	0938	1.1		1.7	2220	1.3
5	SU		1.6	1059	1.2		1.7	2344	1.3
6	M		1.6	1220	1.2		1.8		
7	TU	0057	1.2		1.6	1321	1.1		1.9
8	W	0150	1.0		1.8	1406	1.0		1.9
9	TH	0231	0.9		1.8	1446	0.8		2.0
10	F	0308	0.8		1.9	1523	0.8		2.0
11	SA	0344	0.7		1.9	1558	0.7		2.0
12	SU ●	0418	0.7		2.0	1632	0.7		2.1
13	M	0450	0.7		2.0	1704	0.7		
14	TU		2.1	0521	0.7		2.0	1735	0.7
15	W		2.1	0552	0.7		2.0	1809	0.8
16	TH		2.0	0628	0.7		2.0	1848	0.8
17	F		2.0	0709	0.8		2.0	1934	0.9
18	SA		1.9	0759	0.9		1.9	2031	1.0
19	SU		1.8	0902	1.0		1.9	2143	1.1
20	M		1.8	1020	1.0		1.8	2304	1.1
21	TU		1.8	1141	1.0		1.9		
22	W	0021	1.0		1.9	1252	0.9		2.0
23	TH	0125	0.9		2.0	1350	0.7		2.1
24	F	0220	0.7		2.1	1442	0.6		2.2
25	SA	0310	0.6		2.1	1530	0.6		2.3
26	SU ○	0358	0.5		2.2	1616	0.5		2.3
27	M	0443	0.5		2.2	1701	0.6		
28	TU		2.3	0527	0.5		2.2	1743	0.6
29	W		2.2	0608	0.6		2.1	1825	0.7
30	TH		2.1	0649	0.7		2.1	1906	0.8
31	F		2.0	0729	0.8		2.0	1950	0.9

JUNE

Date	Day	Time	m	Time	m	Time	m	Time	m
1	SA		1.9	0813	0.9		1.9	2039	1.1
2	SU		1.8	0904	1.0		1.8	2137	1.2
3	M		1.6	1006	1.2		1.8	2246	1.3
4	TU		1.6	1116	1.2		1.8	2357	1.3
5	W		1.6	1222	1.2		1.8		
6	TH	0057	1.2		1.6	1315	1.0		1.9
7	F	0145	1.0		1.8	1401	1.0		1.9
8	SA	0227	0.9		1.8	1442	0.9		2.0
9	SU	0307	0.8		1.9	1522	0.8		2.0
10	M ●	0345	0.8		2.0	1600	0.8		2.1
11	TU	0422	0.7		2.0	1638	0.8		2.1
12	W	0500	0.7		2.1	1718	0.7		
13	TH		2.1	0540	0.7		2.1	1759	0.7
14	F		2.1	0622	0.7		2.1	1843	0.8
15	SA		2.0	0708	0.7		2.1	1932	0.8
16	SU		2.0	0759	0.8		2.0	2027	0.9
17	M		1.9	0856	0.8		2.0	2128	0.9
18	TU		1.9	0958	0.9		2.0	2234	1.0
19	W		1.9	1105	0.9		2.0	2344	1.0
20	TH		1.9	1213	0.9		2.0		
21	F	0052	0.9		1.9	1318	0.8		2.1
22	SA	0154	0.8		2.0	1417	0.8		2.1
23	SU	0249	0.7		2.0	1509	0.7		2.1
24	M ○	0339	0.7		2.1	1558	0.7		2.2
25	TU	0427	0.6		2.1	1644	0.7		2.1
26	W	0511	0.6		2.1	1727	0.7		
27	TH		2.1	0553	0.7		2.1	1808	0.8
28	F		2.1	0632	0.7		2.1	1847	0.8
29	SA		2.0	0710	0.8		2.0	1927	0.9
30	SU		1.9	0747	0.9		2.0	2008	1.0

JULY

Date	Day	Time	m	Time	m	Time	m	Time	m
1	M		1.8	0827	0.9		1.9	2052	1.1
2	TU		1.8	0912	1.0		1.8	2143	1.2
3	W		1.7	1004	1.2		1.8	2243	1.2
4	TH		1.6	1106	1.2		1.8	2350	1.2
5	F		1.6	1213	1.2		1.8		
6	SA	0052	1.2		1.7	1312	1.1		1.9
7	SU	0145	1.0		1.8	1403	1.0		1.9
8	M	0232	0.9		1.9	1450	0.9		2.0
9	TU	0317	0.8		2.0	1535	0.8		2.1
10	W ●	0401	0.7		2.1	1620	0.8		2.1
11	TH	0445	0.6		2.1	1705	0.7		
12	F		2.1	0530	0.6		2.1	1750	0.7
13	SA		2.1	0616	0.6		2.2	1837	0.7
14	SU		2.1	0702	0.6		2.2	1925	0.7
15	M		2.1	0750	0.6		2.1	2014	0.7
16	TU		2.0	0840	0.7		2.1	2107	0.8
17	W		2.0	0933	0.8		2.0	2205	0.9
18	TH		1.9	1033	0.9		2.0	2311	1.0
19	F		1.8	1140	1.0		1.9		
20	SA	0023	1.0		1.8	1253	1.0		1.9
21	SU	0133	0.9		1.9	1359	1.0		2.0
22	M	0234	0.9		1.9	1457	0.9		2.0
23	TU	0327	0.8		2.0	1547	0.8		2.1
24	W ○	0414	0.7		2.1	1631	0.8		2.1
25	TH	0457	0.7		2.1	1713	0.8		
26	F		2.1	0535	0.7		2.1	1750	0.8
27	SA		2.0	0612	0.7		2.1	1826	0.8
28	SU		2.0	0646	0.7		2.0	1901	0.8
29	M		2.0	0718	0.8		2.0	1934	0.9
30	TU		1.9	0749	0.9		2.0	2008	1.0
31	W		1.8	0823	0.9		1.9	2046	1.1

AUGUST

Date	Day	Time	m	Time	m	Time	m	Time	m
1	TH		1.8	0902	1.1		1.8	2133	1.2
2	F		1.7	0954	1.2		1.8	2235	1.3
3	SA		1.6	1103	1.3		1.8	2355	1.3
4	SU		1.6	1225	1.3		1.8		
5	M	0110	1.2		1.8	1334	1.2		1.9
6	TU	0208	1.0		1.9	1430	1.0		2.0
7	W	0258	0.8		2.0	1519	0.9		2.1
8	TH ●	0345	0.7		2.1	1606	0.8		2.1
9	F	0431	0.6		2.2	1652	0.7		2.2
10	SA	0517	0.5		2.3	1738	0.6		
11	SU		2.2	0602	0.4		2.3	1823	0.6
12	M		2.2	0647	0.4		2.3	1908	0.6
13	TU		2.2	0732	0.5		2.3	1954	0.6
14	W		2.1	0817	0.6		2.1	2042	0.7
15	TH		2.0	0906	0.8		2.0	2136	0.9
16	F		1.9	1003	0.9		1.9	2241	1.0
17	SA		1.8	1114	1.1		1.8		
18	SU	0001	1.1		1.8	1236	1.2		1.8
19	M	0121	1.1		1.8	1351	1.1		1.9
20	TU	0226	1.0		1.9	1449	1.0		2.0
21	W	0317	0.8		2.0	1536	0.9		2.0
22	TH ○	0359	0.7		2.1	1617	0.8		2.1
23	F	0438	0.7		2.1	1654	0.7		2.1
24	SA	0514	0.6		2.1	1729	0.7		
25	SU		2.0	0547	0.6		2.1	1802	0.7
26	M		2.0	0618	0.7		2.1	1832	0.8
27	TU		2.0	0646	0.7		2.0	1859	0.8
28	W		2.0	0712	0.8		2.0	1927	0.9
29	TH		1.9	0740	0.9		1.9	2000	1.0
30	F		1.8	0815	1.0		1.9	2040	1.1
31	SA		1.8	0901	1.2		1.8	2136	1.3

POOLE HARBOUR *9.2.13*

Dorset 50°40'·93N 01°56'·96W (Ent) ✿✿✿✿✿✿✿✿

CHARTS AC *5601, 2611, 2175*; Imray C4, Y23; Stanfords 7,12, 15; OS 195

TIDES Town Quay –0141, +0114 Dover; ML 1·6; Zone 0 (UT) Daily predictions of the times and hts of LW (but only the hts of HW) are (⟶) for the Standard Port of **POOLE HARBOUR** (near the Ro-Ro terminal); sp and neap curves are above. (The tidal curves (⟶) simplify intermediate calculations.) Secondary Port differences are given below.

Standard Port POOLE HARBOUR (⟶)

Times				Height (metres)			
High Water		Low Water		MHWS	MHWN	MLWN	MLWS
–	–	0500	1100	2·2	1·7	1·2	0·6
–	–	1700	2300				
Differences POOLE HARBOUR ENTRANCE							
–	–	–0025	–0010	0·0	0·0	0·0	0·0
POTTERY PIER							
–	–	+0010	+0010	–0·2	0·0	+0·1	+0·2
CLEAVEL POINT							
–	–	–0005	–0005	–0·1	–0·2	0·0	–0·1
WAREHAM (River Frome)							
–	–	+0130	+0045	0·0	0·0	0·0	+0·3

Double HWs occur, except at nps. The ht of the 2nd HW is always about 1·8m; only the ht of the 1st HW varies from sp to nps. The tide is above Mean Level (1·6m) from about LW+2 to next LW–2. Strong and continuous winds from E to SW may raise sea levels by as much as 0·2m; W to NE winds may lower levels by 0·1m. Barometric pressure effects are also appreciable, see Chapter 7.

SHELTER An excellent hbr with narrow ent; access in all conditions except very strong E/SE winds. Yachts can berth at Dolphin Boat Haven or Poole Quay and, on request, in marinas listed under Facilities. ↓s wherever sheltered from the wind and clear of chans, moorings and shellfish beds; especially in South Deep, off W end of Brownsea Is and off Shipstal Point, all within a Quiet Area (see chartlet and speed limits).

NAVIGATION WPT Poole Bar (No 1 SHM) By, QG, 50°39'·32N 01°55'·16W, 148°/328° from/to Haven Hotel, 1·95M. In strong SE-S winds the Bar is dangerous especially on the ebb. In Studland Bay and close to training bank beware lobster pots. From Poole Bar to Shell Bay a recreational **Boat Chan**, suitable for craft < 3m draught, parallels the W side of the Swash Channel, close to the E of the Training Bank.

East Looe Chan (buoyed) is liable to shift and may have less water than charted; only 1m was reported 1ca ENE of East Looe PHM buoy. 5 groynes to the N are marked by SHM bns, the two most W'ly ones are lit, 2 FG (vert).

Within the hbr the two chans (Middle Ship and North) up to Poole Quay are clearly marked by lateral buoys, lit, with cardinal buoys at divisions. Outside the chans there are extensive shoal or drying areas. High Speed Ferries operate in the area.

Middle Ship Chan is dredged 6·0m to/from the Hamworthy terminal; it is mostly only 80m wide. Leisure craft should keep out of Middle Ship Chan, by using a

Boat Chan which parallels S of the dredged chan between the PHM buoys and, further outboard, stakes with PHM topmarks marking the edge of the bank. Depth is 2·0m in this chan, but 1·5m closer to the stakes. Caution: When large ferries pass, a temporary, but significant reduction in depth may be remedied by closing the PHM buoys.

North Channel, the other option remains usable for yachts/ leisure craft; best water is on the outside of chan bends.

Lulworth gunnery range (see 9.2.10). Yachtsmen cruising to the W should pre-check for activity, as shown in the Hr Mr's office and in the Supplements to this Almanac.

Regulations A 6 knots speed limit applies from Stakes SCM buoy, past Poole Quay and Poole Bridge up to Cobbs Quay in Holes Bay. It also applies within the S half of the hbr which is designated as a Quiet Area (see chartlet). A 4kn speed limit applies within the Dolphin Boat Haven.

A 10 knots speed limit applies to the rest of the hbr, from the seaward app chans (defined by an arc of radius 1400m centred on S Haven Pt, 50°40'·81N 01°56'·99W) westward to the junction of R Frome with R Trent at 02°04'·60W. Speeding fines of up to £1000 can be imposed.

Exemptions. The 10kn speed limit does not apply:
a. From 1 Oct to 31 Mar to vessels in the North, Middle Ship and Wareham Chans.
b. to water-skiers within the water-ski area between Gold Pt and No 82 PHM buoy (Wareham Chan; see chartlet). Permits must be obtained from the Hr Mr.
c. to users of Personal Water Craft (PWC) operating in a designated area N of Brownsea Island. Note: PWCs must not enter the Quiet Area in the S of the hbr, nor linger in the hbr ent. Permits must be obtained from the Hr Mr.

Sandbanks Chain Ferry shows a Fl W lt (rotating) and a B ● above the leading Control cabin by D/N to indicate which way it is going. In fog it sounds 1 long and 2 short blasts every 2 mins. When stationary at night it shows a FW lt; in fog it rings a bell for 5 sec every minute. All non-piloted craft must keep clear of the ferry.

LIGHTS AND MARKS See chartlet and 9.2.4 for main buoys, beacons and lts.

Poole Bridge traffic lights, shown from bridge tr:
● = Do not approach bridge;
Fl ● = Bridge lifting, proceed with caution; ● = Proceed.
Bridge lifts routinely for small craft at: Mon-Fri 0930, 1030, 1230, 1430, 1630, 1830; Sat, Sun & Bank hols : as Mon-Fri, plus 0730; at 2345 daily bridge will also lift if any vessels are waiting. Each lift only permits one cycle of traffic in each direction. Pleasure craft may pass when the bridge lifts on request for a commercial vessel; monitor Ch 14. Bridge will not usually lift during weekday road traffic Rush Hours 0730-0930 and 1630-1830.

RADIO TELEPHONE Call: *Poole Hbr Control* VHF Ch 14 16 (H24). Dolphin Boat Haven Ch 80; Salterns Marina Ch M 80; Parkstone Haven Ch M; Poole YC Haven, call *Pike* Ch M; Poole Bridge, call *PB* Ch 14. Cobbs Quay, call *CQ Base* Ch 80.

TELEPHONE (Dial code 01202) Hr Mr 440233, ▤ 440231; Dolphin Boat Haven 649488; Bridge 674115; MRSC (01305) 760439; ⊖ 01752 234600 (H24); Met (02392) 228844; Marinecall 09068 500457, Police 223954; ℍ 665511.

FACILITIES The following are some of the many facilities:
Marinas (from seaward)
Salterns Marina (300, few visitors) ☎ 709971, ▤ 700398, ≤10m £23, max draft 2·5m, AC, FW, P & D (H24), ME, EI, Ⓔ, Sh, CH, Gas, Gaz, C (5 ton), BH (45 ton), Bar, R, ▣. Appr from No 31 SHM buoy, Fl G 5s.
Parkstone Haven, (Parkstone YC.) ☎ 743610, some ♥ berths, £16; dredged 2m. Access from North Chan near No 35 SHM buoy, Fl G 5s. Appr chan, dredged 2·5m, is marked by SHM buoy (Fl G 3s), 2 PHM and 3 SHM unlit buoys. Ldg daymarks 006°, both Y ◊s; ldg lts, front Iso Y 4s, rear FY. 2 FG and 2FR (vert) on bkwtr hds.
Poole Quay-Dolphin Boat Haven (100 ♥) ☎/▤ 649488, max draft 2·5m, £2·82, AC, FW, Haven Office open 0700-2200 Apr-Sep.
Dorset Yacht Co (56 AB + 6 ♥; 90M + 6♠) ☎ 674531, ▤ 677518, f1·50, P, D, AC, FW, CH, Slip, Gas/Gaz, ME, EI, Sh, C (5 ton), BH (50 ton), Gas, FW; berth not marked by 2FR (vert) and two 2FG (vert). Water taxi, weekends 1/4 to 1/10.

Beyond Poole Bridge:
Gunseeker International Marina (50) ☎ 685335, AC, Sh, D, BH (30 ton), C (36 ton), FW, ME, EI, CH, V, R, Bar;
Cobbs Quay Marina (850, some visitors) ☎ 674299, ▤ 665217, £2, Slip, P, D, Gas, LPG, ▣, SM, FW, AC, ME, EI, Ⓔ, Sh, C (10 ton), CH, R, Bar;
Public Landing Places: On Poole Quay, in Holes Bay and by ferry hards at Sandbanks. **Fuel** Poole Bay Fuels barge (May-Sep 0900-1800; moored off Poole Quay, No 50) P, D, Gas, Gaz, V, Off licence. **Corrals** (S side of Poole Quay adjacent bridge) P & D; **Salterns marina** P & D. **Yacht Clubs: Royal Motor YC** ☎ 707227, M, Bar, R; **Poole Bay YC; Parkstone YC** ☎ 743610 (Parkstone Haven); **Poole YC** ☎ 672687. **Services** A complete range of marine services is available; consult marina/Hr Mr for exact locations. **Town** EC Wed; ⊠, ⑧, ≈, ✈. Ferry to Cherbourg and Channel Islands (all year).

9.2.5 PASSAGE INFORMATION

THE PORTLAND RACE (chart *2255*) South of the Bill lies Portland Race in which severe and very dangerous sea states occur. Even in settled weather it should be carefully avoided by small craft, although at neaps it may be barely perceptible.

The Race occurs at the confluence of two strong S-going tidal streams which run down each side of Portland for almost 10 hours out of 12 at springs. These streams meet the main E-W stream of the Channel, producing large eddies on either side of Portland and a highly confused sea state with heavy overfalls in the Race. The irregular contours of the sea-bed, which shoals abruptly from depths of over 100m some 2M south of the Bill to as little as 9m on Portland Ledge 1M further N, greatly contribute to the violence of the Race. Portland Ledge strongly deflects the flow of water upwards, so that on the flood the Race lies SE of the Bill and vice versa on the ebb. Conditions deteriorate with wind-against-tide, especially at springs; in an E'ly gale against the flood stream the Race may spread eastward to The Shambles bank. The Race normally extends about 2M S of the Bill, but further S in bad weather.

The Tidal Stream chartlets at 9.2.8 show the approx hourly positions of the Race. They are referenced to HW Portland, for the convenience of those leaving or making for Portland/ Weymouth; and to HW Dover for those on passage S of the Bill. The smaller scale chartlets at 9.2.3 show the English Chan streams referenced to HW at Dover and Portsmouth.

Small craft may avoid the Race either by passing clear to seaward of it, between 3 and 5M S of the Bill; or by using the inshore passage if conditions suit. This passage is a stretch of relatively smooth water between 1ca and 3ca off the Bill (depending on wind), which should not however be used at night under power due to lobster pots. Timing is important to catch "slackish" water around the Bill, i.e:

> Westbound = from HW Dover – 1 to HW + 2
> (HW Portland + 4 to HW – 6).
> Eastbound = from HW Dover + 5 to HW – 4
> (HW Portland – 3 to HW + 1).

From either direction, close Portland at least 2M N of the Bill to utilise the S-going stream; once round the Bill, the N-going stream will set a yacht away from the Race area.

PORTLAND TO CHRISTCHURCH BAY (chart *2615*) The Shambles bank is about 3M E of Portland Bill, and should be avoided at all times. In bad weather the sea breaks heavily on it. It is marked by buoys on its E side and at SW end. E of Weymouth are rky ledges extending 3ca offshore as far as Lulworth Cove, which provides a reasonable anch in fine, settled weather and offshore winds; as do Worbarrow Bay and Chapman's Pool (9.2.10).

A firing range extends 5M offshore between Lulworth and St Alban's Hd. Yachts must pass through this area as quickly as possible, when the range is in use, see 9.2.10. Beware Kimmeridge Ledges, which extend over 5ca seaward.

St Alban's Head (107m and conspic) is steep-to and has a dangerous race off it which may extend 3M seaward. The race lies to the E on the flood and to the W on the ebb; the latter is the more dangerous. A narrow passage, at most 5ca wide and very close inshore, avoids the worst of the overfalls. There is an eddy on W side of St Alban's Head, where the stream runs almost continuously SE. 1M S of St Alban's Head the ESE stream begins at HW Portsmouth + 0520, and the WNW stream at HW –0030, with sp rates of 4·75kn.

There is deep water quite close inshore between St Alban's Hd and Anvil Pt (lt). 1M NE of Durlston Hd, Peveril Ledge runs 2½ca seaward, causing quite a bad race which extends nearly 1M eastwards, particularly on W-going stream against a SW wind. Proceeding towards the excellent shelter of Poole Harbour (9.2.13), overfalls may be met off Ballard Pt and Old Harry on the W-going stream. Studland Bay (9.2.11 and chart 2172) is a good anch especially in NW to S winds. Anch about 4ca WNW of Handfast Pt. Avoid foul areas on chart.

Poole Bay offers good sailing in waters sheltered from W and N winds, with no dangers to worry the average yacht. Tidal streams are weak N of a line between Handfast Pt and Hengistbury Hd and within Christchurch Bay. Hengistbury Hd is a dark headland, S of Christchurch hbr (9.2.14), with a groyne extending 1ca S and Beerpan Rks a further 100m E of groyne. Beware lobster pots in this area. Christchurch Ledge extends 2·75M SE from Hengistbury Hd. The tide runs hard over the ledge at sp, and there may be overfalls.

Extract 11

SWANAGE 9.2.11

Dorset 50°36'·81N 01°57'·05W ✵✵✵⊛⚓⚓✿✿

CHARTS AC *5601, 2172, 2610, 2175*; Imray C4; Stanfords 7, 12, 15; OS 195

TIDES HW Sp –0235 & +0125, Np –0515 & +0120 on Dover; ML 1·5
Standard Port POOLE HARBOUR (→)

Times				Height (metres)			
High Water		Low Water		MHWS	MHWN	MLWN	MLWS
—	—	0500	1100	2·2	1·7	1·2	0·6
—	—	1700	2300				
Differences SWANAGE							
—	—	–0045	–0055	–0·2	–0·1	0·0	–0·1

NOTE: From Swanage to Christchurch double HWs occur except at nps. HW differences refer to the higher HW when there are two and are approximate.

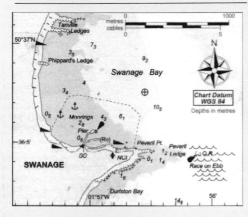

SHELTER Good ⚓ in winds from SW to N, but bad in E/SE winds >F4 due to swell which may persist for 6 hrs after a blow. >F6 holding gets very difficult; Poole is nearest refuge. AB is feasible on S side of pier (open Apr-Oct) subject to wind and sea state; pleasure 'steamers' use the N side.

NAVIGATION WPT 50°36'·73N 01°56'·58W, 054°/234° from/to pier hd, 0·30M. Coming from S beware Peveril Ledge and its Race which can be vicious with a SW wind against the main ebb. It is best to keep 1M seaward of Durlston Head and Peveril Point. On the W side of Swanage Bay, keep clear of Tanville and Phippards Ledges, approx 300m offshore. To the S of the pier are the ruins of an old pier.

LIGHTS AND MARKS The only lts are 2 FR (vert) on the pier; difficult to see due to confusing street lts. Peveril Ledge PHM buoy is unlit and hard to pick out at night due to Anvil Pt lt; keep 0·5M clear of it to the E.

RADIO TELEPHONE None.

TELEPHONE (Dial code 01929) Pier 427058, mobile 0780 1616216; MRSC (01305) 760439; ⊖ 0345 231110 (H24) or (01202) 685157; Marinecall 09068 500457; Police 422004; Dr 422231; Ⓗ 422202.

FACILITIES Pier, L*, FW, AB* £1, £3 for <3hrs; after 2100 gain access to pier from ashore via **Swanage SC** ☎ 422987, Slip, L, FW, Bar, Ⓧ; **Boat Park** (Peveril Pt), Slip, FW, L; **Services**: Diving. **Town** P & D (cans, 1½M), FW, V, R, Bar, ⊠, Ⓑ, ⇌ (bus connection to Wareham), ✈ (Hurn).

ADJACENT ANCHORAGE

STUDLAND BAY, Dorset, **50°38'·73N 01°55'·90W**. AC*2172*, 2175. Tides approx as for Swanage (9.2.11). Shelter is good except in N/E winds. Beware Redend Rocks off S shore. Best ⚓ in about 3m, 3ca NW of The Yards (three strange projections on the chalk cliffs near Handfast Pt).**Village**: EC Thurs; FW, V, R, ⊠, hotel, P&D (cans), No marine facilities. A Historic Wreck (see 9.0.3h) is at 50°39'·70N 01°54'·87W, 4·5ca NNE of Poole Bar Buoy.

Extract 12

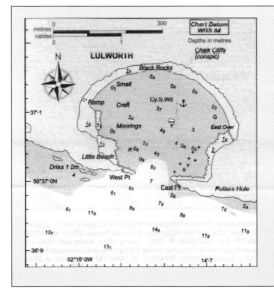

ANCHORAGES BETWEEN PORTLAND AND SWANAGE
Essential to read *Inshore* along the Dorset Coast (P. Bruce)

LULWORTH COVE, Dorset, **50°37'·00N 02°14'·82W**. AC *2172*. HW –0449 on Dover, see 9.2.7. Tides; ML 1·2m. Good shelter in fair weather and offshore winds, but heavy swell enters the cove in S and SW winds; if strong the ⚓ becomes untenable. Enter the cove slightly E of centre. A Y mooring buoy for the range safety launch is in the middle in about 4m. ⚓ in NE part in 2·5m. Holding is poor. 8kn speed limit. Local moorings, village and slip are on W side. Facilities: EC Wed/Sat; FW at tap in car park, Bar, ⊠, R, Slip.

WORBARROW BAY, Dorset, **50°37'·03N 02°12'·08W**. AC *2172*. Tides as Lulworth Cove/Mupe Bay, see 9.2.7. Worbarrow is a 1¼M wide bay, close E of Lulworth Cove. It is easily identified from seaward by the V-shaped gap in the hills at Arish Mell, centre of bay just E of Bindon Hill. Bindon Hill also has a white chalk scar due to cliff falls. Caution: Mupe Rks at W end and other rks 1ca off NW side. ⚓s in about 3m sheltered from W or E winds at appropriate end. The bay lies within Lulworth Ranges (see above); landing prohib at Arish Mell. No lights/facilities.

CHAPMAN'S POOL, Dorset, **50°35'·53N 02°03'·93W**. AC *2172*. Tidal data: interpolate between Mupe Bay (9.2.7) and Swanage (9.2.11). Chapman's Pool, like Worbarrow Bay, Brandy Bay and Kimmeridge Bay, is picturesque and convenient when the wind is off-shore. ⚓ in depths of about 3m in centre of bay to avoid tidal swirl, but beware large unlit Y buoy (for Range Safety boat). From here to St Alban's Hd the stream runs SSE almost continuously due to a back eddy. No lights or facilities.

Extract A

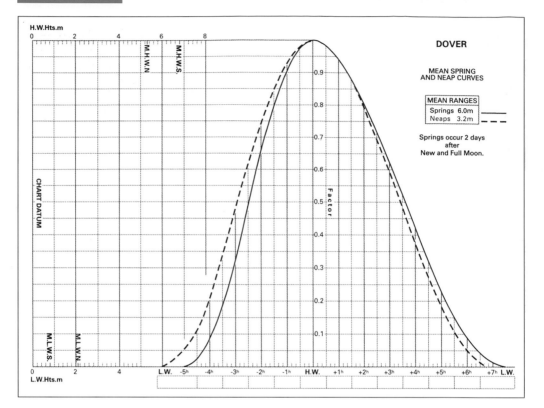

Extract B

H.W.Hts at Secondary Ports

Extract C

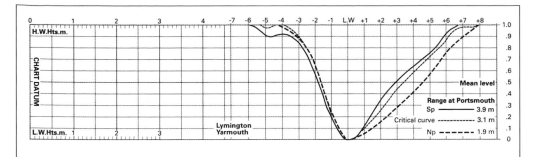

Extract D

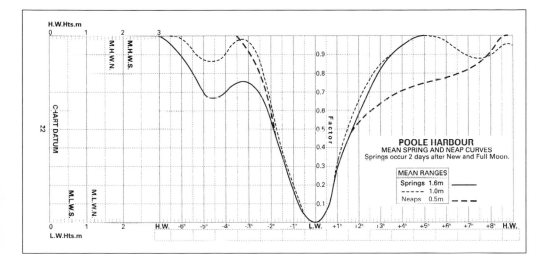

INDEX